Fashion Marketing

Fashion Marketing

Third Edition

Edited by
Mike Easey

A John Wiley & Sons, Ltd., Publication

Blackwell Publishing was acquired by John Wiley & Sons in February 2007. Blackwell's publishing programme has been merged with Wiley's global Scientific, Technical, and Medical business to form Wiley-Blackwell.

Registered office
John Wiley & Sons Ltd, The Atrium, Southern Gate, Chichester, West Sussex, PO19 8SQ, United Kingdom

Editorial offices
9600 Garsington Road, Oxford, OX4 2DQ, United Kingdom
2121 State Avenue, Ames, Iowa 50014-8300, USA

For details of our global editorial offices, for customer services and for information about how to apply for permission to reuse the copyright material in this book please see our website at www.wiley.com/wiley-blackwell.

Library of Congress Cataloging-in-Publication Data
Fashion marketing / edited by Mike Easey. — 3rd ed
    p. cm.
Includes bibliographical references and index.
ISBN 978-1-4051-3953-3 (pbk. : alk. paper) 1. Fashion merchandising. I. Easey, Mike.
HD9940.A2F37 2009
391.0068'8—dc22

                                                              2008030014

A catalogue record for this book is available from the British Library.

Set in 10/12.5 pt Avenir by Charon Tec Ltd (A Macmillan Company), Chennai, India (www.macmillansolutions.com)
Printed in Singapore by Markono Print Media Pte Ltd

1   2009

Contents

List of Contributors

Sheila Atkinson, *MSc, MBA, PGCEd, AMCIM*. Her working experience includes buying and merchandising for the Burton Group plc and management of design education in further education. Sheila has extensive teaching experience in UK and Chinese Universities and has training and consultancy experience in fashion marketing. Sheila Atkinson produced Chapter Six with Mike Easey, on the design and marketing of fashion products.

Mike Easey, *BA (Hons), DipM, MCIM, CertEd*, is Director of Collaborative Ventures in Newcastle Business School at the University of Northumbria. He has worked for three multinationals in marketing research, promotion and marketing planning positions. He is an experienced Marketing Consultant and has undertaken an extensive range of consultancy work including marketing for fashion manufacturers and fashion retailers. He is also a university external examiner in fashion marketing, a QAA Specialist Subject Reviewer in Marketing and a member of the editorial board of the *Journal of Fashion Marketing and Management*. Mike Easey produced Chapters One, Three, Seven and Ten and co-wrote Chapter Five with Christine Sorensen and Chapter Six with Sheila Atkinson.

Patricia Gray, *MSc, Dip MRS, PGCEd*, previously a Lecturer in Marketing Research in Newcastle Business School, is currently working as a Researcher with Newcastle University. Her experience includes numerous consultancy tasks and she has worked in publicity for the arts and for Millward Brown Market and Social Research. Patricia Gray produced Chapter Four on fashion marketing research.

Gaynor Lea-Greenwood, *MA, BA*, is a Senior Lecturer in Fashion Marketing at Manchester Metropolitan University. She has worked at a senior level in the fashion industry including a major role with Miss Selfridge. Along with consultancy experience for fashion retailers, she has extensive knowledge of international sourcing and promotion. She is an active researcher, external examiner for UK Universities and Acting Editor of the editorial board of the *Journal of Fashion Marketing and Management*. Gaynor is currently working on a new textbook on *Fashion Marketing Communications* for Wiley-Blackwell. Gaynor Lea-Greenwood produced Chapter Nine on fashion marketing communications.

Christine Sorensen, *MA, PGDip, BA (Hons) PGCEd, DipM*, is a Senior Lecturer in Marketing in Newcastle Business School. She has worked for three companies in marketing positions including the print industry and franchising. Christine has considerable experience of marketing training for small business and has appeared on radio to discuss developments in promotion. Christine Sorensen produced Chapter Two on the fashion marketing environment and co-wrote Chapter Five with Mike Easey.

John Willans, *MSc, DipM, CertEd*, until his recent retirement, was a Senior Lecturer in Fashion Marketing and Retail Distribution in Newcastle Business School. His background includes work with the retail sector and with textile marketing in Huddersfield. John Willans wrote Chapter Eight on fashion distribution. John is currently working on a new textbook, with Ruth Marciniak, on Fashion Retailing for Wiley-Blackwell.

Preface

If you are interested or involved in fashion you will already be aware that it is an exciting area of constant change, creativity and global commercial activity. However, skills in fashion are not enough to guarantee success, as even when those skills are exceptional there is still the constant risk of failure and bankruptcy. A knowledge of marketing is essential to help ensure success and lessen the possibility of failure. To paraphrase Armani, 'Clothing that is not purchased or worn is not fashion.' A good knowledge of fashion marketing can make the difference between a prototype that lingers in a dark storeroom and a garment that people really want to buy and wear.

Over the last two decades fashion has become a truly global business. Designers no longer work necessarily within manufacturing facilities and, as part of the knowledge industry, they need to be mobile and have the ability to communicate across cultures and business disciplines. Many brands like Gap, Zara and H&M which were just national brands a few years ago are now internationally recognized. Another major force influencing the fashion business is the growth of the Internet. The Internet has influenced the flow of creative ideas, the search for product information, the transparency of pricing and the management of supply chains amongst as well as how and where customers buy garments.

For the designer keen to start his or her own business, this book will offer a guide to most of the major decisions that will enable you to fulfil your creative potential and be a financial success. For the marketer who is interested in fashion, this book will help you understand the special way that marketing needs to be applied to the world of fashion. Established fashion businesses also need to remain competitive by asking questions such as:

◆ What are the major trends we should be monitoring?
◆ How should we set our prices?
◆ What is the most effective way to get our message across about the new product range?
◆ Which colour wash will be the most popular with buyers?

Fashion marketing finds answers to these and many other questions.

This book has a number of special qualities that make it essential reading for anyone involved in fashion.

◆ It deals with contemporary issues in fashion marketing.
◆ It has up-to-date examples of good practice. Over the past 35 years, all other major texts on fashion marketing have been centred on US practice. Fashion is now a global business and that theme is evident in all chapters in this revised edition.
◆ This book is exclusively about fashion marketing. It is not a marketing book with a few fashion examples among the anecdotes about motorcycles, industrial services and banking. It is all about fashion.
◆ There is a unique contribution on range planning which is a practical blend of sound design sense and commercial realism.
◆ There is a constant balance of theory and practice, with examples to illustrate key concepts. Where numerical concepts are included, there are clear worked examples to ensure that the ideas are easily understood and retained.
◆ Each chapter contains an introduction to set the scene and a summary of key points. There are over 50 diagrams to help to explain ideas and a glossary of the main fashion marketing terms is included.
◆ Included within each chapter is a guide to further reading. Keen fashion marketers will therefore be able to use this book as a foundation and springboard to becoming experts in specialist areas such as fashion marketing research or fashion public relations.
◆ A coherent approach to fashion marketing is developed, based on the research, consultancy, working and teaching experiences of a team from a major centre of excellence in fashion marketing in the UK. What you will get is a systematic approach to fashion marketing, not hyperbole or speculation.

How this book is organized

Part A looks at the nature and scope of fashion marketing. In Chapter One the special ingredients that make for good fashion design, care for customers and commercial success are explored. All fashion enthusiasts know of some of the links between fashion and broader social change and Chapter Two identifies those links, showing how fashion marketers are able to anticipate and participate in the process.

Part B is concerned with understanding and researching the consumer. In Chapter Three there is a detailed look at the consumer and what he or she wants from fashion, how ideas and brands are learned and how to paint a comprehensive and sound picture of the 'muse' for the fashion designer. Chapter Four deals with marketing research and shows how to investigate the preferences and behaviour of customers, distribution channels and competitors.

Part C looks at target marketing and the fashion marketing mix. Chapter Five deals with choosing profitable markets to aim at and then gives an overview of possible action to meet customer requirements – the marketing mix. In Chapters Six to Nine, precise coverage is given to the design of marketing programmes to ensure that the right garments (Chapter Six) are correctly priced (Chapter Seven), available at the right time and place (Chapter Eight) and are properly communicated (Chapter Nine). The final chapter deals with planning and co-ordinating the whole fashion marketing process, and setting up a system that works for the consumer, offering good fashion design and delivering profits.

If, like us, you believe that consumers deserve good fashion design and that profits should flow to those who act systematically to make that happen, then join us for the challenge that is fashion marketing.

The book's website

On the book's website, www.blackwellpublishing.com/easey, you will find invaluable on-line resources to support both teaching and learning – all downloadable free of charge. The website has the following features:

- ◆ For fashion marketing tutors, a full set of PowerPoint slides to accompany each chapter.
- ◆ Ideas and exercises for seminars.
- ◆ Access to sample assessment materials.
- ◆ Useful hyperlinks to relevant websites.

Acknowledgements

Fashion is a fascinating subject which stimulates a great many questions, an essential requirement for any academic endeavour. As mainstream marketing educators, the authors of this book brought a range of different expectations and experiences to the area of fashion. All of us have working, teaching, training or consultancy experience in the field of fashion marketing and wanted to write a book that would address real issues and would contribute, in a small way, to make the fashion industry and fashion students more aware of how marketing can enable them to be more effective in their work.

For several years the University of Northumbria has run an undergraduate course in fashion marketing. Our experiences of teaching on this course coupled with the paucity of UK texts on the subject convinced us of the need to write the book. Our research and experiences have led us to challenge the way we think about marketing and recognize the special role of design in the process. In many sectors with creative output, it has long been noted that designers need to know about marketing and marketers need to know about design. It is hoped that this book meets the needs of both groups, though in truth designers may learn more about marketing than vice versa.

Many people have helped me with the second edition of this book via comments on the first and second editions and stimulating conversations and inspirations.

The following people are sincerely thanked for their knowledge, help and friendship: Sheila Atkinson, Christine Sorensen, Patricia Gray, John Willans and Gaynor Lea-Greenwood. My co-authors have been very supportive over the years and have been good colleagues, critics and sources of ideas. Richard Jones, Prof. Christopher Moore, Dr. Sandra Connor, Ruth Marciniak, Prof. Neville Harris, Alan Fyall, Fiona Raeside, Helen Carter and Julie O'Sullivan have all contributed their ideas and friendship over the years. Madeleine Metcalfe at Wiley-Blackwell is due special thanks for her encouragement, patience and tenacity in helping me finish this third edition. Special thanks are also due to my wife Janice for great support.

As usual there is a disclaimer: many people have helped me, but I accept total responsibility for all errors in the book.

Mike Easey
March 2008

Part A
Understanding Fashion Marketing

Chapter One
An Introduction to Fashion Marketing

The global market for apparel, accessories and luxury goods was estimated to be worth US$1217 billion in 2006 and is expected to grow to approximately US$1800 billion by 2011. The company with the largest market share of this vast market is Christian Dior and, despite this great success, the company has approximately 1% of the global market. Global fashion remains one of the largest sectors of world trade that is truly competitive: 1.14 million people were employed in apparel manufacture in the European Union (EU) in 2004 and nearly one-third of all imported clothing bought in the EU in 2007 was manufactured in China. The UK fashion industry is estimated to be worth approximately £22 billion in retail sales value in 2008. Apparel manufacturing industry in the UK employed around 83 000 people in 2006, down from over 200 000 a decade earlier. The above statistics reveal that fashion is a large global business sector going through a period of great change. It is the application of marketing that plays a crucial role in managing this growth and change. This book shows how marketing can be applied to fashion products and services.

This introduction looks at both fashion and marketing and how design and marketing work together in practice. An overview of the fashion marketing process covers the role of marketing in the fashion industry and the ethical issues raised by marketing in this context, with some practical examples of the work of fashion marketers.

1.1 What is fashion?

1.1.1 Fashion is to do with change

Fashion essentially involves change, defined as a succession of short-term trends or fads. From this standpoint there can be fashions in

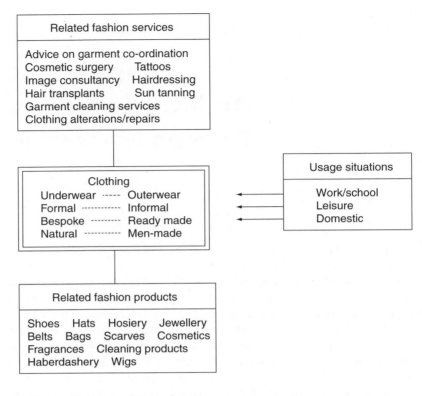

Figure 1.1 Fashion products and services.

almost any human activity from medical treatments to popular music. For the purpose of this book though, the concept of fashion will be taken to deal with the garments and related products and services as shown in Figure 1.1.

Figure 1.1 identifies some major categories of clothing along with their main usage situations, but this list is by no means exhaustive. Fashion marketers should take a broad view of their domain – fashion is not only about clothes.

The competitive ethos of the fashion industry revolves around seasonality. The industry has a vested interest in developing new products for the customer at the expense of existing items: this process is known as planned obsolescence. Planned obsolescence is not confined to the fashion industry, it occurs in several other manufacturing sectors such as the electronics or automobile industries. While the concept of planned obsolescence can be criticized from several perspectives, many customers appreciate the continual change in fashion products and services. Unfortunately, the rate and direction of change are usually slower and less predictable than the fashion industry would like.

1.1.2 Fashion is about creating

In order for the change which is intrinsic to fashion to take place, the industry must continually create new products. Used in another sense, the term fashion means to construct, mould or make. Fashion, therefore, also involves a strong creative and design component. Design skill is essential and can be seen in all products from the made-to-measure suit to the elaborate embroidery on a cardigan. The level of design can vary considerably from a basic item such as a T-shirt to the artistic creations of Coco Chanel, Christian Dior, Yves St Laurent or, in more recent times, Stella McCartney. To some the design of fashion garments can be viewed as an art in its own right, though this is a notion supported more in countries such as France and Italy than in Britain. The majority of garments sold do not come into this category, but the inspiration for the design of many of those garments may have come from works of art.

1.1.3 Fashion and marketing

The continual change, i.e. fashion, involves the exercise of creative design skills which result in products that range from the basic to the rare and elaborate. The creative design personnel provide part of the mechanism by which the industry responds to the need for change. At the same time the ability to identify products that the customer needs and will buy is also essential to the industry. Marketing can help to provide this additional knowledge and the skills needed to ensure that the creative component is used to best advantage, allowing businesses to succeed and grow.

1.2 What is marketing?

Marketing is a business philosophy or way of thinking about the firm from the perspective of the customer or the potential customer. Such a view has much merit as it focuses on the acid test for all business – if we do not meet the needs of our customers we will not survive, let alone thrive. Fashion firms depend upon customers making repeat purchases and the key to such loyalty is the satisfaction of customers' needs with garments which are stylish, durable, easy to care for, comfortable, perceived value for money and all the other criteria deemed relevant by the buyer. For this reason, fashion design personnel should readily appreciate the need to understand the customer's perspective. Most designers have a mental picture of a typical customer. Fashion marketers ask, how typical is that mental picture and does the 'customer' belong to a group of buyers that form a profitable prospect for the company? Notice that the notion of seeing the business from the perspective of the customer does not preclude concern for profit. Indeed, if profit is not actively sought then the firm's ability to meet customers' needs in the long term will be greatly diminished.

Marketing comprises a range of techniques and activities, some of which are highly familiar to the general public. Most people have encountered market researchers and all have seen advertisements. Other less public aspects include product development and branding, pricing, publicity, sales promotion, selling, forecasting and distribution. An overview of the range of fashion marketing activities is given later in this chapter.

Marketing is a management process concerned with anticipating, identifying and satisfying customer needs in order to meet the long-term goals of the organization. Whilst concerned with the organization's relationship with customers it is also concerned with internal organizational factors that affect the achievement of marketing goals.

1.2.1 Is marketing a solution to all business problems?

There are many views of what marketing is and what it does. To the zealots, marketing is the panacea for all business problems and can provide remedies for product failures or falling profits. Clearly, this is naive and does not recognize the interdependence of the many business and creative functions within organizations. Nor does this view fully appreciate the wider marketing environment that confronts all firms when they embark upon marketing activities.

The best marketing plans and activities can be easily and quickly undermined by changes in the economy or in competitors' actions. Such changes cannot always be anticipated, although a framework for monitoring and anticipating change is discussed in Chapter Two. In the fashion industry, which is highly competitive and is characterized by change, the role of good fortune cannot be easily discounted. The fashion industry is well known for the high failure rate of new businesses and the regular price reductions on product lines that have not sold. Such failures are in part a reflection of the enormous risk of fashion, but some are also due to the inadequate or inappropriate application of the marketing process. It is the contention of the authors that, when properly applied, marketing will help to reduce some uncertainty in the fashion industry and cut down the number of business failures.

1.3 What is fashion marketing?

Fashion marketing is the application of a range of techniques and a business philosophy that centres upon the customer and potential customer of clothing and related products and services in order to meet the long-term goals of the organization. It is a major argument of this book that fashion marketing is different from many other areas of marketing. The very nature of fashion, where change is intrinsic, gives different emphasis to marketing activities. Furthermore, the role of design in both leading and reflecting consumer demand results in a variety of approaches to fashion marketing which are explored below.

1.4 Fashion marketing in practice

Within the fashion industry there is enormous variation in the size and structure of businesses serving the needs of customers. From a small business comprising a self-employed knitwear designer to major multinational corporations such as Liz Claiborne or Zara, diversity remains a key feature. With legislative changes and expansion of the EU, the gradual removal of trade barriers on a global scale and the growth of the Internet, the fashion industry is increasingly a global business. This implies considerable variation in the cultural, social and economic perspective of the participants. The consequence of these variations in size, experience and perspective is that the practice of fashion marketing is not uniform at a national level, let alone at an international one.

At the centre of the debate over the role of fashion marketing within firms resides a tension between design and marketing imperatives. Relatively few fashion designers have had formal training in business or marketing, although fortunately this situation is changing in the EU. Similarly, the formal training of marketing personnel can often lack an appreciation of the role of design in business. Training has tended to be separate and this, when coupled with the differing approaches of the two areas, causes divergent views. Design students were traditionally taught to approach problems as though there were no constraints on time or cost so that creativity might flourish. The assumption of much of this training was that creativity flourishes when there is freedom from structural factors.

Spontaneity, eclecticism and the willingness to take risks in challenging the *status quo* are some values central to traditional design training.

Marketing training, by contrast, embraces different values. Marketers are taught to be systematic and analytical in approaching problems. The foundation of a lot of marketing involves the setting of objectives and quantifying inputs and outputs, such as advertising expenditure and market share. Success, marketing students are taught, comes from careful research and planning, not spontaneity or ignoring market realities such as competitor price levels. Owing to a lack of training, marketing personnel often fail to understand the aesthetic dimension of a design or many qualitative aspects of product development.

The above outlines concentrate on differences in perspective between marketing and design personnel but naturally there are areas where they share common values. Good designers and marketing personnel both recognize the need for thorough preparation and the exercise of professional skill, both understand the importance of communication, although with differing emphasis on the visual and process components, and both tend to be in agreement about the functional aspects of clothing, such as whether a garment is waterproof or machine washable.

Starkly put, the designer may see the marketing person as one who constrains freedom and imagination, while the marketer may see the designer as undisciplined and oblivious to costs and profitability. Such views are stereotypes fostered by differing experiences and training, and which are often held by those who do not understand the perspective of both the marketer and the designer. This difference in perspective engenders a range of views about what fashion marketing ought to be. Two views of fashion marketing are shown in Figure 1.2. These views can be labelled design centred and marketing centred, and are detailed below.

Sample statements	Fashion marketing is the same as promotion	Design should be based solely on marketing research
Assumption	Sell what we can make	Make what we can sell
Orientation	Design centred	Marketing centred
Alleged drawbacks	High failure rates Relies on intuition	Bland designs Stifles creativity

Figure 1.2 Two views of fashion marketing.

1.4.1 Design centred: fashion marketing as promotion

According to this view marketing is seen as synonymous with promotion. Adherents of the view state that designers are the real force, and marketers should merely help to sell ideas to the public. Translated into practice this view tends to have all marketing activity carried out by either public relations or advertising departments or agencies. Customers and potential customers are seen as people to be led or inspired by creative styling that is favourably promoted. At the extreme, it is rationalized that the only people who can appreciate creative styling, in a financial sense, are the more wealthy sections of society.

Research within such a perspective is limited to monitoring the activities of others who are thought to be at the forefront of creative change, i.e. film directors, musicians, artists, etc. Many great fashion designers subscribe to this view and have run successful businesses based upon the above assumptions. The principal weakness of this approach is that it depends ultimately on the skill and intuition of the designer in consistently meeting genuine customer needs and consequently earning profit.

1.4.2 Marketing centred: design as a research prescription

Here marketing is dominant and it regards the designer as someone who must respond to the specifications of customer requirements as established by marketing research. Detailed cost constraints may be imposed and sample garments pretested by, for example, retail selectors who may subsequently demand changes to meet their precise needs. Several major retail stores still operate systems not too far removed from this, with merchandisers and selectors exerting considerable control over the designer. The result, according to many, is a certain blandness in the design content of garments available from such retail outlets.

It is argued that marketing constraints have strangled the creative aspects of design. Taking profitability as a measure of popularity, this restrictive prescription for design seems to work for many firms. Whether popular acceptance of fashion designs equates with good design is another matter.

1.4.3 The fashion marketing concept

There is another way to view the relationship between marketing and design, and this is termed the fashion marketing concept. That good fashion design only requires sufficient promotion to succeed is a view

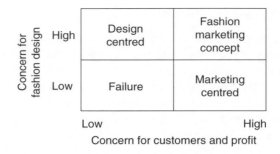

Figure 1.3   The fashion marketing concept.

applicable to a very limited number of businesses – usually those producing expensive garments for an elite market. The alternative view
of fashion design as a function of marketing research fails to recognize either that many people do not know what they will like until
presented with choices, or that their preferences change over time.
For example, many who profess to hate a design seen on the catwalk
may later come to like it when they try the garment themselves or
realize that others have signalled acceptance. Good fashion design
can challenge conventional views. It should be recognized that consumers vary in the conservatism they have towards fashion styles and
also the speed and readiness with which they change their opinions.

A simple model of the interrelationship of fashion design and marketing can be seen above.

In the matrix in Figure 1.3 it can be seen that low concern for
customers, profit and design leads to failure. This occurs as a consequence of overestimating design ability while disregarding customers' preferences and the need for profit.

The fashion marketing concept attempts to embrace the positive
aspects of high concern for design, customers and profit by recognizing the interdependence of marketing and design. If designers understand how marketing can enhance the creative process and marketing
personnel appreciate that within the fashion industry design can lead
as well as respond to customer requirements, progress can be made.
Market researchers can establish the sizing information customers
want on garments and can also analyse reactions to several provisional
illustrations, but they cannot produce detailed styling specifications.
Marketing as applied to the fashion industry must appreciate the
role of design. Some major retailers such as Zara have developed
information systems bringing designers, manufacturing teams and
retail sales staff much closer together enabling customers to be

offered fast fashion at affordable prices and achieving good levels of profit for the company.

This section has discussed a number of approaches to fashion marketing. Many companies have embraced the fashion marketing concept and have demonstrated equal concern for design, customers and profits. In recent years an increasing number of winners of major fashion awards have also achieved success not only in terms of design but also in terms of sales and profit. Thus the fashion marketing concept is not just a theoretical model, it does work in practice and this book sets out to develop it further.

1.5 How fashion marketing can help the fashion industry

The vast output and profits from the fashion industry come not from the designer collections seen on the catwalk but from items sold in high street stores. To put the impact of designers in perspective, one only has to note that the British Fashion Awards' Designer of the Year will often have annual earnings that amount to less than a day's sales for one large retailer in the Arcadia group. Even so, the designer collections are given extensive coverage in the fashion press where each season more than 250 collections are reviewed within a matter of weeks. Reporting and promotion of these collections are suffused within hyperbole, excitement and genuine enthusiasm by many who attend, the catwalk exhibitions being viewed with a range of perceptions from incredulity to sheer entertainment. However, few people see the direct link that some less experienced commentators assert exists between the garments on the catwalk and 'what we will all be wearing next season'. The influence of the designer collections on everyday apparel purchases is complex and will be considered in later chapters on the fashion consumer, product design and fashion promotion.

The main concern of fashion marketers is therefore the design and sale of garments to the majority of the public, for that reason, the techniques described in this book will concentrate on high street fashion rather than haute couture.

Many people in the fashion industry have aspirations to run their own business. Indeed, the industry is characterized by many small firms and regrettably many failures. This book embraces the fashion marketing needs of people starting their own business; it does not, however, extend to all the needs of small businesses, particularly the financial and legal aspects of new ventures. For the new entrepreneur the chapter on marketing research will provide a sound basis on which to start building a business plan. The marketing component of the business plan is covered in the last chapter of this book.

Medium and large businesses are also catered for. The need for co-operation and communication between the various levels of distribution in this sector is so important that manufacturer, wholesaler, importer and exporter will all benefit from understanding the structural aspects of the marketing of clothing and related products and services. Many of the principles and techniques described in detail as applicable to the UK are transferable to other markets. For example, UK mass media data are given in the chapter on fashion promotion, but criteria for designing campaigns and selecting media are also given; these criteria are readily transferable.

1.6 What fashion marketers do: five examples

To give an overview of the sort of activities that fashion marketing personnel engage in, five examples will be given. A key point to note is that job titles do not always accurately reflect what people do. In fact, few people are called fashion marketing managers, but many carry out functions that are fashion marketing, e.g. those with job titles such as selector, merchandiser, sales executive or public relations consultant.

1.6.1 Fashion marketing research

A fashion marketing researcher may investigate the market shares of competitors and trends in those shares. Through a group discussion with potential consumers they may discover that a possible brand name has negative connotations and needs rethinking.

1.6.2 Fashion product management

A design manager may be concerned with producing a range of shirts for a major retailer. The shirts must co-ordinate with other garments such as jackets, trousers and ties, all of which may be provided by other manufacturers. The design manager must collect and pass on information to ensure that designers are adequately briefed. Later the manager will be required to sell the designs at a presentation to the retailer, usually in the face of fierce competition. The design manager's knowledge of the retailer's customers and an awareness of his or her own company costs will enable an effective marketing function.

1.6.3 Fashion promotion

A manufacturer of corporate workwear may have produced a range of clothes suitable for staff working in small independent restaurants. After careful research and planning the manufacturer may decide that a brochure is needed as part of the promotional effort. The brief to be given to the person preparing visual and textual material for the brochure will include an estimate of the number of brochures needed and a list of addresses – essential fashion marketing tasks.

1.6.4 Fashion distribution

An owner of a retail outlet selling her own specially designed millinery wishes to expand. She needs to research a few options including franchising her business, obtaining concessions in selected department stores and linking with a leading womenswear designer to produce new complementary ranges each season. Marketing research and analysis of the status of the business along with the preparation of a future marketing strategy are the major fashion marketing activities needed here.

1.6.5 Fashion product positioning and pricing

A major retailer discovers that a competitor is selling imported silk lingerie similar in design and quality to its own, but at prices that are 20% lower. A fashion marketing decision must be made about the positioning and pricing of the product, taking into consideration the strategic goals of the company as well as the price sensitivity of its customers.

1.7 Ethical issues in fashion marketing

The practice of fashion marketing is often criticized. These criticisms can be classified into two types, the micro-issues and the macro-issues.

Micro-issues concern particular products and services where consumers may feel that they have not been fairly treated or that they have been misled. Most customers have bought clothing that has fallen below expectations by, for example, coming apart at the seams or shrinking in the wash. These problems may occur due to poor quality control or at worst a callous attitude towards customers. Sadly, the view of customers as mere punters to be exploited does exist in some parts of the fashion industry but it is a short-sighted attitude as lack of repeat business, legal redress and negative word of mouth are all possible consequences. Given the number of items of clothing bought each year, however, some errors are inevitable and the issue really revolves around how the seller deals with the complaint. According to the fashion marketing concept we should be concerned about long-term consumer welfare as this is the key to building and retaining profitable custom.

The quick and fair correction of genuine errors reinforces the message to the customer that the retailer cares about long-term customer welfare. Unfortunately, some staff are placed in positions where their own interests may not coincide with those of the firm or the customer – those who work on a commission only basis, for example. Such practices should be condemned as they lead to an undermining of public confidence in the fashion industry.

Macro-issues are broader and emerge not from the conscious conspiracy of individuals or groups of individuals but as unintended or unanticipated consequences of certain activities.

The most obvious example is the criticism that the bulk of the fashion industry is lacking in sensitivity to environmental issues in that it encourages a throw-away society, conspicuous consumption and unnecessary use of packaging. Marks and Spencer plc can lay claim to a serious attempt to address some environmental concerns with their 'Plan A'. The Marks and Spencer 'Plan A because there is no Plan B' involves a £200 million eco-plan to become carbon neutral by 2012, to extend their sustainable fabric sourcing and to set new standards in ethical trading. Other attempts to address such concerns, although on a relatively small scale, include the so-called 'environmentally friendly' or 'green' fibres and recycled wool.

However, the charge of encouraging a throw-away society is a problem that is likely to recur with sharper and move vehement focus in the future. The public response to the various anti-fur campaigns run by PETA, Lynx and others since the 1980s has reduced the market for fur products in many countries and has transformed a status symbol of the rich to an item of derision. 'Green' issues in fashion marketing are examined further in Chapter Two.

Another example of a macro-issue is the use of particular models to show garments in advertising material or on the catwalk. Critics allege that this can cause damage ranging from supporting an image of women as mere sex objects to acting as a contributory factor in dietary problems of adolescent females. The over-representation of young, tall and slim female models raises many issues, not least of which is the sensitivity of some promoters to the responses of the audience. The Madrid Fashion Week has banned models with a body mass index (BMI) of below 18.5; this is a BMI that is regarded as unhealthy by the World Health Organization. The use of wider ranges of body shapes and sizes has been effectively used by Dove in their campaign for real beauty. The non-response or excuse of 'We have to do it, because everyone else does it' from some fashion companies may reveal an unwillingness to research other less potentially harmful ways of promotion. In an industry with an abundance of creative talent, it is surprising to find such pockets of conservatism.

1.8 An overview of the fashion marketing process

Fashion marketing can be viewed as a process and Figure 1.4 illustrates that process. It also gives an indication of the structure of this book and how various parts link together.

All firms operate within a wider commercial environment that influences their activities. Changes in value added tax may inhibit demand for certain garments whereas a fall in unemployment may stimulate demand for workwear. These two simple examples illustrate how changes in the marketing environment can have significant effects on the operation of fashion firms. The marketing environment and how to analyse it are covered in Chapter Two.

Central to the concept of fashion marketing is the role of the customer and Chapters Three and Four deal with understanding and researching the fashion purchaser. In Chapter Three the behaviour of consumers will be discussed. In particular, there will be an examination of the reasons why people buy particular garments: what influences them and what criteria they use. Clothing may be an expression of how people wish others to see them, it may denote membership

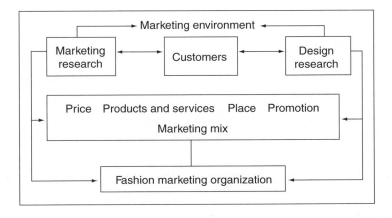

Figure 1.4 The fashion marketing process.

of a certain group or represent a particular lifestyle. To understand customers' aspirations and expectations about clothing fully, relevant psychological and sociological factors are examined in Chapter Three.

Chapter Four takes the understanding of customers' behaviour one step further by looking at how data concerning this behaviour are obtained, namely marketing research. This research can also involve the study of competitors and analysis of the company's own marketing efforts.

In Figure 1.4 the term marketing mix is used to describe the combination of variables used by the fashion marketer to meet the needs of specific groups of customers known as target markets. The selection of target markets and the management of the marketing mix are discussed in Chapters Five to Ten of this book.

Here is an example of how a variable may be adjusted using an example concerning price. A firm may decide to charge low prices and sell large quantities making a small profit on each item, but a large profit in total. A consequence of charging low prices may be that certain outlets are selected because their image is compatible with low prices. The concept of the marketing mix and target marketing are dealt with in Chapter Five. The actual components of the marketing mix are known for the sake of simplicity as the four Ps, i.e. Price, Product, Place and Promotion, and these are covered in Chapters Six to Nine. The role of design research, integral to product design and development, is covered in Chapter Six.

Putting all aspects of the marketing mix together to achieve the goals of the organization is the most important marketing task. Activities must be planned, co-ordinated and implemented effectively, and the results monitored. The final chapter deals with fashion marketing planning.

1.9 Summary

This chapter has introduced and defined fashion and marketing, and how fashion marketing:

- ◆ emphasizes the importance of design;
- ◆ aims to meet customers' needs;
- ◆ helps to achieve corporate goals.

There followed an examination of the practical side of fashion marketing:

- ◆ how fashion marketers work;
- ◆ the ethical issues.

The chapter concluded by:

* examining the business environment, and the place of fashion marketing within it;
* introducing the ideas of marketing research and consumer behaviour;
* outlining the concepts of target marketing and the fashion marketing mix.

Further reading

Baker, M.J. (2007), *Marketing Management and Strategy*, 4th Revised Edition, Palgrave MacMillan, Basingstoke.

Barthes, R. (2006), *The Language of Fashion*, Berg Limited, New York.

Brassington, F. and Pettitt, S. (2006), *Principles of Marketing*, 4th Edition, Financial Times/Prentice Hall, London.

Costantino, M. (1998), *Fashion Files: Marketing and PR*, Batsford, London.

Davis, F. (1994), *Fashion, Culture and Identity*, University of Chicago Press, Chicago, IL.

Hines, T. and Bruce, M. (2006), *Fashion Marketing: Contemporary Issues*, 2nd Edition, Butterworth-Heinemann, Oxford.

Jones, R. (2006), *The Apparel Industry*, 2nd Revised Edition, Blackwell Publishing, Oxford.

McDowell, C. (2003), *Fashion Today*, Phaidon Press, Oxford.

Tomlinson, A. (1990), *Consumption Identity and Style: Marketing Meanings and the Packaging of Pleasure*, Routledge, London.

Tungate, M. (2005), *Fashion Brands: Branding Style from Armani to Zara*, Kogan Page Ltd, London.

Chapter Two
The Fashion Market and the Marketing Environment

2.1 Introduction

A market is a place for buying and selling, for exchanging goods and services, usually for money. The fashion market is unusual because until early in the twentieth century it was almost solely the domain of kings, queens, aristocrats and other important people. As will be seen, great changes, mainly due to technology and increasing globalization, mean that we now have a fashion marketplace open to everyone.

Fashion can be a reflection of the time, from the utilitarian clothing of the war years to the yuppie look of the buoyant 1980s. Fashion also can be a reflection of individuals. Clothes are often chosen to reflect among other factors our age, gender, lifestyle and personality.

Because fashion is both a reflective and yet creative discipline, it is necessary for fashion marketers to be aware of the factors surrounding the market and develop a broad understanding of the issues that can affect the garments that are seen in any high street store.

2.2 The development of the fashion market

2.2.1 Origins of the modern fashion market

Until relatively recently, fashion had always been élitist and was used by its adopters to show that they were above the common people. Even the inventions of the eighteenth and nineteenth centuries; the spinning jenny, the water frame and the sewing machine have not had as great an effect on the market as have cultural changes and the explosion of the media during the twentieth century.

The end of World War I, in 1918, really marked the start of mass fashion. Style began to be influenced by the fashion designers of Paris, Milan, New York and London. In the 1930s film personalities and later pop stars all played their part in spreading or even starting fashion trends.

Some fashion styles are more easily explained than others. World War II forced hemlines up because of a shortage of material. In the 1950s newer freer styles made corsets less and less necessary. However, other fashions are less easily explained and are regarded by some as merely a whim or the market just looking for a change.

Technology played its part in advancing mass production methods, so that from the 1930s onwards ordinary people could buy copies of designer fashions from high street stores within weeks of the big fashion shows.

The media started to become an important influence in the late 1970s. People became more selective in what suited them, and magazines and books advised them on creating their own style. Designers could no longer dictate the styles as they had up to the 1960s. 'Street fashion' styles, developed by young people themselves in towns and cities, also affected designer clothes.

London was at the forefront of the fashion scene in the 1960s and early 1970s. Mary Quant was in her heyday and her clothing was famous the world over. It was the time of Carnaby Street, and Biba made famous by Barbara Hulanicki.

The influence of royalty on fashion made a comeback with the Princess of Wales in the 1980s as many women copied the lace and ruffles which she wore.

While not the first to introduce lifestyle segmentation to the market, George Davies, then chief executive of the Next chain, is undoubtedly the best known. His retailing phenomenon, targeting a particular age and lifestyle group, exploded onto the marketplace and had many other high street retailers following suit.

Changes towards a healthier lifestyle advocated by the medical profession and the increase in leisure time have encouraged people to take up more sport, particularly jogging and aerobics. Membership of health clubs and gyms has increased in recent years. So the clothing from this and other activities has moved into everyday wear.

The future for the fashion industry is mapped out, perhaps more than at any time in its history. Influences from the demographic structure, concern for the environment and further adoption of new technologies are all inevitable. These factors could stifle designers if they are not careful or could offer them greater challenges than any they have had to face so far.

2.2.2 Recent developments in the fashion market

Consumer demand for clothing is now more fragmented and discerning. Retailers are wary of carrying high levels of stock, major demographic changes are occurring, and many different styles and fabrics are available. These have all resulted in the mass market for clothing being fragmented and are eroding the advantages of long-run manufacture.

Previously the UK textile industry had a reputation for being dictatorial and short on choice. This was blamed on the nature of the relationship between retailers and manufacturers. Clothing retailing was dominated by a few large groups who exercised enormous power in the wholesale market for garments and fabrics. Retailers emphasized basic garments with very little fashion content, and Marks and Spencer in particular set very detailed specifications for fabrics, making-up and quality. Manufacturers such as Courtaulds and Carrington Viyella geared their production to large volumes of basic fabrics for a few major customers. It became uneconomic to deal with orders that either were small or required much design detail. Competition among retail chains was over the price and quality of garments.

Since then the market share of the multiple retailers (such as Bhs, Debenhams and Marks and Spencer) has been affected firstly by the emergence of smaller specialist chains (Benetton, Next) then grocery supermarkets ('George' at Asda and Tesco). Mintel 2005 estimates that 'George' sales in 2004 (excluding VAT) were £1.07 billion and that non-specialist retailers of this type enjoyed an increase in sales of 13% from 2003 to 2004, with this rising trend continuing. Further European retailers (Zara, H&M) have also gained market share in the UK by importing low-cost garments. To avoid competing with the abundance of low-cost imports, the big retailers have responded by increasing the speed with which they introduce fashion and style changes. This, in turn, has forced suppliers to manufacture shorter runs of garments with higher design and fashion content. In some parts of the market there has been a distinct shift in retail competition away from an emphasis on garment price to non-price factors, such as design, quality and fashion. However, this non-price competition has had only a limited success with even Marks and Spencer and its strong 'British Made' slogan, turning to importing more cheaply from overseas. Value retailers such as Matalan, Primark and TK Maxx, who have attracted the more price conscious shopper, have enjoyed considerable success in other sectors of the market (Table 2.1).

Table 2.1 UK trade in clothing (£ million), 2001–2005

	2001	2002	2003	2004	2005
Imports	9160	9806	10341	10884	11543
Exports	2592	2506	2713	2729	2679
Balance of trade	−6568	−7300	−7628	−8155	−8864
% change year on year		11.1	4.5	6.9	8.9

Source: HM Customs and Excise. © Crown copyright material is reproduced with the permission of the Controller of HMSO (and the Queen's Printer for Scotland).

2.3 The fashion market: size and structure

2.3.1 Structure of the fashion market

Apart from technology, another reason why fashion is now available to the masses is that there are several levels at which fashion clothing functions, as shown in Figure 2.1:

Figure 2.1 Levels of fashion.

◆ Haute couture houses are the major fashion houses of the world, run by recognized, internationally famous designers. They show their collections at least twice a year and sell individual garments for thousands of pounds. For many designers the catwalk shows are essentially a publicity exercise for the many goods that are sold under their name such as perfume and accessories.

◆ Designer wear is shown at pret à porter. The move into ready-to-wear clothing by designers meant that they could offer their stylish designs and high quality to a wider audience. The garments are still highly priced, although in hundreds of pounds sterling rather than thousands. They are to be found in the designers' shops, independent stores and some of the more exclusive department stores. Designs are not unique, but are still produced in limited numbers and, although some garments are produced abroad, there is very strict quality control.

◆ Mass market or street fashion is the market area in which most people buy their clothes. New fashions can be in the high street stores extremely quickly and what the customers lose in exclusivity they can make up for in value for money. This is one area of the market that is undergoing many changes and this chapter will look at how it is being affected.

This three-tier view of the market is perhaps oversimplistic as there are many strata and price levels between the ones mentioned. Many customers do not stick to any one level when buying their clothes.

The more affluent will buy several haute couture outfits but turn to designer wear for every day. Women who mostly buy designer ready-to-wear may occasionally splash out on a couture dress for a very special occasion. Those who generally only buy mass market clothing may still buy designer wear occasionally, if only from the discounted rail. In the early twenty-first century celebrity fashion icons have moved to mixing their outfits with some designer pieces and some from high street stores. At times it is difficult to identify the origin of our clothing and to decide who has the power in the marketplace. Is it the fibre and fabric industry that, after all, make the cloth for the garments? Is it the designers? Or perhaps the retailers are the power base in the market? Ultimately it should be the customer, but traditionally the fashion market has been one where the customer was dictated to and so merely followed along almost blindly.

The fashion flow chart in Figure 2.2 illustrates the flow of goods between the various participants in the marketplace. Later it will be seen that there is even more choice in deciding where the goods will be manufactured (see Section 2.5.2).

2.3.2 Size of the fashion market

All three levels of the market have shown some growth in domestic clothing demand in recent years. Growth of the total UK market for

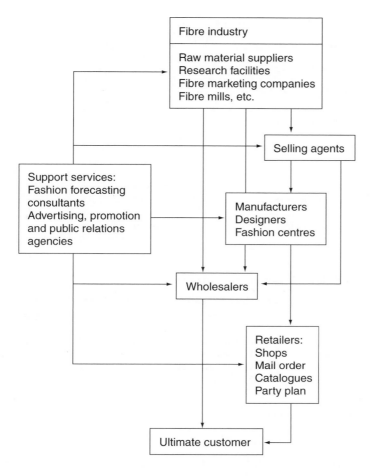

Figure 2.2 Fashion flow chart.

clothing has grown by over 16% from 1994 to 2004 and retail sales for 2006 are predicted to be nearly 50 billion (Table 2.2).

UK imports now greatly exceed exports, having increased from £9.1 billion to £11.5 billion from 2001 to 2005 with the main traders being Hong Kong, China and Turkey (see Table 2.1). UK exports have remained steady at about £2.5 billion per annum over the same period with about 73% of this output going to other European countries. As less UK manufactured clothes are sold in the home market the proportion of goods being exported is actually increasing. The figures become more complex as UK manufacturers are developing their own production facilities overseas to take advantage of lower wages and production costs (Table 2.3).

Table 2.2 Some major developments in fashion

Pre-nineteenth century	Fashions only for the rich and powerful
1918 onwards	Start of mass fashion
1930s	Film personalities influencing popular clothing
1939–1945	World War II – raised hemlines
1950s and 1960s	Freer styles, fewer control garments
1970s to 1990s	Growth of multi-nationals and mass media influence
1990s	Increase in branded and designer label goods
2000 onwards	Growth of electronic shopping
2002 onwards	Increasing influx of cheap foreign manufactured clothing

Table 2.3 Consumer spending on clothes

	Consumer Expenditure at Current Prices in £ Million					
	2000	**2001**	**2002**	**2003**	**2004**	**2005**
Clothing	31048	32103	33927	35689	37112	38067
Footwear	4431	4719	5165	5466	5680	5661
Total	35479	36822	39092	41155	42792	43728
% change on year	+6.3	+3.8	+6.2	+5.3	+4.0	+2.2

Source: Consumption, The Blue Book 2006.

2.3.3 Employment in the fashion sector

Employment in the manufacturing of clothing textiles and leather production in the UK has now fallen to rank 24th out of the 25 categories of manufacturing industry recorded by the Government. Two main factors have reduced the numbers employed in the sector in recent years to only 132000 in 2006 (Table 2.4). New technologies have reduced the need for many workers, particularly in the more skilled areas of pattern cutting as much of this can be computerized. The computer systems still need to be manned by a skilled workforce, but retraining has to be done and still there will be redundancies.

The far more important factor has been the stiff level of cheap competition from abroad. With an inability to raise prices in the face of a depressed domestic market and crippled by large debts, many firms have had to make savage cuts in their labour force and investment plans as the alternative to going out of business. In the late 1990s many major UK clothing manufacturers suffered as their customers

Table 2.4 Recent decline in employment figures in textile clothing and footwear industries (in '000s, in June each year)

1998	1999	2000	2001	2002	2003	2004	2005	2006
331	304	273	230	205	169	149	136	132

Source: ONS.

Table 2.5 Production output indices of total manufacturing industries and textiles, leather and clothing industries in the UK (index 2002 = 100, 2001, 2005)

	2001	2002	2003	2004	2005
Total manufacturing industries	103.2	100.0	100.1	101.9	101.3
Textiles, leather and clothing	108.1	100.0	98.1	87.0	83.2

Source: Monthly Digest of Statistics.

Table 2.6 Production of textile and textile products in UK, 2000–2006 (index 2003 = 100)

2000	2001	2002	2003	2004	2005	2006
122.4	107.2	99.7	100	98.1	90	89

Source: ONS.

chose to source garments from cheaper overseas suppliers. The UK clothing industry is made up of small, medium and large manufacturers. The smaller manufacturers feed off the larger companies by offering specialist finishing services. As the larger retailers turn to overseas manufacturing or supplying, so the vulnerable smaller companies suffer. Table 2.5 shows the fortunes of the fashion industry in the context of the decline in manufacturing (Table 2.6).

2.3.4 The current role of London in the fashion business

Fashion centres of the world have always included London, even before the era of Carnaby Street and Mary Quant, but recently designers have been choosing not to show in London. Now that London Fashion Week no longer has the financial backing of the French Chambre Syndicale (the French organization that decides which fashion houses may join the ranks of the haute couturiers), the number of exhibitions has declined. With it no longer being a requirement to show in London, designers have taken the opportunity to save the expense of showing at yet another fashion week, instead concentrating on the ones which they feel will be most prestigious and best covered by the media.

This shift away from London is of concern to the industry, particularly for the knock-on effect that it will have on everything from employment to tourism. Cities which are taking a more prominent role in the fashion year are New York, Tokyo and, new to the list, Shanghai.

2.3.5 The British High Street

In contrast to Italy and most of the rest of Europe, UK has a much more consolidated market sector with only a few players as the big earners. Mintel (2005) stated that the top five UK retailers account for almost 45% of sales. The leading players by turnover being Marks and Spencer, Next, Arcadia Group (comprising Top Shop, Etam, Wallis, Dorothy Perkins, Burton, Miss Selfridge, Outfit and Evans), Matalan and Bhs. This dominance of the big players makes it hard for independent stores to get a foothold into the marketplace. It is hard to compete on price when dealing with high rents and cheap imported clothes.

2.4 Marketing environment

Fashion is ultimately about change. Every season there are new fashions that lead to obsolescence of last year's clothes. Many of these changes are brought about by designers trying to create something new to satisfy customers, but others are because of influences beyond the control of designers or manufacturers. These are all gathered together in what is called the marketing environment, as shown in Figure 2.3. Some changes occur very slowly while others can affect the market much more quickly; some are within a company's control and others are way beyond it.

2.5 Micro-marketing environment

Factors which ideally are within companies' control are to a greater or lesser extent their suppliers, marketing intermediaries (which help to get the goods from the factory to the consumer) and the consumers themselves. For customers the providers of fashion may seem to have a variety of sources, for instance the designer who has the idea for

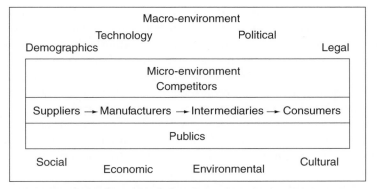

Adapted from Kotler, P. (1994), *Marketing Management*, 8th edn.,
Prentice Hall International, New Jersey.

Figure 2.3 The marketing environment. Adapted from Kotler, P. (1994), *Marketing Management*, 8th Edition, Prentice Hall International, NJ.

the style, the manufacturer who makes up the garment or the retailer to whom the consumer goes to buy the garment.

2.5.1 Designers

While Paris is often thought of as the fashion capital of the world in fact there are five main cities supplying designs and new ideas to the international market.

Paris is historically seen as the fashion capital and has the edge on many other cities as its fashion industry is taken very seriously by government and citizens alike. The haute couture designers are protected by the French Chambre Syndicale, which has strict codes of practice for any designer wishing to style him- or herself as an haute couture house. The main French designers are Yves St Laurent, Chanel (now run by Karl Lagerfeld), Christian Dior, Pierre Cardin, Jean Paul Gaultier, Sonia Rykiel and Christian Lacroix. The British are also making an impact in France, with Julian MacDonald and John Galliano securing senior designing roles in French fashion houses.

Milan is the other fashion capital of Europe, and Italians have always taken fashion very seriously. There are probably fewer well-known designers, such as Giorgio Armani, Franco Moschino, Muicca Prada, Emanuel Ungaro and Versace, now headed by Donatella, sister to the founder Gianni who was tragically murdered in 1997, but Italy is a country whose people and retail set-up, with many more independent stores, is a successful environment for young designers.

London is no longer the focal point of fashion that it once was, though it still produces many internationally influential designers. Many are quite small fish by international standards but others have their designs bought by the rich and famous from all over the world. Although London is no longer a major centre, the UK clothing industry is still significant and exports are actually growing in contrast to internal sales. The city also retains many successful designers such as Bruce Oldfield, Jasper Conran, Matthew Williamson, Alexander McQueen, Dame Vivienne Westwood, Paul Smith, Katharine Hamnett, Joseph Ettedgui, Rifat Ozbek, Amanda Wakely, Betty Jackson and Caroline Charles.

In America the major centre is New York. To a considerable extent American fashions are confined to the home market, although all the big names are known and bought internationally. American designers include Ralph Lauren, Calvin Klein, Oscar de la Renta, Marc Jacobs, Vera Wang and Donna Karan.

Tokyo, the centre of the Japanese clothing market, has a reputation for a distinct style and for almost a lack of colour. There has been considerable growth in recent years at the top end of the Japanese clothing market by designers, especially since 1981 when Comme des Garçons and Yamamoto took Paris by storm. This is a fashion city that is destined to continue to grow with such designers as Yohji Yamamoto, Comme des Garçons (Miss Rei Kawakubo), Issey Miyake, Junya Wantanabe and Kenzo.

The Middle East is now considered the sixth fashion terminus of the world, not because any designs come from here but because it is where the submerged 11% of the fashion industry goes. Much clothing is bought by women either within or while on holiday from such places as Dubai, the United Arab Emirates, Kuwait, Bahrain and Saudi Arabia.

The overall market pattern now is that designers either make for themselves or subcontract to British or overseas manufacturers. Likewise retailers have their own designers and make them up in their own factories, subcontract their own designs to home or overseas manufacturers, or buy garments designed and made up by other companies.

2.5.2 International sourcing

The UK clothing industry is being squeezed further between the highly price-sensitive volume market which gets its supplies from low-wage economies and the quality end of the market which is increasingly supplied from Europe. The level of imports to the UK from the relatively high-cost producers on the continent has finally succumbed to pressure from other parts of the world and is decreasing.

Supplies come from three main sources:

1. UK, Europe and just beyond (Germany, France, Italy, Portugal, Eire, Turkey and more recently Romania) making up about 20% of UK clothing imports. Italy has traditionally been the major player here with Germany and France in close second place.
2. The Far East (Hong Kong, China, South Korea, Thailand, Taiwan, Malaysia, Indonesia and Mauritius). The two major players here are Hong Kong and China. They contribute, almost equally, to the 30% of clothing entering the UK from the Far East.
3. Asia (India, Bangladesh and Sri Lanka). These main three players contribute to more than 12% of UK clothing and accessory imports. Predictions that the reduction of quotas for Chinese goods would have a negative impact on these countries do not seem to have held true so far.

The greatest increase in supply has come from China and this is only expected to increase further now that quotas have been all but dropped to the UK and most of the rest of the world. However this does not seem to have affected UK exports suggesting there are different ranges of products being trade such as knitwear, rainwear and high-quality tailored items.

Imports from eastern European countries such as Romania have been seen to rise, as they have benefited from preferential access by the European Union (EU) in order to aid their economic restructuring prior to the abandonment of Multi-Fibre Agreement (MFA) quotas.

The days when Marks and Spencer used to boast that its garments were almost all produced in the UK, have long gone and they have suffered from criticism by some of the groups discussed later in Section 2.5.9.

2.5.3 Manufacturers

In the late 1990s and early 2000s a gloomy picture was painted as a result of the move towards global sourcing. Several larger clothing companies such as J. Baird Ltd closed factories and others such as Dewhurst in the north-east of England who relied on a few major customers such as Marks and Spencer have suffered from this loss of business.

There has been a reduction in the clothing manufacturing industry in the UK and many foreign companies have changed from both designing and manufacturing to one of merely cut, make and trim (CMT) for other people's designs. Other parts of this chapter look at the way forward for the UK manufacturing industry. There is undoubtedly a role that it can play in the international sourcing market if it exploits the strengths of flexibility and quality and moves away from competing on price alone. It is in these areas that the UK is still exporting its fashions, although Table 2.5 illustrates the changing fortunes in the import and export of clothing. Clothing manufacturers have had to improve their manufacturing methods. There has been severe cost cutting in some areas coupled with an increased emphasis on good design in other areas.

2.5.4 Marketing intermediaries

These are the main channels that help to get the goods from the manufacturer to the consumer. A detailed consideration of marketing intermediaries is given in Chapter Eight. Their roles can be many and varied. The main ones are:

- retailers,
- agents,
- distributors,
- wholesalers,
- advertising agencies,
- market research agencies.

The intermediary having the greatest influence on the clothing market is the retailer group. British clothes retailing is unique in that 70% of garment sales come from only 17 retail chains. The larger chains have taken an increasing share of the growing clothing market at the expense of the smaller firms. In 2004 the Arcadia group (formerly Burton), which included Dorothy Perkins, Top Shop, Top Man, Miss Selfridge, Wallis, Evans, Burtons and Outfit, had sales, estimated by Mintel, of £1527 million from their clothing outlets numbering more than 2000. Supermarkets have had an increase in the share of the clothing market; however, the largest market share still goes to Marks and Spencer despite the company's recent difficulties from which 2006 seemed to be a turning point. In Italy, by comparison, 95% of clothes are sold by single shops.

On the whole, competition, particularly on price, has intensified since the 1990s. Customers are increasingly looking for value for money; but are not totally driven by price; they also want good design, comfort and quality.

Companies have had to rationalize and restructure to combat increasing competition, cheaper imports and changing customer expectations. In consequence, many womenswear multiples have been forced to segment markets more effectively, making their customers much more aware of the markets that are being catered for. This has led and will increasingly lead to a narrowing of product ranges.

Retailers always need to be aware of how demographic factors can affect their core 15- to 29-year-old customer and adjust their offering accordingly. Demographic changes often force retailers to reposition themselves in the marketplace as was seen a few years ago when Top Shop, suffering from a reduction in the number of 15–20 year olds, decided to increase the age of their target customer upward. Targeting certain groups in terms of age and, often as important, lifestyle will become ever more crucial. Research into market trends and close co-operation with chosen target groups can help retailers. As the 'middle youth' market of women in their forties continue their youthful interest in fashion, there are opportunities for some retailers to try to keep customers loyal for longer. Others, such as H&M, have professed concern that the presence of too wide a target market in their stores could alienate their core younger customers.

2.5.5 Fashion predictors

For the consumer it must be quite baffling to understand how each year designers, manufacturers and retailers all seem to know what styles and colours will be in fashion. The reality is that since the 1970s there have been companies who specialize in fashion prediction and act as consultants to interested parties in the fashion world.

Companies such as the Paris-based organizations Peclers and Promostyl, France, and London-based Worth Global Style Network (WGSN) sell their predictions on styles, colour and the market for the coming season or even further in advance for up to 18 months. There are at least 10 main organizations of this type in the world, although some specialize in specific markets such as childrenswear. Their predictions are not all identical, although there are usually many similarities between them.

These predictions help manufacturers and retail buyers alike to make and stock the fashions; styles and colours that will be 'the fashion' for a coming season. However, at the end of the day the final decision rests with the customer in deciding whether to buy or not.

2.5.6 Consumers

Once fashion was dictated to consumers and there was little choice but to accept what was on offer. The tables are beginning to turn and the consumer has more power to accept or reject fashions. Recognizing this, clothing producers are researching the market more to see what will be acceptable before filling the stores with goods that just end up being discounted at sale time.

Consumers of all descriptions are more fashion educated and consequently more fashion conscious. They are demanding products that are designed to perform in special ways. Most want to express their personalities through their appearance and therefore their choice of clothing. The increasing numbers of working women want garments designed for their particular needs. They understand fashion cycles and they know when a style has become tired. Manufacturers must constantly research and develop new fibres, fabrics and uses for these to keep up with the consumer's higher level of ability to select from the vast choices on offer.

However, there are other changes in the marketplace affecting consumers' attitudes, values and priorities. They are suffering some degree of fashion fatigue. For some the desire to acquire is more muted and rather than spending their income on fashion clothing they prefer to choose from a much wider range of products, services and leisure pursuits.

In the past, fashion styles, types of garments and advertising were all deeply influenced and directed by the interests and needs of the young consumer. Now that the increasing numbers of older consumers are becoming a market to be reckoned with, things must change or opportunities will be lost. The trend is towards people dressing more to please themselves. They won't be dictated to. People are more self-reliant and cautious and careful for their individuality. They are putting more emphasis on self. Recognition of the new fashion consumer may mean that the fashion models of today will have the opportunity of a longer career than they first imagined. Elle McPherson's modelling career saw no sign of ending as she entered her forties and Twiggy who started her modelling career in the 1960s is still popular, with the turn around of Marks and Spencer being largely attributed to using her in their advertising. To a small degree the shape of the fashion model is showing signs of change with more magazines producing features using size 16+ models. This trend probably started with the then somewhat voluptuous Sophie Dahl being heavily featured in fashion magazines and on posters, although now at a size 10 she has ditched the trend herself.

2.5.7 Competition within the fashion market

Consumers today are presented with a bewildering array of choice, yet it is probably in the clothing market more than any other that the consumer complains that he or she cannot find what they want. The clothing producers and retailers are working hard to correct this, but increasing competition and very small margins have made many firms wary of too much investment and experimentation. The high street stores have had to work much harder at tempting consumers and at times it seemed as if price cuts were their only weapon.

However, much of the major competition happens at the sourcing of goods rather than in the stores, as summarized in Figure 2.4. It

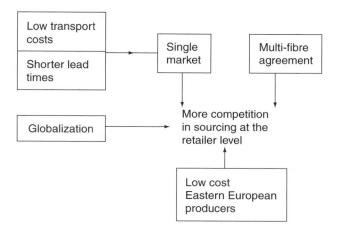

Figure 2.4 Competitive forces in fashion sourcing.

has been mentioned that globalization and sourcing from wherever cheapest is increasingly becoming the trend, particularly among European competitors. This is enabling them to keep overall costs down, while offering merchandise of good design and quality.

Since the opening of the single European market, competition from continental clothing producers has increased further, partly because of lower transport costs and shorter lead times. With a single MFA quota for the EU, the highly concentrated and accessible British clothing market has become even more of a target than it was previously.

There are also concerns about increased low-cost competition from some eastern European countries whose pleas for special treatment of their exports to the EU are showing sings of success. Now that Poland, Hungary and the Czech Republic have joined the EU, they too have gained free access to this vital market as will Turkey which is a candidate country. The clothing industries in these countries, in conjunction with EU companies, have undergone major restructuring and re-equipping. This has enabled them to present some formidable competition.

2.5.8 Direct and indirect competition for fashion products

Marketers have to realize that with increased choice consumers have many different ways to spend their money. In the western world people rarely need to buy clothes out of pure necessity. A woman does not merely choose between one dress and another; she also may choose between a new dress or hiring one, or making one or even to spend her money on something completely different like a handbag or entertainment. A man may choose between one jacket and another, or he may choose between a jacket and some new golf clubs.

When consumers have to choose between similar goods such as one shirt or another, the garments, stores or manufacturers can be described as being in direct competition. However, when the goods are different, but perhaps fulfil similar needs, like the woman choosing between buying and hiring a dress, then the stores and manufacturers are deemed to be in indirect competition.

2.5.9 Publics

There are many groups of publics that can affect a company's success, notably the financial institutions, unions and pressure groups to name but a few. The concept of fashion marketing publics is developed further in Chapter Eight within the context of fashion promotion.

Perhaps one of the most powerful groups to affect the fashion market is the media. A report in the fashion press after a designer shows a collection can have disastrous results. It is for this reason that some fashion editors have been criticized for having too much power and influence on the market. Whether true or not, much time and effort is spent between fashion editor and designer to try to maintain good relations between the two. It is hoped that this courting may result in a favourable article at a critical time.

While many national newspapers have strong fashion pages, the two most recognized fashion magazines in the UK are *Vogue* and *Elle*. Both are seen as essential reading for the woman or man who wants to know the important people and events in the fashion world. Powerful as these magazines are, neither has the overwhelming importance of the 92-year-old publication and premier daily newspaper for the women's fashion and retail industry in the USA as Women's Wear Daily, whose editor John Fairchild has long been regarded as a fashion guru.

Another force which seems to be having an impact is the pressure groups, concerned with the use of cheap labour and unethical practices. Anti-sweatshop campaign groups, in particular Labour Behind the Label, No Sweat and Tearfund have criticized manufactures whose production practices are deemed unethical. Their concerns have been taken up by the media and many retailers are now taking a much closer interest into the conditions under which their garments are being made.

2.6 Macro-marketing environment

Factors considered within the macro-environment affect not only the company, but all the other members of its micro-environment, namely

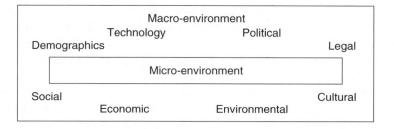

Figure 2.5 The macro-environment.

its suppliers, consumers, etc. These generally have a much wider influence and their effects become apparent more slowly than factors within the company. Factors within the macro-environment are cultural and social, political and legal, demographic, technological and environmental (Figure 2.5).

The inter-relationship of macro-environmental factors is most easily discerned in matters of world tension. Political, legal, social and economic matters become entwined to exert a great impact upon general levels of consumption. Consumer confidence was thought to have been dented by the Gulf War in 1991, which, although now over, has influenced consumer thinking. The war and terrorist activities in London have also affected the market as tourists stayed away for fear of terrorist action, which has particularly influenced more upmarket brands and retailers such as Jaeger and Austin Reed.

2.6.1 Political and legal

Politics and law might seem a world away from fashion but both can have extensive consequences for manufacturers. With such globalized sourcing of suppliers, world political events can aid or hamper the acquisition of supplies. A new legal requirement, be it in the product or the methods of manufacture, can have a make or break effect for some companies.

The General Agreement on Tariffs and Trade and the Multi-Fibre Agreement

The Arrangement Regarding International Trade in Textile, popularly known as the MFA, is an international agreement that regulated imports of textile and clothing products into western industrialized countries from low cost, mainly developing countries. Operating under the auspices of the General Agreement on Tariffs and Trade (GATT), the MFA currently has 43 signatories, the EU counting as one. Until January 2005, under the system most imports of textiles and clothing into developed countries were subject to detailed quantitative ceilings, implemented through a combination of import and export licences. The MFA was therefore unique in international regulation of trade in industrial products in that it was a formal departure from the free trade principles of GATT. Especially as there is no regulation on exports from industrialized countries to low-cost producers and there are no regulations between the EU and USA.

Originally signed in 1973, the MFA has been renewed on several occasions, most recently in 1994 in Uruguay where an agreement was made to phase out the quotas over a 10-year period which ended on 1 January 2005. This regulated, gradual dismantling of three decades of protection for western textile and clothing industries has had a huge impact on the UK clothing market, probably even more so than for some of its other EU partner's countries for whom imports from developing countries as well as exports to them would grow. However during 2005 imports from China quickly grew by more than 100% for many items and so the EU set up its own quotas to control the influx of Chinese clothing and footwear. In a hurry to beat the deadline for new quotas, Chinese manufacturers speeded up imports and quickly exceeded their full years' quota. Consequently 75 million items of Chinese manufactured clothing were held in European ports until a resolution for their release was reached in August 2005. Whilst, many of the items were school uniform required by retailers for sales prior to the autumn school term, there was also a large amount of underwear leading to the dispute being called the 'Bra Wars'. These new agreed quotas will last until 2007.

Legal aspects: children's nightwear and other safety considerations

All children's nightdresses and dressing gowns, including threads and trimmings, have to comply with British Standard BS 5722. Those which do not must be labelled 'keep away from fire'. While manufacturers had two years to comply completely with this standard, some were still taken unawares.

Hoods on children's coats and jackets can no longer be drawn by a cord for fear of strangulation or being caught in something such as a fairground roundabout, which could result in the child being dragged along by the cord.

Minimum wage

The introduction of the minimum wage in 1995 undoubtedly affected UK clothing manufacturers. Labour costs in North Africa and the Far

East showed a widening gap from UK labour costs and many British clothing manufacturers set up their own units abroad, initially favouring Morocco, Tunisia and Sri Lanka, and more recently moving further afield mainly to China. British and European manufacturers also have to conform to a more stringent set of legal obligations and working standards than many other countries.

Copyright

Any design is the creative work of the designer – it is an original and priced as such. Imitation can be said to be the highest form of flattery, but it is unlikely that any designers who have had their creations copied would agree.

There are essentially two types of copying, either of a logo or of a design, as shown in Figure 2.6. Both are very frustrating and often it is too late to do anything about it when, or if, the copying is discovered.

Logo copying might be imitations of the Lacoste crocodile, Mickey Mouse T-shirts or the copy of a registered design feature such as the Levi's stitching marks. Copies of this type are an infringement of trademark and the perpetrator can be sued.

Design copying can happen in one of two ways: first, before the garment is on general release, the thief can sketch designs at a fashion show, or steal the design sketches, computer tapes or discs from the designer's place of work, or even steal the actual garments. This can mean that the copies get into the shops at the same time as or even before the original. Secondly, designs can be copied once they are already in the stores.

Copies are usually cheaper and of inferior quality to the original and can give the original designer many problems. First, they will lose sales to the cheaper versions. At first sight the copies may not seem

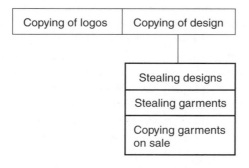

Figure 2.6 Copying of fashion.

any different to the unsuspecting buyer who usually would go for the cheaper version. Frequently it is only after wearing the garment or more particularly washing it that the quality differences become apparent. Fabrics do not wash or clean as well and seams will not hold as well. These quality differences can lead the original designer to get an unjustly poor reputation among the consumers who think that they are buying original labels.

Retailers could be criticized for encouraging this practice. Now that goods can be produced very quickly, high street stores pride themselves on having high fashion 'copies' available within their stores only days after they have been seen on the catwalks. Fashion magazines often have features, such as the *Sunday Times*' Style magazine's 'skinted and minted', showing their readers how to get a designer look at a fraction of the price by buying from high street stores. It is very difficult to decide at what point these items are blatant copies or merely following a fashion trend.

Copying of designs is not new. In 1975 the Fashion Design Protection Association was set up by Achilleas Constantinou of Ariella Fashion after he saw many of his designs in stores that he knew his company had not supplied. This was subsequently taken up by the British Clothing Industry Association (BCIA) who lobbied to get the Department of Trade and Industry to bring out the Copyright Designs and Patents Act in 1988. The aim of this Act is 'to protect creativity without restricting competition'. Designers are encouraged to claim copyright of their designs by signing and dating their original drawings. However, designs are often copied and sold in other countries without the designer ever knowing, although the effect might be felt in decreased sales and reputation. So these laudable efforts have not really solved the problem. Aside from the practical difficulties of time and cost in pursuing legal actions against the suppliers, there is still the problem of deciding when a fashion house is merely following a trend and when it is breaking the law.

One solution, used by Levi's, is to monitor the market outlets constantly, to make life harder for the counterfeiters. This may not be possible for a smaller company, especially when any monitoring has to be done internationally. Most of the copies are made abroad, to enable cheaper manufacture and avoid copyright laws. Another tactic used by Levi's is to tightly control the distribution of their red label tag stitched into all their jeans. They count out an exact number for their manufacturers and require exactly that number of pairs of jeans back from them, so preventing the manufacturer from producing overruns and selling them as originals.

Such is the problem that in November 1999 the Consumer Affairs Minister, Dr Kim Howells, attended the Sports Industries Federation

'War on Counterfeiting' conference in London. He pledged to 'Crack down on the "Mafia Gangsters" who peddle counterfeit sportswear costing the economy billions of pounds. Consumers need to know that fake goods are dangerous and damaging and rarely last as long as the genuine article'. Many companies are trying to do this crackdown themselves. Mulberry, the Bond Street producer of original leather handbag designs, took out 17 legal actions against retailers for copying their designs; only one reached court as the other 16 were all settled out of court. In all cases Mulberry won, either compensation or at least the withdrawal and destruction of stock.

2.6.2 Technological

As in all areas of industry new technology is making great inroads to improve quality of life and increase speed and quality of manufacture. In the area of fashion and clothing there have been many inventions. Some have had only minor effects on the market, whereas others have or are about to revolutionize them.

Other innovations in fabric technology are in the introduction of a variety of different properties in fabrics. Available in stores is heat-sensitive hosiery to keep the wearer warm or cold; moisturizing hosiery and underwear with a built-in fragrance capable of surviving up to 40 washes.

Fibres and fabrics

Lycra is not a fabric. The trademark Lycra is the property of the US-based chemical company Du Pont and is an Elastane fibre that lends itself to whichever fabric it is mixed with. Lycra is therefore an additive that gives knitted and woven textiles the quality of lasting stretch and recovery. It was first developed in 1959 and its first real use in garments was in the 1960s in ski wear and men's cord trousers. It was really not until the 1980s that it took off in knitted garments.

Lycra has become a household name associated with dancewear, swimwear, hosiery, cling-to-fit fashion separates such as leggings and vest dresses, in fact anything knitted. Lycra overcomes problems of fit and movement for body-hugging designs. Manufacturers obviously benefit from associations with a consumer recognizable brand in premium, superior quality garments and fabrics.

Such is the swimwear market's reliance on Lycra that swimwear designers do not design their collections until they have received Du Pont's own fashion forecasts.

Lycra is now being mixed with woven fabrics for outerwear and tailoring to take advantage of such benefits as improved appearance, better drape and less wrinkling. There is more development into adding Lycra to other cloth to create a wide diversity of fabrics. This has resulted in all kinds of finishes for fabrics using Lycra such as bubble, cire, shiny, matt, satin finish or printed.

The development of Lycra into other clothing, notably sportswear, has led to the increase of interest and sales in sportswear for professional, hobby and leisure purposes.

The clothing industry is extremely labour intensive, but installation of modern machinery fitted with the latest electronic controls is helping to improve productivity.

In the sportswear clothing field there have been huge developments in energy transfer fabrics which transfer heat away from the body so allowing sportsmen and -women to remain cool during their activity.

Computers

The dramatic increase in the use of computers has not passed by the fashion world, as shown in Figure 2.7. One of the main uses of computer systems is that of computer-aided design (CAD). The implication that this can have on the speed of transition of goods from design to the shop floor is quite phenomenal. It also has great implications for the employment sector in this industry. It may be the saviour of the UK clothing industry if it is accepted quickly enough.

A CAD system can perform a wide variety of tasks:

- The programmer designs a motif.
- The motif can be enlarged to any size, and duplicated to cover a piece of cloth. This can then be viewed on the computer screen to see how the design will look on the draped fabric.

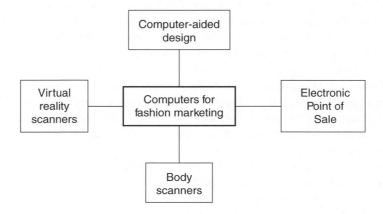

Figure 2.7 Computers in fashion marketing.

- The fabric can be tried in different colourways.
- The fabric can then be printed either directly onto the fabric using a bubble jet printer, or for larger lengths of fabric a printing layout can be produced.
- The operator can then design a garment, perhaps a blouse, by selecting different sleeves, collar, yoke, length, etc.
- The software will then print out a paper pattern to any basic measurements given.
- It can also plan a layout for the pattern pieces to achieve the optimum use of the fabric.

There is no reason why all these tasks cannot be performed by one skilled computer operator; however, the question today must be whether we need to train designers or computer operators. Although in 1992 only 150 out of 9000 fashion companies in the UK were using these systems to design garments, this number has increased dramatically, particularly as the systems become more flexible and prices are reduced.

These programmes can dramatically speed up the time it takes for a garment to get into the stores. They are also very cost effective both in terms of time saved and in minimizing fabric wastage. Perhaps the biggest saving that these systems can offer is in the area of pattern making and grading.

Some high street retailers like to deal with designers using this system as they can easily ask for adjustments to be made without delaying delivery time. So decisions are made more quickly and the buyer has more choice and influence.

Made-to-measure has been used as a means of producing garments since the inception of clothing. Since the industrial revolution, standardized sizing has gained prominence as it brings affordable garments to many markets. With growing populations comes diversity, the need for flexibility and the desire for better fitting clothes for all, not just those who can afford it. CAD can take a customer's measurements and reproduce designs or patterns for many different garments, quickly and accurately. It also can grade patterns for different sizes.

A further development in technology for the clothing market is for use in the made-to-measure market, where a system like a body scanner can be used to measure body size and shape within seconds to provide electronic tailoring.

In the future, virtual reality could transform the fashion business. There would be no need for supermodels or scrambles to get the front row at the fashion show. Designers could have the model they wanted parading around their salons, while clients could view whole couture collections in the comfort of their own homes.

Another major computerized invention for the retailer is EPoS (Electronic Point of Sale). This is very familiar in our supermarkets where bar codes are scanned to give the price. The bar codes can also tell the clothing retailer such information as size of garment, colour and how long it has been in stock. This information can then go into a central system that controls stock, and can, if necessary, rapidly reorder.

Computerized links with suppliers are growing in importance, speeding up order processing and improving the accuracy of transactions. The use of computers and EPoS has become very important in retail success in data capture at the point of sale, management of the merchandise and links with suppliers. Those retailers who have invested in these systems will fare best in the future.

Internet

With 86% of all homes in the UK having Internet access in 2006, clothes shopping via the web is predicted to continue to increase from the estimated 4.1 billion or 1.8% of retail sales estimated by Mintel (2005). While most fashion retailers now have established websites, but there are mixed fortunes in terms of online purchases. The tactile dimension of clothing purchases, the salience of colour matching with skin tones and the variability in sizing are all factors that continue to inhibit the use of the Internet by some customers. In addition, many consumers still express concerns about the security of passing credit card details over the Internet. The body scanner mentioned above could be used to see whether the clothes available via a website will fit the consumer before a purchase is made. Companies that have been most successful such as Next use a multi-channel format of store, catalogue and website. Other successes have been amongst those who specialize in selling online such as Asos with their celebrity inspired fashions or Figleaves with lingerie.

Television shopping

Still in its infancy, shopping via interactive television direct from the armchair has a similar potential to change how we buy clothing. However, growth of this area is limited by the same inhibitors as those connected with Internet shopping. Figures from Mintel (2003) estimate sales to be worth £395 million and only take a 2.7% share of the total home-shopping market.

Body scanners

Body scanners are a way of collecting 3D data about a consumer's body shape and size. By standing, fully clothed, in a booth or pod, up to 3000 body measurements can be taken in a matter of seconds by cameras and lasers. Minutes later an accurate true to scale 3D body model can be produced. This technology is already being put to a variety of uses. Whilst mass production companies can now ensure that their garments more closely fit the average consumer, the greater benefits will be made by the made-to-measure market for which measurement is both quick and accurate. Retailers are also finding uses for this technology. Selfridges, on Oxford Street, London, offer body scanning in order to produce custom-fit jeans. The customer can choose the fabric, rise and leg style and be assured of a perfect fitting pair of jeans. In some Gap stores consumers can use the body scanner to help them find which brands and sizes will offer the best fit. There are even predictions that body scanners could eliminate the need for changing rooms. The one market where they could reap most benefits are in clothing purchased online. Internet sales still suffer from consumer dissatisfaction due to poor fit and consumers frequently do not bother to return goods that don't fit, they just don't bother shopping with that company again. In time consumers could have their own body scan on their computer they could 'try on' clothes from participating online retailers. Early efforts in this area have been made by some organization such as Landsend to offer 'My Virtual Model™'. An attractive mannequin can be programmed to assume a customer's shape, skin tone, hairstyle and facial features, and customers can try clothes on their model to check fit and co-ordination of different outfits. Clearly this is more fun than accurate but as a tool for getting the customer involved with the merchandise it is very effective.

2.6.3 Demographics

This is the study of changes in the size and make-up of the population. While these changes occur slowly and can be predicted well in advance, only the foolish manufacturer ignores the effect they might have on business. The UK has begun to undergo a quite radical change in the make-up of its population and many of these changes will have strong repercussions on the fashion clothing market.

Customer size

As a nation we are changing shape and businesses are being forced to cope with the larger customer. Adult obesity rates have almost quadrupled in the past 25 years and now 22% of Britons are obese, classed as having a body mass index of over 30, and three-quarters are overweight. The implications for the fashion industry are obvious in terms of sizes, stock levels and styling. Not only are people heavier but the average height for both men and women has increased by 10 mm. This has implications for all sorts of goods and services such as transport, furniture and clothing.

Many clothing manufacturers are offering goods in a wider range of sizes or a more generous cut, although some have pandered to their customers' vanity and disguised the increase in size, Marks and Spencer have admitted that a size 12 made in the 1980s is not exactly the same as the equivalent size now. Even high fashion retailers targeting the younger consumer are realizing the need to cater for a broader range of sizes. Top Shop now offers a selection of their clothing up to size 16 and Next up to size 22, although availability is greater online or in the directory.

Apart from offering a wider range of sizes, some stores have a special own range in store, e.g. Bhs's range 'Extra', and H&M's range BiB. Many stores, including Marks and Spencer, also have petite ranges and New Look has a range for women over 5'7". There are also more retailers catering solely for the larger customer. High and Mighty, as the name suggests, is a growing chain for men. Dawn French has an upmarket store in South Molton Street in London for women sized 16 and upwards. If the trend continues the time may come when it is the size 10s who are complaining that they cannot find anything to wear.

An ironic contrast, however, is the concern for people, particularly women, who try to stay extremely thin or have eating disorders. For them, stores are stocking jeans in sizes 6, 4 and sometimes even smaller.

Changes in the family

The much quoted statistic of the family with 2.4 children has changed. In recent years it has fluctuated around the 1.8 mark. Couples are tending to marry later and start a family later. This gives them the opportunity to become more financially stable, to get further on in their careers and to have more disposable income to spend on their children, some of it on clothing. More exclusive children's clothing shops have, like many others, suffered during the recession of the early 1990s. However, there is still a substantial designer market for childrenswear whether the garments are bought as gifts from generous grandparents or as regular clothing by more financially indulgent parents.

With more people remarrying and starting a second family in their late thirties and early forties, there is a need for maternity wear for the more mature expectant mother, who may also be working at the time. Whilst the high street caters quite well for the younger mother within high street stores such as New Look and H&M, there are several successful companies who sell mainly via catalogue or online. JoJo, Maman, Bebe and Isabella Oliver offer more upmarket ranges with a high design element to cater for the more mature and more affluent mother to be. These mothers will also want to keep a youthful appearance consistent with their young children so there are other market opportunities for post-natal ranges. Further details about the role of the family in purchasing behaviour are given in Chapter Three.

Age changes in the population

The British population is forecast to rise by less than 2% between 2005 and 2010, but the significant impact on the clothing sector is the large changes to the structure of the population. Not withstanding minor fluctuations, the long-term decline in the number of 15–24 year olds, high spenders on clothing, continues, albeit slowly. Table 2.7 illustrates how different age ranges will be affected.

Children

Over the past 15 years there have been fluctuations in the size of the population in different children's age bands. However, it is estimated that, despite the increasing trend for women to be older when they

Table 2.7 Population trends (male and female), Great Britain (in '000s)

Age range	% Change 2000–2005	2005–2010	2010–2015
0–4	−3.48	+2.15	+0.64
5–9	−6.39	−3.27	+2.15
10–14	−0.72	−6.36	−3.34
15–19	+9.14	−1.94	−6.25
20–24	+11.39	+7.75	−1.60
25–29	−7.88	+10.77	+6.88
30–34	−9.36	−7.52	+9.79
35–39	+0.84	−9.34	−7.70
40–44	+12.98	+0.65	−9.33
45–59	+5.57	+4.29	+6.91
60–64	+7.37	+20.58	−8.33
65–74	+2.19	+7.56	+15.68
75–84	+5.41	+1.86	+8.10
85+	+5.08	+16.87	+12.15
Total	+2.25	+2.34	+2.27

Source: Adapted from Government Actuary.

have their first child or even the move towards having a 'second family' with a new partner, there will be little growth in the children's market.

However, changes in the children's market can still present many opportunities for clothing and footwear demand for infants. Many retailers have recognized this and the market is very competitive. Retailers can best compete by offering good styles and designs with good value for money. The premium end of the market shows room for some expansion with many children's only label such as Miniman and Oilily, plus many adult designer labels offering diffusion children's ranges such as Baby Dior, Moschino, Armani, Ted Baker and DKNY.

The 10–14 years of age children's market remains underdeveloped in retail terms at present. Marks and Spencer have all but withdrawn their attempt to appeal to teenagers. Next fare better but sell most of the teen boys range online or via the Next Directory. The one apparent success with stand-alone stores was Tammy Girl a younger extension of the Etam range. Now under the control of Philip Green, owner of the Arcadia group and Bhs, Tammy would appear to have been demoted and is now only offered within the Bhs stores, reinforcing the opinion that this is a very difficult sector at which to win. The increasing interest in sportswear and sportswear labels would suggest that it is the sports outfitters that are best satisfying this group.

Traditional core market aged 15–34

The traditional core market for clothing suppliers, that of men and women between the ages of 15 and 34, declined rapidly between 1990 and 2000 when stores for whom the lower end of this market was key, such as Miss Selfridge, suffered as they saw their customer base drop by about a twelfth. This age group has remained fairly steady since then. Whilst the high spending 15–34 year olds will continue to remain steady in numbers as a group until 2010, there will be a drop in the 30 year olds at the top end of this market. There may be some consolation in the fact that the 20-year-old group will grow slightly, although they also have most demands on their finances with mortgages and many are starting to have families.

The mature market

In 2005 almost 56% of all inhabitants in Britain were aged 35 years or older. By 2010 the number of 45–54 year olds is expected to rise more rapidly than any other age group. Previously people of this age would have been grouped together with older consumers who traditionally spend less on clothing, particularly men, than consumers in their late teens, twenties and thirties. They bought fewer garments and often spent less per garment than younger people. But emerging from this group is the new 'middle youth' market as they are sometimes referred to, who have a greater interest in health, fashion and shopping, and whose members, particularly the women, are a potentially lucrative market for the retailer who can offer the right formula.

Going against this tradition of being the lowest spenders on clothing, in recent years, the spending of the 55–64 year olds has risen dramatically, particularly that of women. This increase is expected to continue as they benefit from inheritance money from older relatives.

Most older groups, particularly towards the higher end of the age bracket, are not as interested in fashion as in comfort and quality of clothes. They buy fewer and lower priced items than younger people. However, price is now becoming less significant and service levels are of increasing importance. There are now more magazines aimed at them and a somewhat improved choice of merchandise in the shops. Such people are influenced in their fashion attitudes by their growing affluence and are more aware of different styles. This is mainly due to having been brought up in the post-war boom years. Retailers aiming to serve this older market are responding with updated classic ranges, particularly for women. There is, however, still an opportunity to stimulate more menswear sales to older consumers by updating ranges and retail presentation.

2.6.4 The social and cultural environments

These can cover a wide range of issues, but are basically the society-wide influences, values and changes that can affect the market.

Leisure activities

Changes in the amount and types of leisure activity have resulted in a move away from formal codes of dress to much more casual styling. The increased amount of leisure time that many people have, due to shorter working hours, more electronic help in the home and convenience foods, has led to a need for more clothing to wear in these leisure hours.

Leisure wear, particularly in the guise of sportswear, has become a style to wear during the whole day for most ages and socio-economic groups. Nearly everyone wears some form of sportswear, be it T-shirts, sweatshirts, jogger bottoms or polo shirts. Tracksuits and trainers are almost a social uniform, in some parts of the market, for many daily activities such as shopping, housework, looking after children, dog walking and of course sports activities themselves.

The role of work

The market for menswear and womenswear is very different in terms of the occupational status of consumers. As far as the 'working wardrobe' is concerned a wearer's occupation influences both his or her garment needs and how much they can actually spend. Changes over time in the occupations that comprise the labour market can therefore have a major effect on the overall size and composition of the domestic clothing market. The relationship between the structure of the labour market, socio-economic groups and purchasing is developed further in Chapter Three.

The past 20 years has seen a gradual increase of working women to now make up just over 70% of the workforce. Less free time, more disposable income and a need for clothing for work all have implications for the clothing market. Although many of these women work part time, it is still be the case that working women have less free time in which to shop, but more disposable income. The desire to dress smartly, along with the desire for financial status, results in more spending on clothes for different occasions.

Women in supervisory jobs tend to spend well above the national average on their wardrobe. While there are still very few women in professional and higher managerial jobs, they do tend to spend more on their outerwear than the national average for women and are a small and highly lucrative market.

Economically inactive women spend well below average on clothing but cover a broad spectrum of ages, purchasing power and reasons for not working, for instance they may be students, pensioners, unemployed or women whose husbands have well-paid jobs.

For working men there has been a long-term shift from blue-collar to white-collar work, which one might think would stimulate consumption. Now that the UK is enjoying high levels of employment and the steep rise in unemployment during the recession is over, sales of formal workwear have not returned to their previous levels. This is partly due to fashion changes, but pressure on the finances of many of its core customers can also be a strong contributory factor.

Seasonal factors

Clothing producers and retailers have always found that demand for their goods is subject to the vagaries of the weather and the seasons. New ranges are introduced at certain times of the year in the expectation that the weather will be as normal. In the past few years the weather has been quite 'unseasonal' on many occasions. Summers have either arrived early and lasted longer than expected or even appear not to have arrived at all. Winters have been milder and suppliers have often found themselves with the wrong stock for the weather. This has led to a loss of profits either through lost sales due to shortages of clothing or through heavy discounting to get rid of leftover end-of-season stock. When viewing figures seasonally, it is necessary to look at several years together to avoid the bias of the extreme vagaries of the weather although as a trend we are buying less heavy overcoats and more summer wear.

Clothing sales are generally very low in January and February with only around 6% of the total annual consumer sales. Childrenswear is particularly weak here, whereas in September sales of school clothing make this month the second most important sales period for childrenswear. June is far more important than September for menswear and womenswear. This is the beginning of summer and the holiday season when around 10% of womenswear is bought, with menswear sales just slightly lower.

The largest amount of clothing is bought in December with 17% of total annual spending taking place. A large part of these sales is for gifts. This month is especially important for menswear as men very often receive clothing as gifts. Even the high volume of sales in the January sales in no way matches the bumper sales period before Christmas.

2.6.5 'Green' and ethical issues

As many consumers are accepting the concept of conserving and recycling in other areas such as washing powders and paper, so they may soon be questioning the need for constant renewal and replacement of clothing to follow fashion. To the environmentalist an industry that advocates continual change and ensures inbuilt obsolescence in its products is far from attractive.

To satisfy the environmentally conscious consumer the pace of fashion changes must slow down. The emphasis needs to shift from short-term fads to durable styles, comfort, quality and real innovations in fabrics and style that add to garments. There is already pressure to develop 'green fabrics' with demand for more organic cotton and an increased use of hemp but 'green clothing' is also likely to become an increasingly important issue. There will be a need for the recycling of fibres and fabrics, and production of biodegradable clothing.

Since successful companies need to recognize and anticipate consumer needs and desires, research and development into these environmental issues should be happening now.

Aligned to the concern of fabrics themselves is a concern over manufacturing conditions now that so many garments come from countries where wages are low and working conditions can be bad.

Green issues: the response of retailers

There have been several attempts to launch environmental clothing ranges by labels such as Esprit and Claus Steilmann, but the high-profile attempts by some parts of the fashion industry to become greener have yet to have any significant impact. At the retail end of the business, the major chain stores are examining how they can run their stores in a more environmentally friendly way. Most of their efforts may appear minor, but in total they could be quite significant.

Environmental efforts include:

- the use of recycled paper for till rolls;
- using recycled plastic and actually recycling garment overbags;
- recycling hangers and not offering them to the customer, but returning them to the clothing manufacturer to use again;
- using less packaging: Marks and Spencer now use virtually no extra packaging for most of its garments, a far cry from when jumpers were all packed in cardboard and cellophane;
- using fewer hardwoods for fittings in store design;
- using more energy efficient transport, etc.

Hoechst, a European polyester and fibre manufacturer, was the first fibre company to gain a certificate under EMAS, the European Eco-Management and Audit Scheme. The review of its environmental practices led to a comprehensive report on energy and water consumption, production emissions and recycling.

Marks and Spencer, in particular, are taking environmental concerns into account. They are aiming to keep abreast of such issues and take them into consideration in their buying decisions and operational areas.

Second-hand clothing

In some high street shopping centres charity shops seem to be almost as common as new clothing shops. The huge increase in the number of these and second-hand clothing outlets can be explained in many ways. As people buy more new clothing the second-hand clothing shops are an obvious place for them to dispose of their unwanted fashions from last season. Economic reasons could lead us to assume that lack of money means that the only clothing some people can afford is from the second-hand market. Or it could be that more environmentally conscious people are preferring to buy second hand and so recycling clothing rather than always buying new. The retro look of the late 1990s meant that second-hand clothes shops were a good source of desirable genuinely fashionable items.

One 'new' trend for the 2000s, partly fuelled by its popularity at red carpet events such as the Oscars, is vintage clothing. Be it a 1950s Dior dress or a 1970s Vivienne Westwood T-shirt, period pieces by well-known designers are becoming much sought after. Top Shop on Oxford Street, London, has a whole floor devoted to vintage clothing and several of London's famous markets such as Portobello Road are good hunting grounds for second-hand/recycled/vintage clothes. Many new websites have been launched devoted to the buying and selling of garments from another era. Ebay, whilst not exclusively selling clothing and accessories, plays a big part in this desire for recycled fashion.

Environmentally friendly fabrics

During the late 1980s, when there was a sudden focus on environmental issues, the textile industry was forced to improve its processes as a result of increased legislation. It had become evident that environmental damage was being caused by gaseous and liquid emissions from the industrial processes of many producers, including textiles.

New legislation covers, among other things, the wet processing activities such as dyeing and finishing. Already, many firms are spending large sums to reduce gaseous emissions from their processes and are investing in systems for recycling dyestuffs and other chemicals and even water.

There is much misinformation in the media that natural fibre fabrics are best, leading many people to think that natural fibres are good for the environment and synthetics are automatically bad. Most of this thinking is based on negative perceptions of the chemical industry. Although natural fibres biodegrade more easily, some give off toxic gases as they do so. Some processes for making synthetic fibres are actually friendlier to the environment than those for making natural fibres, especially when energy and water usage are taken into consideration.

It is not only the manufacture of the fabrics that is of concern, but how they biodegrade after disposal. Germany's leading clothing producers have been working on a range of biodegradable garments.

While the textile industry is usually blamed for the unfriendly emissions and wastage, it is arguable that the clothing manufacturers and fashion designers should really be blamed. They are the ones who dictate that strong dyed fabrics are required or non-crease products that need to be made from the thermoplastic properties of synthetics. The clothing and textile industries need to integrate their efforts for the future.

Whilst the consumer does not often consider the manufacturing processes, the desire for organic products, popular among food stuffs, has also moved into clothing. The use of organically grown natural fibres fulfils the needs of those with sensitive skin who react to chemicals and those with a greater environmental conscience.

Fair trade

With such a large proportion of clothing imported from overseas, concerns are growing regarding the working conditions within factories in some Asian countries. Large organizations such as Marks and Spencer and Nike have been accused of outsourcing to factories using the so-called 'sweatshop' labour. Often employing children, long working days in potentially unsafe and uncomfortable conditions are demanded in return for very low pay. Companies need to be able to reassure their customers that goods are manufactured ethically and fairly by closely monitoring the factories that supply them.

Some smaller organizations use overseas labour not for their low wages and ability to mass produce, but for the special skills that people can offer in hand-made garments.

'Green' fashions

Green fashion can be viewed in several different ways. On a simple level there is a growing movement against labels and conspicuous consumption. Some people are shying away from dressiness and are returning to basic clothing. Basics are usually part of traditional workwear – they have a high degree of functionality, and are simply cut and built to last. Doctor Marten boots and denim jeans are items of clothing that could be considered to be following the green ethos of less consumption as they are classic items that will not date and will only need replacing when they have worn out. Some of these views are shown in Figure 2.8.

In the late 1980s we also had the 'ecology look'. Fabrics were natural in both feel and colour. T-shirts available from the designer shop to the local chain store were adorned with environmental messages. Coming at a time when consumers had had enough of overt consumerism and the Yuppie look, the ecology look fitted in nicely as a contrast to the structured silhouettes and wide shoulders of the previous fashion.

The controversy over who is to blame for the less environmentally friendly fabrics, designer or textile manufacturer has not gone unnoticed by some designers. Most denim producers have replaced traditional chemical finishing by using pumice stone to achieve a stonewashed fabric finish. These new fabrics and processes will cost the consumer more. As with many environmentally friendly products there is a conflict of interest. Consumers and retailers seem to want

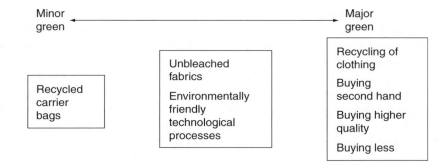

Minor green ←————————————————→ Major green

Recycled carrier bags

Unbleached fabrics

Environmentally friendly technological processes

Recycling of clothing

Buying second hand

Buying higher quality

Buying less

Figure 2.8   How 'green' can you be in fashion?

new, environmentally sustaining products but are reluctant to pay for the additional cost involved.

Friends of the Earth have produced ranges of 'green' fashions using unbleached, undyed cotton. This satisfied the ecology issue but not the fashion issue, and sales have been rather limited. They were avoiding the issue by not using any processes rather than finding 'green' solutions to enable fabrics to be used for fashion items.

The next logical stage is for designers to now take these issues on board. Many, such as Katharine Hamnett, are concerned about the fabrics they use and are developing more environmentally friendly fabrics. It has taken time for these to 'trickle down' to appear in the garments stocked in high street shops and they still do not constitute a large part of what we buy. One company, Edun, set up by Bono and Alison Hewson aims to offer a clothing line for people with a social conscience. They use organic fabrics, made up in environmentally friendly factories with ethical working conditions.

Paris held the first 'Ethical Fashion Show' in 2004 offering a platform for ethical and environmental designers around the world to showcase their clothing and accessories. Now an annual event, up to 50 designers show to the increasing number of distributors who want to sell designs that are ethically produced and environmentally friendly.

Another environmental concern for consumers is the risk of skin cancer that depletion of the ozone layer and excessive exposure to the sun may bring about. New ranges of beach and swimwear offering UV protection of up to 97% are being seen at holiday resorts, offering even more opportunity for Lycra.

2.6.6 Economy

General economic factors such as income, employment and home ownership have just as great an effect on the clothing industry as on other product groups. Consumer expenditure on new clothing is very dependent on the general state of the economy measured by the gross national product (GNP), their employment status and their disposable income. There are many other factors that influence the shape of the market for clothing and footwear. Consumer spending is influenced by some economic factors mentioned above while lifestyle changes that occur, such as getting married, having children, children leaving home and retirement, all alter people's requirements and aspirations for clothing and footwear. Clothing is one area where in recent years there has been price deflation, sales growth in volume is exceeding sales growth by value, people aren't buying less clothes but the clothes are becoming cheaper. In the 1960, households spent on average 10.3% of their income on clothing. This fell to less than 6% in the late 1990s and have more or less stayed at that figure ever since. This relatively low figure can be accounted for by the ability of manufacturers and retailers to source from around the world and constantly respond to competitive pressure on prices.

Recession versus 'feel good factor'

In the late 1980s and continuing into the early 1990s the UK was in a recession that was mirrored throughout the world. Increasing unemployment and high interest rates led consumers to be wary of spending more than was necessary. This in turn led to more frugal spending on clothing and a partial rejection of fashions that require a total new look, causing a move towards more classic styles that will last beyond the next season.

By the late 1990s there was discussion in the media of a 'feel good factor' in the economy, but this did not necessarily reach the clothing stores, many of which had somewhat lost their direction and positioning in terms of consumer needs. In the new millennium people may feel the benefit of low inflation rates, easily available credit and a consumer confidence that their standard of living will stay the same or get better. This can lead to more spending but with clothing, and the price deflation experienced in the market, more items purchased do not necessarily relate to more spending overall.

Unemployment

Local spending power can be greatly influenced by unemployment, which varies considerably from region to region within the UK. The retail sector of whole towns can be devastated by the closure of a large local employer.

Table 2.8 House price increases, 1997–2006
(index 1997 = 100)

Year	Standard Price	Index
1997	68 042	100.0
1998	71 704	105.4
1999	81 595	119.9
2000	84 293	123.9
2001	90 590	133.1
2002	106 195	156.1
2003	129 450	190.3
2004	157 091	230.9
2005	162 783	239.2
2006	177 962	261.5

Source: Adapted from Halifax UK House Price
Index.

Home ownership

Home ownership has been increasing steadily since the end of World
War II. However, as interest rates rose, the cost of mortgages greatly
increased for a time, putting pressure on owner-occupied households.
Even as rates began to fall again, consumer caution and the switch to
saving spare cash may not result in the anticipated increase in spending. With average house prices having risen more than two and a half
times over the past 10 years, homeowners have gained in confidence
as they have seen the price of their house rise (Table 2.8). Coupled
with relatively low interest rates homeowners have been able to
spend more on themselves. They are more willing to access the equity
in their homes by remortgaging. Conversely high house prices mean
that it is hard to get a foothold onto the property ladder for first time
buyers. They are having to save hard for a deposit and then take out
large mortgages to buy even the most modest property.

Credit cards

There is concern that consumers and their willingness to take out
personal loans and credit will follow the pattern of the 1980s. At that
time consumers were more willing to borrow when their homes rose
in value and were confident to extend their personal loans in the
knowledge that their assets were appreciating in value faster than the
rate of inflation. However, as the rise in interest rates caused depres-
sion of the housing market, and the value of some properties fell, the
banks, so willing to lend in the 1980s, restricted credit. Spending on
plastic cards has increased over four times the amount spent 10 years

ago, although this does include debit as well as credit cards. Usage of store cards as consumers have realized the high interest rates being charged or as they are converted into store credit cards, likes Marks and Spencer, where purchases can be made in other stores using a Marks and Spencer credit/store card.

The rest of Europe does not have the same love of credit cards and willingness to go into debt as the British, having a much greater reluctance to take on the high levels of debt as seen in the UK.

European Monetary Union

In January 1999, 11 of the 15 EU members at that time joined the European Monetary Union (EMU) and now have a single currency – the Euro. Currently, the UK Government does not feel that the economy fulfils the five economic tests set out by the Maastricht Treaty, and so UK membership is still on hold. The likely addition of the UK to the EMU in the next few years will mean that stores will trade in the Euro. UK retailers will gain the chance to trade more easily in a wider European market although this will also mean more competition. It will be possible for EU consumers to easily buy throughout Europe and the world via the Internet.

Exchange rates

Both exports and imports are greatly affected by the strength of the pound. Since the late 1990s sterling was particularly strong, making imported clothing cheaper and hampering clothing exports by increasing their costs in foreign markets.

2.7 Trends in the marketing environment

Trends are relatively slow-moving changes in the marketplace that can occur for a variety of reasons, and businesses ignore them at their peril. Sometimes trends are business led and sometimes consumers lead the way. General fashions can change very quickly and go from one extreme to another whereas trends in clothing fashion tend to be slower and build upon themselves rather than ignore what went before.

2.7.1 Styles and consumer preferences

While there probably will always be people who are interested in high fashion there has been a noticeable move away from status and image dressing. Consumers still demand fashion, but they are requiring more understated styles that combine realism, comfort and practicality.

Changing work and lifestyles, with more time for leisure pursuits, are speeding the change from formal wear to a more casual look and sportswear. There is an increasing blur of divisions between active wear and fashion. Sometimes the sports store and boutique seem to be carrying almost the same merchandise.

The explosion in sportswear sales has been accompanied by a sharp rise in demand for other casual garments. Sales of conventional jumpers and cardigans have suffered a severe contraction as casual knitwear such as T-shirts and sweatshirts have grown in popularity.

Demand for womenswear is as crucial as ever to the health of the domestic clothing market. Demographic changes have already been mentioned and these will quickly affect the relevant markets. First, the upper end of the children's market should be considered. Secondly, customers in their late forties and fifties represent a great opportunity.

These changes and the long-term weather pattern are encouraging lighter weight clothing and trans-seasonal clothes, where many people no longer have a winter and summer wardrobe, but use the same clothes year-round. There are two distinct shifts in clothes labelling. Many manufacturers are continuing to manufacture or source under their own brand, such as Dorothy Perkins, Next or Karen Millen. Other stores are using and promoting the clothing designers themselves or bringing in strong brand names, particularly in the area of sports clothing. Some of these issues concerning taste preferences and seasonal aspects are developed further in Chapter Six in the context of product development.

2.7.2 Manufacturing

Retailers are increasingly under pressure to carry less stock in the interests of greater efficiency, and to offer the customer more choice, more often. This means that suppliers are required to deliver shorter runs of merchandise more frequently than in the past.

Too many manufacturers have also been taking a back seat and relying on retailers to keep them in touch with customers' demands. In the future the most successful manufacturers will be those who invest in market research, design and technology.

2.7.3 Trends in fibres and fabrics

Performance and versatility are becoming increasingly important. Customers are beginning to seek out specially engineered high-tech, high-performance fibres and fabrics such as Lycra and the tactile fabrics and ask for them by name. They are looking for fabrics to fulfil not only a fashion or style function, but also a clearly defined performance need.

Polyester and cotton are still the most widely used fibres, either on their own or as the dominant (50% or more) fibre in a blend; however, natural fibres are still more popular, and it is expected that their use, often for reasons of cost and handling properties, will rise further. Polyester is gradually losing ground and more cotton-rich blends are being used. Wool is still popular but for cost reasons it is again bought more as a blend than a pure fabric.

The main area of development in fabrics is still in blending stretch Elastane yarns. They are being applied to a much wider range of fabrics either for fashion effect in body-hugging styling or for comfort and recovery in outerwear and tailoring.

Microfibres such as superfine polyesters and polyamides in new forms and applications, especially in blends with other fibres and knitwear, are likely to remain the main area of interest for some time to come.

Changes in the pattern of shopping

Despite current government policy to limit the increase in out-of-town developments, the trend is towards large drive to shopping malls and complexes. This shopping trend is supplemented by the growth in catalogues and may be joined by a move towards electronic shopping.

2.8 Summary

- ◆ This is a time of change for the clothing market. The companies who survive will be the ones who initiate change and adapt. There is not much scope for those who are slow and lag behind. In the medium term there seems little prospect of a return to the high rates of growth in clothing sales seen during much of the 1980s.
- ◆ Unless they can offer the discounted prices and high value that customers are looking for, many companies will find that they can only survive by moving away from these price-sensitive parts of the market into segments where quality, design, variety and quick response to changes in fashion and consumer tastes matter more than price. Although now with an expectation of low prices, it will be hard for customers to accept much in the way of price increases as spare income has already been allocated to other things. If anything they are

moving the other way, demanding more quality and styling from retailers whilst still keeping prices low.

- In terms of clothing people are growing older later and there will be opportunities for producers and retailers who can meet the demand from older and more discerning customers who are looking for the current fashion styling in their clothing but adapted more closely to their needs such as better quality, more comfortable styling and well-informed friendly service.
- The market is not changing very much in overall size but there will be major demographic growth in certain areas. Age bands offering significant scope for sales are among the young adults (20–24) and 45–54 year olds.
- There is an increasing interest in designer labels resulting in more diffused lines and more mixing of labels and clothing at very different price points.
- Garments manufactured overseas are dominating the UK High Street. To compete the UK has to offer a quick response, meaning low stock levels for the retailer, especially as the seasons become less distinct and retailers want to offer more frequent seasonal ranges.
- Customers are choosing to buy their clothes from wherever suits them best, be it high street stores, out of town shopping malls, supermarkets, catalogues or via the Internet.
- Fashion is moving into an era where marketing techniques will be more influential than ever before. Clothing producers need to be far more aware of consumer needs. To a large extent fashion still leads, but consumers are beginning to exert more leverage in the issue. No longer will they merely wear what is dictated to them. The customer is becoming king.

Further reading

Blythe, J. (2006), *Principles and Practice of Marketing*, Thomson, London.

Brassington, F. and Pettitt, S. (2005), *Essentials of Marketing*, Prentice Hall, Harlow.

Hines, T. and Bruce, M. (2001), *Fashion Marketing: Contemporary Issues*, Butterworth-Heinemann, Oxford.

Mintel Reports: Value Clothing Retailing (May 2005); Clothing Retailing (July 2005); Keynote Reports: Clothing Manufacturing (May 2006); Clothing and Footwear Industry (March 2006).

Oldroyd, M. (2003/2004), *CIM Coursebook Marketing Environment*, Butterworth-Heinemann, Oxford.

Part B
Understanding and Researching the Fashion Purchaser

Chapter Three
The Fashion Consumer and Organizational Buyer

3.1 Introduction

This chapter is concerned with the behaviour of fashion consumers and organizations that purchase fashion products and services. The relevance of fashion buyer behaviour is examined and links with marketing research, market segmentation and the marketing mix are established.

An outline of consumers' decision-making is given. The types of decision made by consumers are described and the stages in the decision process are discussed. From the perspective of the buyer as a problem solver the chapter then focuses on the consumer as an individual. The main psychological variables relevant to fashion consumption are identified and outlined. For example, an understanding of the perceptual process allows us to comprehend more easily why some fashion promotional messages are more effective than others.

Fashion goods enable people to show identification with, or separation from, certain social groups. Clothing can be a symbol of belonging or alienation. To understand the fashion consumer, the broader social forces that help to shape individual buying behaviour are assessed. These social dimensions include the family, social stratification, opinion leadership and cultural factors. Some people are more ready to adopt new fashions than others, and the study of diffusion and opinion leadership helps us to understand why this occurs and what may be done to facilitate the process.

Fashion firms not only sell to fashion consumers, they also sell to other firms in the industry. An obvious form of organizational buying is sales within the fashion distribution channel and this is described in Chapter Eight. Another area of organizational buying of relevance is that of the corporate consumer, for instance the purchase of uniforms and distinctive clothing as part of a company's image. The nature of organizational buying will be outlined, and differences and similarities with consumers will be highlighted.

3.2 Why study the fashion buyer?

A central component of the definition of fashion marketing is satisfying customers' needs profitably. To achieve that it is necessary to understand consumers, their needs and wants, and how they will respond to various marketing efforts.

Everyone interested in fashion marketing brings a particular quality to their studies, i.e. their experiences as a fashion consumer. That experience is a mixed blessing. The benefits are that concepts from consumer behaviour can be understood and readily applied to one's own clothing purchases. The main drawback is the temptation to generalize and assume that all other fashion consumers behave as we do. The unfortunate fact is that the study of fashion marketing will probably change buying behaviour and make the expert fashion marketer atypical. Greater knowledge of products and promotional processes coupled with enthusiasm for fashion mean that there is a dislocation from typical consumers. Interestingly, many serious market research companies exclude marketing personnel as survey respondents because of their tendency to be atypical.

As will be seen when looking at social processes in consumer behaviour, people tend to live within fairly narrow social networks. They interact with others of similar social status and sets of interests. For fashion marketers, the danger is that these narrow social networks reinforce 'world views' of what is good about fashion and this becomes the explanation of what all consumers want. The key point is that opinions should never be accepted without question and that fashion marketing decisions should be based on evidence about the market, and not just on introspection.

Each consumer is unique and that is a good reason to trust sound marketing research rather than hunches based on the extrapolation of personal motives. As a starting point for marketing research hunches are useful when they are regarded as ideas to be tested. Therefore we can ask:

'Do many people share this view?'
'How many?'
'Do they have any other views that are more strongly held?'

For example, a fashion designer may be inspired by the reflection that business travel for the female executive would be enhanced by a small range of light flexible garments that do not crease. This inspiration may come from the designer or from his or her friends. The next stage is to determine via marketing research, how many women engage in business travel and of those, how many feel that the current clothing market does not meet their precise requirements. Chapter Four provides detailed coverage of marketing research techniques used to measure the behaviour of the fashion consumer.

3.2.1 The role of consumer behaviour in marketing

Consumer behaviour provides a range of concepts to help fashion marketers think about their customers, and marketing research provides the techniques to measure those concepts. Consumer behaviour is also closely integrated with all other aspects of fashion marketing, but most notably with the selection of target markets and the development of marketing mixes. An overview is given in Figure 3.1.

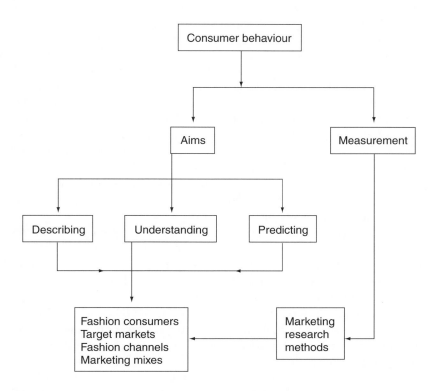

Figure 3.1 The role of consumer behaviour in fashion marketing.

3.2.2 Consumer behaviour and target marketing

As mentioned earlier each consumer is unique. Besides bespoke tailoring and couture items, most fashion marketing is concerned with the provision of standardized garments aimed at particular groups of consumers. All consumers are different from other consumers, but, and this is not contradictory, they are similar to some other consumers. The marketing of volume clothing demands that groups of consumers with similar needs be identified and then supplied with similar products. Chapter Five considers the nature of target marketing further, but for the moment the links with buyer behaviour will be noted.

If the total market for clothing is considered it can easily be seen that it really comprises many smaller segments, each with specialized needs. Obvious bases for the segments include age, gender and income. Less obvious, but as important, may be segments based on psychological or social characteristics that are common to significant numbers of consumers. For example, consumers differ in their levels of aspiration and also in the relationship they see between clothing and the achievement of social mobility. Throughout the twentieth century there were times when conspicuous consumption became a widely used mechanism for emphasizing new distinctions that emerged from changes in wealth and occupational structure. For example, the power dressing phase of the 1980s was followed by the 'dress-down Friday' phase of the 1990s and was succeeded by some companies reintroducing smart dress codes for work in the early 2000s. Socially aspirant groups will often seek clothing to support and reinforce their changing status. The fashion designer of the twenty-first century must meet these needs in a way that engages these social aspirations, yet is sensitive to the prevailing values concerning overt displays of wealth and social distinction. It is the understanding of these types of consumer needs that is the essence of consumer behaviour and the subsequent identification of suitable target markets for fashion firms.

Changes in social structure, or demographics, as identified in Chapter Two, cause new market threats and opportunities and therefore different targeting imperatives. For example, the increasing interest in environmental issues has been accompanied by a whole range of views from ardent advocates to strident opponents. Numerous research studies undertaken between the late 1980s and 2007 have demonstrated that the majority of consumers are concerned about environmental issues. However, there are also large differences among social groups in terms of how much extra they are prepared to pay for products in support of those beliefs. Within the fashion market, consumers can be categorized according to attitudes held on environmental matters. Clearly, if significant numbers with purchasing power are active supporters of environmental issues, then they probably would be most interested in recycled or recyclable fabrics and fibres and in long-lasting clothing that is manufactured and can be cared for in an environmentally friendly manner.

Investigation of consumer behaviour is sometimes designed specifically to identify particular groups of consumer with fashion interests and buying behaviour in common. The later section on lifestyles will outline one such approach to market segmentation.

3.2.3 Consumer behaviour and the marketing mix

The study of consumer behaviour not only provides a framework for identifying consumer needs and target markets, but it also enables the anticipation of consumer responses to marketing action. When studying the consumer the interest lies not only in describing what is the case, but also in predicting future behaviour.

The marketing mix is the combination of elements that a fashion marketer offers to a target market. It comprises decisions made about products, prices, promotion, services and distribution that are assembled in a coherent manner to represent the firm's offering to the consumer. A detailed discussion of the marketing mix is given in Chapter Five. For the present a consideration of links between consumer behaviour and some elements of the marketing mix will be given.

Consumer behaviour and products

Products are bought because they meet needs. These needs may be mainly physiological such as the requirement for warmth or may include social needs such as the desire to be thought sexually attractive. A psychological need, for example, may relate to vanity and self-image and be manifest in a desire to perceive oneself as smaller or larger than reality. Styling skill can create garments that emphasize or reduce the aspect size as wished, but a limited amount of 'psychological sizing' also can play a part. For example, a well-known bra manufacturer produces its leading brand with labels that are one size larger. The assumption is that some consumers derive satisfaction and confidence from a size label that flatters aspirations or a particular self-image. A similar situation exists with the sizing of boxer shorts where it is well known that very few men want the label small when buying or receiving underwear. Another example relates to perceptions and garment sizing where some women desire to see themselves as a smaller size and manufacturers respond accordingly by classifying what is really a size 18 dress as a 16.

It is not the contention of this book that such examples are to be advocated. Indeed, we would argue that much time and effort is wasted at the retail level and that the net effect upon the consumer is probably counterproductive. When market researchers claim that the majority of British women do not accurately know their own bra size, one wonders whether this ignorance is not perpetuated by the absence of an industry standard on sizing.

Consumer behaviour and promotion

The promotion of fashion items requires an understanding of consumers' media habits so that the correct media can be chosen. Understanding consumer behaviour enables the selection of appropriate promotional messages. For example, fashion photography often seeks to reflect a particular lifestyle that the consumer can identify with and then perceive the product as a vehicle to the attainment of that lifestyle. The use of celebrities in advertisements also enables fashion firms to reach certain target audiences and influence consumers via the process of identification. Further consideration of the use of celebrities in fashion promotion is given in Chapter Nine.

Consumer behaviour and price

Price for many people is a major indicator of quality. Style and design are sometimes difficult to judge, especially for the untrained. Therefore some consumers take surrogate indicators of quality and in particular price. An understanding of the perceptual process and how consumers learn about prices and value is helpful in constructing a pricing policy.

Consumer behaviour and distribution

The choice of an appropriate distribution channel and designing elements within that channel should be based on an understanding of the fashion consumer. Knowing when, where and how consumers wish to buy are fairly obvious applications. Understanding and matching self-images and store images and creating particular store atmospheres to encourage certain moods need research and ideas from consumer behaviour.

3.3 Fashion consumer decision-making

One main way of examining consumer behaviour is to take the view of the consumer as a problem solver. The requirement for clothing, however it is driven, is seen as a problem for the consumer to solve, usually by exchanging money with a seller. The problem-solving perspective raises many questions that will be addressed; they concern the types of decision fashion consumers must make, the various stages of the decision process consumers progress through and major factors that influence those decisions.

3.3.1 Types of consumer decision

It is tempting to see the purchase of a garment as just one decision, to buy or not to buy. However, it can be useful to break the larger decision down into several separate decisions that collectively comprise the buy or no buy decision. For instance, consumers must decide the following matters:

- How to find out about new styles?
- What style, colour and size to buy?
- Where to buy from?
- How to pay?
- Which bills to pay promptly?
- When to buy?
- How many items to buy?
- Will any accessories need to be purchased?
- Whether to shop alone or accompanied?
- Whether to try the garment on?
- Whether to order an out of stock size or colour option?
- Which sales assistant to approach for help?
- What to do if the product is unsatisfactory?
- What will be the reaction of significant others to the purchase?
- Whether or not to purchase online or mail order?
- If buying online or mail order, how to arrange delivery?

If fashion marketers see consumer decisions as a series of smaller related problems to be solved, then the benefit comes in terms of planning activities to ensure that the consumer is helped when help is needed. For example, a consumer may not be bothered about trying a blouse on if she knows she can easily exchange it later for another size if needed.

Alternatively, another customer may dislike the whole process of shopping for clothes and appreciate speedy service with advice and nearby displays of matching accessories. Marketing research is necessary to determine which decisions are important to the particular target market of the fashion firm.

3.3.2 Consumer involvement

Another way to look at consumer decisions is the level of involvement the consumer has in the decision. Consumers differ considerably in terms of their interest in fashion. Even those people who are very interested in fashion may be more interested in some types of garment than in others. A common way consumer theorists have classified consumer decisions is into high- and low-involvement purchases. This classification, in part, reflects different theoretical paradigms, although some significant attempts at synthesis have emerged over recent years.

The level of involvement depends on the person, the purchase object and the time and place of purchase. For one consumer, the purchase of a pair of socks may involve considerable deliberation and visiting several stores to make comparisons in order to obtain a product that meets fairly precise specifications in terms of colour, size and construction. For another consumer, the purchase of socks may be relegated to a simple commodity purchase undertaken with little conscious thinking through and they may be selected along with other low-involvement purchases in a supermarket.

The implication for fashion marketers is to find out the level of involvement of the target market or markets and design the marketing mix accordingly. A central issue is the provision of marketing information to consumers who may or may not want or use it. A connection between low-level involvement and impulse buying can be shown and this has a bearing on the relative proportion of the promotional budget that goes on in-store promotions rather than on advertising. If consumers do not really pay much attention to information about some fashion products, but simply make decisions in the store, it would be more productive to concentrate promotional efforts in-store.

3.3.3 The decision process

As shown earlier, the consumer decision to buy may be seen as a series of smaller decisions. It also can be shown as consumer progression through a number of discrete stages. Most models of consumer behaviour use the stages or near equivalents as shown in Figure 3.2.

The various phases will be briefly outlined. First, problem recognition occurs when a consumer becomes aware that a need for clothing arises. This may be triggered by garments wearing out, comments from others about how unfashionable existing garments are, a change of social status prompting or facilitating purchase or a change in

Problem recognition

↓

Information search

↓

Evaluation of alternatives

↓

Purchase

↓

Post-purchase evaluation

Figure 3.2 The consumer decision process.

aspirations or taste. The extent to which fashion marketers are able to influence problem recognition is fiercely debated.

Whether marketers create needs is the question often asked. Blackwell *et al.* (2006) argue that marketers do not create needs, they show consumers better ways of satisfying pre-existing needs. For example, high-status needs can be satisfied by any number of different purchases or activities. The fact that a fashion advertiser captures the imagination of some consumers and secures purchases probably has more to do with the understanding of those needs and careful design of a message than the creation of the needs in the first place. Many powerful social forces operate in society of which advertising is only one and one not often held in very high regard. Advertising both reflects and influences societal values towards consumption. If it were truly able to create needs and exert such a powerful influence then it has been an outstanding failure in the world of fashion.

Having become aware of a need, the consumer reflects on the situation and can decide to proceed with the purchase process and collect information, defer the purchase or conclude that the problem is insignificant or cannot be solved. In deciding to proceed, the consumer reviews information already held in memory. This includes knowledge of brands and stores where solutions may be found. Inexperience or unsatisfactory prior purchases may cause external information sources to be consulted. External sources include personal sources such as friends, neutral sources such as a television programme on eveningwear, or fashion marketing sources such as a window display or a poster advertisement. These three main external types of information sources are usually regarded with different degrees of credibility by the consumer.

When sufficient information is held by the consumer about possible solutions then evaluations take place and a choice is made. The nature of the evaluations varies from individual to individual. Some consumers have extensive repertoires of buying criteria, whereas others have limited and often vague mechanisms for making decisions. The process of making an evaluation may involve the mental ranking or rating of alternatives or simply eliminating items that fail to meet a certain threshold. At times consumers can suffer what is described as information overload where there are too many possibilities or too much information has been presented. An awareness of consumer information needs and the provision of information in an appropriate manner via facts and advice from sales staff or brochures can help the consumer to make a choice. The decisions made by a consumer at the time of purchase have been mentioned earlier and the sales effort to influence purchase is covered in Chapter Nine.

After a purchase consumers may engage in a process of evaluation of the product and to an extent their own efficiency as a consumer. Systematic evaluation is most unlikely except where items are bought primarily for their functional characteristics, such as hiking boots where protection and durability may be closely scrutinized. The extent of evaluation seems related to how socially conspicuous the item is, how central the product is to the self-image of the consumer, the particular consumer orientation and also to the purchase price. For most consumers, the evaluation can involve seeking comments from others perceived to be significant.

Fashion marketers should be interested in this post-purchase behaviour as it can relate directly to repeat purchases, the level of customer complaints and word-of-mouth communications about the firm. The law of effect in psychology states simply that behaviour that is rewarded is likely to be repeated. Satisfied customers are likely to become regular customers. The goal of fashion marketing is to move customers along the continuum from the promiscuous to the insistent, as shown in Figure 3.3.

Careful monitoring of customer complaints can lead to the early correction of faults and avoidance of some future complaints. Sensitive handling of genuine complaints can also help retain goodwill and avoid negative word-of-mouth communication. As research indicates that consumers are more likely to pass on negative rather than positive information about products, onae dissatisfied customer may lead to many more with negative attitudes towards the store or brand.

The above discussion of the decision process has shown the need to consider factors beyond the immediate concerns of the consumer when trying to understand and predict the behaviour of the fashion consumer. The factors to be considered may be

Promiscuous – will shop around for the best deal
Occasional – will sometimes buy from us
Loyal   – will usually buy from us
Insistent   – will only buy from us

Figure 3.3 Types of customer.

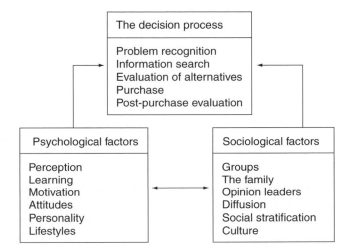

Figure 3.4 A model of consumer behaviour.

grouped under the broad headings of psychological and sociological factors. Psychological factors are taken from the study of individual behaviour while sociological factors are based on the understanding that much consumer behaviour takes place as part of a group process and involves social interaction and patterns of influence. Figure 3.4 illustrates the main explanatory variables related to the decision process.

3.4 Psychological processes

3.4.1 The buyer's perceptual process

Perception is the process whereby buyers select, organize and interpret simple stimuli into a meaningful and coherent picture of the world. To explain this process further, a distinction between sensation and perception must be made. Sensation refers to the responses of our sense organs to simple stimuli, whereas perception is the psychological consequence of sensation. An analogy would be to compare a photograph with a painting: the photograph is the 'reality', whereas the painting is a very personal view of 'reality'.

For the fashion consumer, the stimuli presented in a busy fashion store are a bewildering array of sensations that must be made sense of. The consumer goes through a number of stages in the perceptual process that can be seen as steps in filtering and distilling marketing stimuli into a unique marketing experience. The stages in this perceptual filtering and distilling process are:

◆ selective exposure;
◆ selective attention;
◆ selective distortion;
◆ selective retention.

Selective exposure

Age or income can impose some constraints on the exposure to certain stores or media, as can the more deliberate choice by the consumer. This process, where there is a narrowing of the opportunities for experience of the total range of marketing stimuli, is known as selective exposure. Examples of marketing stimuli subject to selective exposure are the fashion page in a daily newspaper, advertisements, brochures and store window displays. The task for fashion marketers is to ensure that the correct media and location for retail outlets are selected to maximize the opportunities for selective exposure.

Selective attention

Selective attention is the next stage, and the range of possibilities is further narrowed when the consumer pays attention only to some marketing stimuli and not to others. Consumer factors that determine consumer attention to marketing stimuli are existing attitudes, attention span, emotional states, motives and expectancy. The last point is illustrated by the following well-known saying (Figure 3.5):

> A stitch in time
> time saves nine

Figure 3.5

Many people will have 'read' the above statement and not have noticed the double use of the word 'time'; they will have perceived what they expected to see rather than the reality. Existing attitudes and prejudice similarly influence how we perceive marketing messages. Items which are promoted as designer label or sale items may attract attention or may even be screened out by the consumer depending on prior attitudes. Thus the importance of determining consumer predispositions, via marketing research, before designing marketing messages is underlined.

Some factors under the control of the fashion marketer can influence whether the marketing message gains the attention of the consumer. The size and intensity of a message (i.e. very loud) plus novelty, contrast, repetition and movement can all enhance the chances of gaining attention. Thus advertisements in the first 10% of a magazine such as *Company* or *GQ* have a higher potential readership than the latter part of the same magazine. Similarly, a black and white advertisement in a glossy magazine, which is surrounded by colour advertisements, stands a good chance of gaining attention because of the contrast.

Selective distortion

Having gained the consumer's attention the next perceptual filter for the marketer to penetrate is selective distortion. Consumers interpret stimuli in a manner that is consistent with existing attitudes. The perceptual process operates in such a way as to enable and maintain a coherent view of the world; too many contradictions to existing views make the management of everyday life irksome. That is not to say that changing consumers' perceptions is impossible, just that before embarking upon change marketers need to discover the starting points and the strength with which existing views are held. An example of the distorting effect of the perceptual process is easily noted when considering the stereotypes that are brought to bear in judging garments by country of origin. To most British consumers the labels 'Made in France' or 'Designed in Italy' have connotations of higher design content and quality than an item made in a developing country. These connotations can have such an influence that they may, and often do, override the judgements that would emerge in a blind test.

Selective retention

The final perceptual filter is selective retention. This refers to the phenomenon of consumers remembering information about fashion marketers and their products in a highly subjective way. An important aspect of perception is that the consumer interprets information in terms of current priorities and concerns to such an extent that the individual in effect rewrites their personal history. The main driving force behind this selective retention is a need for consistent and, sometimes, easy explanations for our feelings and past behaviour. In this process good and bad aspects of some items may become exaggerated with, for example, nostalgia for some so-called golden age of fashion when there was 'real pride and skill in tailoring, unlike today'. The close associations that many people have between blue jeans and youth have been recognized by the jeans manufacturers in the targeting of middle-aged consumers with the use of suitable music in advertisements to evoke the nostalgia.

3.4.2 Learning

The fashion consumer is not born with a knowledge of fashion brands, of criteria for judging garments, a knowledge of stores or prices, preferences for certain styles or fabrics or even how to care for garments. All this information has to be learned. Consumer learning is any relatively permanent change in buying behaviour that is a result of practice or experience. Two main sources for consumer learning are the family and peer groups. However, much learning occurs through consumer experience with fashion marketers, their products and promotional methods.

Many explanations of consumer learning are given in the marketing literature, most of which can be classified as association learning or cognitive learning. Although the two main types of theory compete to explain behaviour, neither category is sufficient to explain all learning that occurs. The following discussion presents aspects of both approaches.

Association learning

Association learning occurs when a marketing stimulus and the consumer response are repeatedly paired. Much low-level learning such as brand names occurs at this level. A key explanatory theory for this type of learning is known as the law of effect. When behaviour is rewarded, it will tend to be repeated and when it is punished or not rewarded, it will tend to diminish in frequency. Therefore we have a simple explanation for repeat buying and brand loyalty. The consumer who buys a particular brand of shirt and finds that it meets his criteria in terms of being stylish, comfortable, durable and value for money will tend to buy the same brand again. The main lesson for fashion marketers is to identify the relevant buying criteria of the consumer and produce products to meet those criteria. Another consumer who finds that the skirt she purchased three weeks ago is starting to come apart at the seams will probably avoid buying another skirt from that supplier. Yet, another customer may learn to avoid certain shoe shops as the sales assistants, paid primarily by commission, all compete to serve the customer and do not allow adequate time for browsing.

An interesting aspect of association learning is the notion of shaping behaviour. This notion allows marketers the opportunity to influence consumers and help them learn more complex forms of behaviour. By selectively rewarding closer and closer approximations to the final goal sought by the marketer, consumer learning is modified. In the section in Chapter Seven on pricing the link between sales discounts and consumer behaviour is described. Some consumers learn, because of regular retailer action, to defer purchase until sale time, as they are rewarded by lower prices.

Shaping behaviour, when effectively planned, permits the fashion retailer to alter behaviour in other ways. Suppose the retailer introduces a new range of cotton underwear with Lycra, the goal is to encourage the consumer to buy several pairs. To launch the range and encourage a trial with minimum risk and maximum reward a coupon offering a discount may be offered. The consumer who buys the product receives another coupon as well, this time of lower value than the initial coupon. The second coupon should induce another purchase at reduced cost, but without coupon support. If the product performance meets expectations, then the beginning of brand loyalty has been shaped. It should be stressed that the main reward should come from the product and not the coupon, otherwise the consumer learns something else, only to buy from the retailer when an incentive is offered.

Cognitive learning

Cognitive learning theories approach the problem of consumer learning by assuming consumers reason and reflect upon the relationship between marketing stimuli and consumer response. Clearly all consumers do think about some purchases in detail and may engage in mental processes to try to reach a reasoned conclusion before purchasing. Inexperience, previous dissatisfaction, expense and high-involvement clothing items are most usually linked with cognitive learning. The cognitive approach concentrates on the thinking through of different courses and the identification of the decision criteria and rules used by consumers. Knowing how consumers make connections between product features and their buying criteria is obviously helpful for marketing staff in order to provide the right information at the right time. The concentration on the information processing aspect of learning will be developed further in Section 3.4.3.

3.4.3 Consumer attitudes

Attitudes are a learned orientation or predisposition to a given situation, person, object or idea resulting in a tendency to respond favourably or unfavourably. There are three main components to an attitude: the cognitive, affective and conative. The cognitive dimension refers to knowledge or information possessed about the fashion product, service, image, store or prices; the knowledge possessed by the consumer may not be accurate or complete, but it is what is believed to be the truth by the consumer. The affective dimension is concerned with consumer feelings about fashion marketing offerings and is measured in terms such as like and dislike or good and bad. The conative aspect provides the behavioural aspect of attitudes and is usually expressed in terms of an intention, or not, to buy within a specified time. Thus a consumer may know of a new range from Missonia and of the colours, prices and sizes available; the consumer may like the new range and moreover intends to purchase a new sweater within the next seven days.

Fashion marketers are interested in consumer attitudes as they are seen to be closely linked to behaviour. A simple model of the link between attitudes and buying behaviour is shown in Figure 3.6.

The model below oversimplifies matters somewhat as it is argued that sometimes attitudes emerge or become manifest after purchase. Other writers contend that liking may precede knowledge in certain

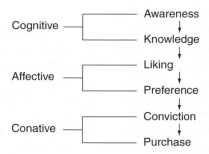

Figure 3.6 Attitude components and buying behaviour.

circumstances. Several attitude theories offer competing explanations for the same phenomenon. It is clear that predicting behaviour from simple measurements of attitudinal components is a problematic and contentious area. Numerous studies have shown that positive attitudes towards fashion products do not always result in higher sales. The work of Ajzen and Fishbein (1980) suggests that the crucial factors to consider are the measurement of the attitude towards the act of purchase and the identification of normative beliefs. For example, a consumer may like the designs of Jean Paul Gaultier and have very positive attitudes towards the designs and cut of the garments. However, the same consumer may not buy because of negative attitudes towards the price or a belief that his or her close friends may not like the styling. Techniques for measuring attitudes are described in Chapter Four.

When considering the point that attitudes emerge and/or change after purchase, it should be noted that post-purchase experience with garments can lead to attitude change, both positive and negative. Festinger (1957) proposed that there is a tendency to seek consonance or harmony of thoughts, feelings and behaviour. Post-purchase doubt over a new garment or dissonance then becomes a motivating state of affairs and the consumer acts to reduce dissonance. Dissonance can be reduced in a number of ways, including:

- changing behaviour (e.g. exchanging the garment for another colour);
- changing attitudes (e.g. deciding that the brand is perhaps not as good as previously thought);
- revoking the decision (e.g. asking for a refund);
- seeking extra consonant information (e.g. asking a friend for reassurance of the wisdom of the choice made);
- avoiding dissonant information (e.g. not visiting other shops in case a lower price is seen for the same item).

A considerable amount of the early research on attitudes was conducted in the USA at the Universities of Yale and Columbia. Much of this research still provides a useful framework for the practising fashion marketer, and its findings are useful in the design of advertising efforts. Some of this work has been incorporated in Chapter Nine.

3.4.4 Consumer motivation

Motivation is the inner force that drives and energizes consumers towards goals. Motivation incorporates need arousal, causing the drive that leads instrumental behaviour to reduce the drive.

Consumer motivation is a complex matter to understand for many reasons. First, motives are inferred, a consumer motive cannot be seen or observed; what is noted is behaviour and then an assumption about the underlying behaviour is made. An important distinction should be made between merely describing behaviour and explaining behaviour. Saying, for example, that a customer buys low-cut tops, because she is the sort of person who likes to reveal her cleavage is mere description, whereas, for example, a particular purchaser of a Prada jacket may be said to be satisfying status needs, especially if the brand name is prominently shown on the garment.

Motivation is a complex concept as similar motives may find expression in different behaviour. Just as in the example above, a status-seeking consumer bought a Prada jacket, other people will seek different brands or may find non-fashion products or activities to satisfy status needs. Furthermore, people may buy the same product, but for different motives. Another purchaser of a Prada jacket may do so primarily for warmth and protection (a physiological motive) or for social motives, e.g. to be accepted by a particular group of friends.

Motives may change over time with, for example, a change in social status. The arrival of a child is often accompanied by a change in motivation towards clothing purchases for most women. Another consideration is that many motives may simultaneously affect purchasing behaviour. Sometimes the motives operate to make the consumer positive towards the clothing item, whereas at other times there can be motive conflict. An example of motive conflict could be a person attracted to the purchase of a coat that will satisfy status needs, but at the same time repelled as the coat may not be warm enough to satisfy a physiological need.

There are several ways of classifying motives and these are described below. Motives can be placed along a continuum from rational to emotional. Buying a waterproof hat clearly has a strong rational element; an evening dress costing several thousand pounds that will be worn only once is obviously near the other end of the continuum. Another question to consider is whether the consumer is conscious of all the motives impelling choice. Freudian theory likens the personality to an iceberg where people are only partly aware of their motives. Many consumers may be unaware of or unwilling to admit to some of the motives that cause them to buy or avoid certain garments. It is easier for many people to assert that an item was bought because it looks nice than to admit that it was bought to impress others. The measurement of consumer motivation is problematic and some qualitative techniques for measuring motives are outlined in Chapter Four.

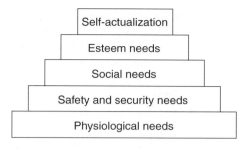

Figure 3.7 Maslow's hierarchy of needs.

A widely cited classification system for motivation was developed by Abraham Maslow. Maslow, a psychologist, stated that motives were organized in a hierarchy and that only when lower-level needs were satisfied did higher-level needs become important (Figure 3.7).

Thus the consumer on a limited income will be concerned with perhaps the functional aspects, such as warmth, of low-cost clothing before matters of social acceptance assume importance. Social needs include the need to belong and be accepted by others. Esteem needs are the need for the consumer to think well of themselves and have others hold a high opinion of them. Self-actualization, for Maslow, was the desire to grow psychologically and it embraces creativity and achievement. For one person knitting needles and some wool may enable self-actualization, whereas for another the participation in the design process by suggesting colours or styling aspects of a garment enables self-actualization. Some clothing purchases may satisfy needs at more than one level, e.g. a Barbour waxed jacket may satisfy the need for warmth and protection from the elements as well as enabling acceptance by a group who are similarly dressed. The translation of product features into specific benefits related to motives is a key selling task and this is described in more detail in Chapter Nine.

3.4.5 Consumer personality

Personality is the particular configuration of qualities that make a person unique. Two main approaches to personality will be considered, psychographics and the self-concept.

Earlier approaches to consumer behaviour concentrated on consumer personality traits and tried to discover consumer types. The hope was that having identified certain types of consumer, buyer behaviour could be predicted and fashion products could be produced and promoted accordingly. Unfortunately, the correlation between personality type and buying behaviour was very small and this approach was succeeded by one which based consumers not on traits, but on activities, interests and opinions (AIOs). This is known as psychographics or lifestyles. Typically consumers are asked a large number of questions, usually based on a Likert scale, as described in Chapter Four, of general and specific questions relating to AIOs. Examples of such questions are 'I believe regular exercise is essential for good health' (general) and 'I go swimming at least once a week' (specific). The answers to these questions are then analysed together with demographic, purchasing and media data about consumers to derive distinct groupings, or types who have AIOs in common. Some interesting analyses have been undertaken linking clothing lifestyle groups with geo-demographics and this work will be discussed later in this chapter.

These lifestyle groups are given names and can be the basis of target marketing efforts or used as a platform for advertising copy design or store design. The major drawback to lifestyle analysis is the lack of theoretical underpinning or measures of reliability or validity of much of the work undertaken. Evidence suggests that general lifestyle analysis is less useful and that research is best conducted into specific products and related areas such as health, beauty and fashion. Some labels given to the groups are plainly insulting to consumers, such as apathetics or dowdies, and at worst are little more than promotional aids for advertising agencies trying to sell their services to retailers and manufacturers. Recent work by Mintel and TGI on fashion lifestyles in Europe examined the incidence of eight lifestyle categories (Big Spenders, Label Admirers, Well Dressed, Stylish, Fashion Conscious, Shopaholics, Individualists and Practical) across four EU countries (UK, Germany, France and Spain). Marked differences were found between Germany and France, for instance where Germans were over-represented as Big Spenders and Label Admirers, whereas French consumers were over-represented as stylish and fashion conscious. The clear implication of this research for retailers is that the influence of culture means lifestyle marketing is perhaps not easily transferred across national boundaries. When done systematically, lifestyle analysis can offer real insights into buying behaviour, but there is no consensus on methodologies and the technique is expensive and needs to be undertaken continuously.

Analysis of the self-concept is another major strand of research from the area of consumer personality studies. The dimensions of the self-concept include:

- the self-image, which is how the person sees him- or herself;
- the ideal self-image, which is how the person would like to see him or herself;

- the social self-image, which is how the person thinks others see him or her;
- the ideal social self-image, which is how the person would like others to see him or her.

In addition, the self-concept is influenced by situational factors such as who the 'others' are and the context of buying. Thus there seem many 'selves', although there is an enduring sense of continuity and sameness that provides coherence for the consumer and this is known as identity. It should be noted that consumers do not always accurately perceive themselves or the reactions of others towards them. The main tool for measuring the self-concept is the semantic differential scale and that is described in Chapter Four.

For the fashion marketer, the self-concept represents a promising area as clothing is an obvious way in which a consumer may express him- or herself and show how they would like others to judge them. Consumers buy clothes both to maintain and to enhance the self, depending on the ascendency or salience of the self versus ideal self-image. Self-images are affected by many factors, but most notably by age and social class. Perceived opportunities and/or the lack of opportunities can influence not only images of the self, but also the value placed upon the self, namely self-esteem.

3.5 Sociological aspects of consumer behaviour

Consumers are social creatures, who form groups and interact in relation to goals. Consumer behaviour when viewed from a sociological perspective is more than a simple aggregation of individual acts, for the patterns and processes of both individual acts and wider social changes are profound in their impact on fashion marketing. Several social dimensions of consumer behaviour will be examined and these relate particularly to the process of influence over choice and to the basis for segmenting markets.

3.5.1 Social groups

A group may be defined as two or more people who bear a psychological relationship to one another and who interact in relation to a common purpose. People do not just form groups, they form groups for reasons such as to satisfy social needs, for mutual protection and enhancement or to check attitudes and perceptions. The price of group membership is conformity to norms, a norm being a shared expectation of behaviour. Norms are essential to groups as they

Figure 3.8 Escada store.

enable stability and provide a framework within which identities may be expressed and common goals can be pursued.

For many aspects of life there is uncertainty and groups provide a mechanism to check that uncertainty. This checking function is apparent in clothing purchases where the advice and support of friends is sought to check, among other things, the appropriateness of styling of garments and whether the items represent good value for money. Group members do not usually dress identically, but for specific occasions there are norms or unwritten rules about the range of garments and stores that would be considered acceptable. For example, a group of friends may all visit an Escada store (Figure 3.8), but not necessarily buy the same items within that store. The young man whose friends usually wear blue denim clothes doesn't turn up to meet his friends wearing a suit without the anticipation of a little teasing.

The mechanisms of maintaining conformity are rewards for compliance and punishments for deviance. Much of the control is exercised by non-verbal means or joking and teasing. These methods allow group members to retain dignity and comply without the great risk that would follow from blunt verbal demands. Norms for dress are most explicit for formal occasions where the expectations may be printed on invitations. Many workplaces have dress codes, although these vary in specificity from the rigidly prescriptive uniform through the broad list of exclusions to the vague hints about dress related to status within the organization.

The anticipation of the reactions of others can be a key factor in the choice of clothing. Consumers may not accurately anticipate those reactions or may lack confidence and rely upon friends to advise and accompany them on shopping trips. Everybody differs in their social needs and those with the highest needs will tend to conform the most. The discussion so far has concentrated on face-to-face groups where conformity is often greater.

Consumers also belong to many groups that are not face to face; they also may aspire to belong to certain groups and still further wish to distance themselves from others. Everyone belongs to automatic groups by virtue of age, gender, race, religion, etc. and with membership come sets of expectations of how one ought to dress. Two women may both have legs that are flattered by short skirts, but if one woman is in her fifties and the other in her early twenties, the social influences and pressures to conform may be markedly different.

Groups that individuals identify with are known as reference groups and as noted they can be positive, negative or aspirational. An example of negative reference group influence may be a young man not buying a well-known brand of boot because he thinks they are worn by skinheads and racists. Aspirational reference group influence is most apparent when people apply to join new organizations – for instance most people take care over their job interview outfit. Similarly, parents sending children to school for the first time will make an effort to dress their child in a way that will enable him or her to be accepted quickly. Reference group influence is important not only for styles of fashion products, but also for endorsements and rejections of particular brands. Teenage purchases of trainers are influenced by what brands are regarded as 'in' and what is considered 'out' by the reference group.

3.5.2 Opinion leadership

Opinion leadership refers to the degree of influence exerted where a consumer is faced with a choice. Many people discuss clothing and fashion advertising as a normal part of social interaction. The influence of others is accepted under certain circumstances. When little information about garments or stores is possessed or when the information is out of date, consumers seek information from others. Opinions are also sought where products are highly visible such as outerwear or where the garment involves risk because it may be expensive, go quickly out of fashion or simply prove unpopular with significant others. Opinion

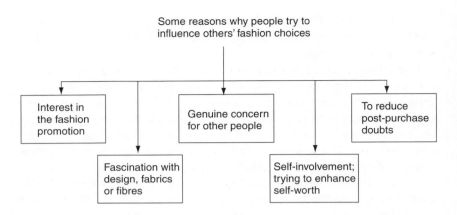

Figure 3.9 Opinion leadership.

leaders exist in all groups and indeed the role may change according to the issue facing the group; one person may exert much influence over the choice of where to dine, whereas another group member may have sway over which are the best clothing stores to visit.

Celebrity influence is a particular type of opinion leadership. Evidence on celebrity influence shows that it is most powerful when the celebrity selected has credibility, is attractive, is trustworthy and is likeable. The enduring involvement of many leading fashion houses with clothing celebrities at the Oscar Awards is testimony to their belief in the power of such influence. Further examples of celebrity influence and their use in fashion promotion are discussed further in Chapter Nine.

There are many reasons why people try to influence others about fashion products and services, as shown in Figure 3.9. There may be genuine concern for the well-being of a friend and advice is given on obtaining value for money by visiting particular stores. The influencer or opinion leader may talk about fashion products because he or she is fascinated by the design or fabrics used. Sometimes a fashion message via advertising or public relations may prompt discussion and generate much media coverage. Dolce & Gabbana, Sisley, Puma, Benetton and Wonderbra have all used advertisements at times that have provoked strong public reactions. At other times opinion leaders may talk about clothing as a way of establishing self-worth by claims to superior knowledge or taste. In addition, the opinion leader may discuss an item of clothing as a way of reducing his or her dissonance (see earlier).

Fashion marketers often hope to use opinion leadership as a way of encouraging the diffusion of a product range. If opinion leaders can be identified and targeted with promotional efforts, then the hope is that the message will be distributed via word-of-mouth communications. Fashion media personnel perform an important role in the word-of-mouth process and the marketing efforts directed at them will be discussed in Chapter Nine, particularly with regard to public relations, trade fairs and exhibitions.

3.5.3 The family

The family is the basic social group and the main mechanism by which social values and aspirations are transmitted. The family is important to the fashion marketer because families share finite financial resources and media exposure, and they make some purchases either collectively or in anticipation of the reaction of other family members. Paying attention to the role of the family is important when it is realized that the person buying the item of clothing may not be the wearer. For example, about half of all male underwear in the UK and a significant proportion of knitwear for men are purchased by women.

Families, as defined by government statisticians, are persons related by blood, marriage or adoption who reside together. It is tempting to view the family as in decline when newspaper headlines about divorce rates are considered. However, the family remains a strong institution in British society, most people get married and the majority of those do not get divorced. Over the long term, divorce is a factor that has had a major influence upon the lives of many people and is often accompanied by a reduced purchasing capacity for either or both former marriage partners.

The family life cycle is an attempt to classify people according to the age of the head of household, marital status, and the age and number of children. Early models of the family life cycle, by Wells and Gubar, omitted the occurrence of divorce and made the assumption that everyone followed the same route from birth to old age, namely single, married without children, married with children, etc. Later models of the family life cycle have recognized the role of divorce, but there is still a need to account for the extent of cohabitation, the number of people who remain single all their lives and alternative lifestyles.

Modelling the progress of people through time via the family life cycle is useful for two major reasons. People at the same stage of the life cycle may, because of similar demands upon income, constitute target markets for companies. The fashion retailer Next grew dramatically during the early 1980s by recognizing and responding to a demographic change connected with the family life cycle. Further, knowledge of how many people are at a certain stage in the life cycle enables predictions for future demand. For instance, knowing the marriage rate and the fertility rate, some fairly accurate estimates can be made about the number of births over the next few years. This information is vital for manufacturers of baby clothes and stores such as babyGAP and Gapkids.

Family decision-making is important for fashion marketers, for it is important to know how decisions are made and who exerts influence over the clothing decisions made by families. Three stages of the purchasing process are relevant: initiation, information search and purchase decision. It may be within a family that the female notices that an item of clothing needs replacing, and she also may collect information via reading magazines or clothing catalogues to narrow the choice. In the same family the male may be the sole wage earner and he may be the person sanctioning the purchase. If such a pattern of decision-making were typical for the target market, then there would be clear implications about which media should be used for advertising.

Family decisions can be classified according to the degree of influence that husbands and wives exert for given product choices. Four types can be considered: husband-dominated, wife-dominated, joint and autonomic. Joint refers to equal influence and a shared decision and purchase. For example a couple may shop together to purchase a new suit for the husband. Autonomic refers to an equal number of decisions made, but those decisions are made separately. Autonomic decisions are perhaps best illustrated by gift purchases, where a female may buy some jewellery herself, but also receives other items purchased by her husband. The factors related to joint decision-making are higher-priced items and where the couple is younger. Whether young couples are more egalitarian or simply less knowledgeable about one another's needs is a matter to be determined by longitudinal research.

Family decision-making requires more research, in particular into the role of children in influencing clothing purchases. Changes in the level of participation in the labour market by married women and relative earnings of males and females mean continuous research is necessary in this area. Discovering the actual level of influence within families is problematic as influence is not always accurately discerned by the participants or even revealed to market researchers. The gender of the interviewer, the presence of the other party, and vanity and modesty from both partners can conspire to make this important research task very difficult to undertake.

3.5.4 Social stratification

All known human societies are stratified. Stratification refers to divisions of people according to their economic position in society, whether

Table 3.1 Socio-economic groups

Class	%	Description
A	4.0	Upper middle class Higher managerial, administrative and professional
B	21.9	Middle class Intermediate managerial, administrative and professional
C1	29.0	Lower middle class Supervisory, clerical or junior managerial, administrative or professional
C2	20.7	Skilled working class Skilled manual workers
D	16.2	Working class Semi-skilled and unskilled manual workers
E	8.1	Those at the lowest level of subsistence Includes most pensioners and the unemployed

Source: National Readership Survey (NRS Ltd), January to December 2006.

they are aware of that position or not. In the UK the main method of determining social stratification or social class is based on occupation. The most widely used system in the fashion market is the National Readership Survey using A, B, C1, C2, D and E. Table 3.1 gives a brief outline of this system.

This system is not the only system nor is the basis of classification uncontradicted, but it is the most widely used system and can be useful in explaining some of the vagaries found in fashion purchasing. A thorough exposition and critique of theories of social class is beyond the scope of this book; however, its impact is undeniably pervasive. A simple model of the influence of social class is that a person's position in the social structure, as determined by occupation, is associated with purchasing power, sets of aspirations and constraints and membership of social groups, all of which lead to patterns of consumption. The process is not only one way, as how somebody's income is spent can be relevant to some of the causal factors. Savings can be one factor in social mobility, though how particular clothing purchases, in themselves, influence social class is both less clear and less powerful.

The links between clothing purchases and social class are less clear than in the past. Photographs from the 1920s and 1930s reveal that clothing was an easy way to depict class. Hats, in particular, were markers of social status. Nowadays, because of the fragmentation of styles, the range of choice available and the change in classes themselves, clothing is no longer an unambiguous guide to class.

Socio-economic groups have all changed, partly on account of the changing occupational structure of the country – while far fewer workers are employed in large-scale manufacturing operations, the service sector has grown dramatically. To give one stark example, in 1907 over 7 million people worked in production industries in the UK and in 2007 the figure was around 3 million. The provision of better health care, education and higher standards of living through the twentieth century have changed all social classes. Class differences at the beginning of the twenty-first century are not the same as the class differences that prevailed a hundred years ago, but that is not to argue that a convergence of class values, attitudes and behaviour has occurred.

Class remains a significant discriminator of consumer behaviour. Although it is not a linear relationship, there is a link between class and income, and the prospects of increases in income. People do not wear rank overtly via their clothing as in the armed forces, but ways are found by many to indicate status. Within social classes, distinctions can be made between creative professional people such as advertising copywriters and accountants in how they dress. The former may tend to favour less formal attire at work whereas the latter tend to dress more conservatively.

Many working-class people may reach their earnings peak early in their career, whereas many middle-class occupations have incremental salary scales. Such experiences, coupled with different entitlements to, and discretion over, holidays, pensions schemes and other 'perks', are associated with different 'world views'. The daily experience of work impacts on these views where, for example, a manager may exercise discretion and make decisions, and a manual employee may work to a rigid work schedule almost like a robot. Workplace tasks, rules or norms may place restrictions upon clothing that can be worn depending upon a person's position. Where uniforms have to be worn it is usually the lower levels that wear them – even the Japanese companies excuse their senior managers from the need to wear overalls. In consequence, clothing worn during the person's leisure time may be chosen to express a distance from, or affinity to, work identity. Class differences are evident in media use, store selection, ownership and use of credit cards and bank accounts, and annual expenditure on clothing and footwear per person.

3.5.5 Geodemographics

Related to social class is a newer system of classifying consumers based upon where they live. A small number of proprietary systems exist based upon the census and categories of neighbourhoods.

One such system is ACORN, which stands for A Classification Of Residential Neighbourhoods and is owned by CACI; Pinpoint is another. These systems are derived from statistical analysis of census variables to discover residential areas, usually census enumeration districts comprising about 150 households and approximately 450 people, that are distinct in composition.

The census data can be linked to survey data on purchasing behaviour and information on media usage. Knowing the postcode of a respondent, the market researcher can determine the geodemographic category. ACORN has 5 categories and 17 related groups. The categories are Wealthy Achievers, Urban Prosperity, Comfortably Off, Moderate Means and Hard Pressed. Among the categories in Urban Prosperity category there are groups known as Prosperous Professionals, Educated Urbanites and Aspiring Singles. The owner of the ACORN system is CACI and the hyperlink is: http://www.caci.co.uk.

Geodemographic data have been used by marketers for target marketing, media planning, setting sales targets by area, forecasting, market testing and selecting new locations for outlets. Among fashion firms, the heavy users are the mail order firms, although retailers such as House of Fraser are involved. Geodemographics presents a promising future for marketing, especially when demographic data are interlaced with psychographic data. However, a number of major criticisms can made of geodemographics. First, it relies on census material that, at best, will be at least one-year-old when it is first used and up to 11 years old before the next census material is readily available. The owners of these systems claim they are able to update their databases to take account of changes in the housing mix and local economies. The systems are in competition and currently are much more expensive than data from secondary sources. Geodemographics is not equally predictive of buying behaviour across all product categories. A geodemographic category is a composite of a number of variables such as class, age, ethnic origin and housing amenities, and critics assert that it is either social class subdivision by another name or a statistical artefact looking for a theory.

An interesting recent development is the combination of geodemographics with lifestyles, particularly those focused on fashion segments. One commercial system developed by Experian and TNS has categorized every adult in the UK into 1 of 20 female and 15 male categories called the Mosiac Fashion Segments. The categories are based on attitudes and shopping behaviour in relation to fashion and these are linked to the census and location data. An example of a female is 'Annabel' a type 12 female described as 'best-dressed fashionistas', aged 18–25, often living with parents, interested in designer labels, quality and style and shopping at River Island and Independent

Stores. A male example is 'Stephen' a type 6 described as 'a mainstream father' aged 35–46 who shops at Next and Debenhams, he doesn't rate brands and quality is not a high priority for him, but he does like to spend money on clothing for his children. The actual profiles available give much more detail than that above and readers can access the full dataset via the hyperlink: http://www.business-strategies.co.uk/.

Fashion marketers obviously need better tools for analysis and planning, and geodemographics combined with fashion lifestyles represents a significant advance, but it is not a panacea or even a clear successor to alternative methods of analysis. To ask some obvious questions, why should the type of dwelling have any bearing on the purchase of clothing? Does the buyer of a leather coat live in an inner city flat, an affluent suburb or a rural setting?

3.5.6 Diffusion of innovation

An innovation can be defined in a number of ways. Innovation can be anything that is new to the company, so it could include 'copying' a method of merchandising or a new style of garment. An innovation also can be taken to mean anything that has been taken up by only a small proportion of the market, usually 10% or less, or an item that has only been on the market for a short time. For the purposes of this discussion an innovation will be taken as anything the consumer perceives to be new, thus it could include an 'old' product introduced into a new market.

Obviously different individuals will adopt new fashion products with differing degrees of enthusiasm and at different times. The process by which the acceptance of an innovation is spread by communication to members of a social system is known as diffusion. Diffusion refers to how an innovation is spread among consumers (groups) over time, whereas adoption refers to individual acceptance of new products. Rogers (1983), after an extensive literature review, proposed a scheme whereby consumers are classified on the basis of the time when they adopt any innovation. Rogers' scheme is obviously arbitrary with regard to percentages, and therefore ideal types are presented in Table 3.2. The scheme is based on the common-sense notion that most users do not adopt the innovation simultaneously. Another way of looking at the issue is to conceive the process as being segmentation over time.

Instead of trying to find characteristics of the above five groups, modern research efforts have focused on the differences between innovators and non-innovators. In practice this means researchers have combined innovators and early adopters and compared them with

Table 3.2 A classification of adopters of innovations

Innovators	2.5%
Early adopters	13.5%
Early majority	34%
Late majority	34%
Laggards	16%

Table 3.3 Comparison of opinion leaders and innovators

	Acceptor	Rejector
Active	Opinion leader	Opinion leader
Passive	Innovator	Innovator

the rest. Innovators tend to be more open-minded, inner- rather than other-directed, and younger rather than older. They also tend to be higher than non-innovators in terms of income, education, social mobility, and reading magazines and newspapers. Non-innovators tend to watch more television and perceive more risk in the purchase of new products than do innovators.

There is only limited, and contested, evidence of the super-innovator, i.e. a person who is an innovator across several unrelated product areas. As with opinion leadership, the evidence suggests there is moderate overlap depending on product interests. Therefore we may find an innovator for fashion products to be an innovator for other aspects of appearance, but not necessarily for food or electronic items.

There is often a tendency to equate the innovator and the opinion leader. They may indeed be the same, but there are differences, as shown in Table 3.3. Opinion leaders are active since they tend to communicate with others, positively and negatively, about their purchases.

Fashion marketers are interested in the factors that influence the rate of diffusion, so that appropriate marketing action may be taken to overcome obstacles of speed during the process.

The main factors that influence the rate of diffusion are:

◆ *Relative advantage*: The more immediate and important the benefits, the faster the rate of diffusion in terms of lower cost or long product life.
◆ *Compatibility*: The innovation must match cultural values, beliefs and expectations. An example of a compatibility issue, when first introduced, was the *Next Directory*, one of the first major paid-for catalogues. More recent examples compatibility

concerns are ethical use of labour and the use of sustainable raw materials in garment manufacture.

◆ *Possibility of trials*: The ability to try on garments or easily exchange those that cannot be tried on, i.e. mail order items, is a key factor.

◆ *Observability or communicability*: Ease with which information about an innovation is transmitted.

◆ *The complexity of the innovation*: The more complex, in terms of understanding and use, the slower the diffusion. Newer synthetic fabrics or garments that have complicated care or cleaning requirements are examples.

◆ *Perceived risk*: The greater the risk the slower the diffusion. Risk can be financial, physical or social. In addition, a perception may exist that a delay in purchasing will lead to lower prices.

◆ *Type of target market*: Some groups are more willing to accept change than others, e.g. the young, the affluent or the highly educated.

◆ *Type of decision*: Depends on whether the purchase of the innovation is an individual or a collective decision.

◆ Marketing effort: The rate of diffusion is not completely beyond the control of the firm selling it. Greater promotional spending can speed the diffusion process.

Knowledge of diffusion of innovation may aid planning, particularly concerning setting targets over time and forecasting. The diffusion process is directly related to the product life cycle concept discussed in Chapter Six. The key roles of the innovator and early adopter are examined from the perspective of product planning in Chapter Six and in relation to promotion in Chapter Nine.

3.6 The organizational buyer

The discussion so far has concentrated upon the retail consumer of fashion. It should be remembered that a significant amount of fashion marketing effort is directed at organizations, be they manufacturers or retailers, who buy to sell on, or companies who purchase garments for consumption by their staff. All of the concepts discussed so far have a bearing upon organizational buying, for organizational buyers are still humans with needs and attitudes, who also conform to social norms like consumers. However, there are some differences that do influence behaviour and these points will be addressed.

It is argued that because organizational buyers buy in bulk, are better trained and better informed, are accountable for their decisions and are often part of a buying team they are more rational than consumers. Organizational buying usually involves more formality with regard to explicit buying criteria or vendor rating systems and unlike most consumer buying, there is often negotiation over products and prices. Given the greater concentration in fashion retailing that has occurred in recent years (see Chapter Eight), organizational buyers are subject to personal forms of promotion, more so than consumers who receive mass communications and have impersonal relations with suppliers.

The preceding arguments support the view that organizational buyers are more rational. However, there is another perspective that argues otherwise. Because organizational buyers are spending someone else's money they may be less careful than the consumer would be with his or her own money. Fashion is concerned with personal taste and the consumer needs only to be certain about his or her purchases, whereas the organizational buyer faces greater uncertainty in the anticipation of the needs of an assortment of others. This multiple responsibility for buying can, under some circumstances, lead to careless action, as personal accountability may be diffused via committees or teams. The extent of supplier loyalty displayed by retailers and manufacturers could be taken as being counterindicative of a more rational approach to buying than that of the consumer who shows no loyalty to any brand or retailer.

Clearly the arguments about relative rationality cannot be easily resolved, but the point to note is that both types of buyer are influenced by psychological and sociological processes which are expressed in buying decisions. Key structural factors that enable fashion marketers to determine specific approaches to organizational buyers are developed further in Chapters Six to Nine, where the relationships between the organizations are explored in relation to the marketing mix.

3.7 Summary

This chapter has introduced the concept of buyer behaviour in the fashion market. It has dealt with:

- the importance of understanding buyers;
- how individual customers make decisions;
- what types of decision they must make;
- psychological influences on customer decision-making;
- how fashion marketers classify customers and sociological influences;
- a comparison of organizational and consumer buying.

Further reading

Ajzen, I. and Fishbein, M. (1980), *Understanding Attitudes and Predicting Social Behavior*, Prentice Hall, Englewood Cliffs, NJ.

Blackwell, R.D. *et al.* (2006), *Consumer Behavior*, 10th Edition, Thomson Business and Economics, Mason, OH.

East, R. *et al.* (2008), *Consumer Behaviour*, Sage, London.

Evans, M.J. *et al.* (2006), *Consumer Behaviour*, John Wiley and Sons, Chichester.

Festinger, L. (1957), *A Theory of Cognitive Dissonance*, Stanford University Press, Stanford, CA.

Peter, J.P. and Olsen, J.C. (2008), *Consumer Behaviour and Marketing Strategy*, 8th Edition, McGraw-Hill, London.

Rogers, E.M. (1983), *Diffusion of Innovations*, 3rd Edition, The Free Press, New York.

Schiffman, L.G. and Kanuk, L.L. (2007) *Consumer Behavior*, 9th Edition, Pearson Prentice Hall, Upper Saddle River, NJ.

Solomon, M.R. (2007), *Consumer Behavior: Buying, Having, and Being*, Prentice Hall, Harlow.

Solomon, M.R. and Rabolt, N.J. (2004), *Consumer Behavior: In Fashion*, Prentice Hall, Upper Saddle River, NJ.

Chapter Four
Fashion Marketing Research

4.1 Introduction

The purpose of this chapter is to provide an introduction to some of the main concepts and decisions involved in the research process, as well as the main techniques used in survey research.

Most adults in the UK have had some experience of marketing research, usually through contact with the 'lady with the clipboard' in street surveys. As such, the main emphasis of this chapter will be on the decisions that must be made as part of survey design; from the definition of the research problem to the design of the questionnaire and data collection. The application of marketing research to product development and fashion forecasting international marketing research issues and the impact of the Internet will also be considered.

4.2 The purpose of marketing research

4.2.1 What is marketing research?

Kotler (2000) defines marketing research as 'the systematic design, analysis and reporting of data and findings relevant to a specific marketing situation facing the company'.

It is often asked whether there is a difference between market research and marketing research. The difference is in the scope of an investigation, as shown in Figure 4.1. Market research is used to refer to research into a specific market, investigating such aspects as market size, market trends, competitor analysis, and so on. Marketing research is a much broader concept, covering investigation into all aspects of the marketing of goods or services, such as product research and development, pricing research, advertising research,

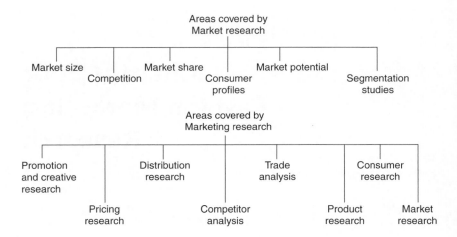

Figure 4.1 Comparison of market research and marketing research.

distribution research, as well as all the aspects of market analysis covered by market research.

4.2.2 Why is information necessary?

In today's fierce market economy the risks faced by businesses are great. Aggressive competitors pose serious threats for both large and small businesses in the constant fight to maintain and increase their market share. To maximize opportunities the successful business person must make the right decisions at the right time. The consequence of making the wrong decision can be financial ruin.

Without the gift of clairvoyance, such decisions are problematic. An understanding of the market and the needs and wants of your consumers now and in the future are rarely based on intuition alone. Sound market information provides the basis for marketing decisions. Marketing research, properly designed and implemented, will provide this information.

4.2.3 Marketing research as part of a marketing information system

The wealth of information flowing into a company has to be organized so that it reaches the right people. Successful companies operate marketing information systems (MIS) to gather accurate, up-to-date information, analyse it and disseminate the results to appropriate decision-makers in time to allow the company to maximize its opportunities and to avoid potential threats. Along with other information producing departments within the company (sales, accounts, etc.), marketing research can assist management in the decision-making process across the full range of marketing activities, from description of a market segment to prediction of future trends.

4.2.4 The scope of marketing research

There is no area of marketing activity to which the techniques of marketing research cannot be applied. Marketing research can provide information on the size and structure of a specific market as well as information about current trends, consumer preferences, a competitor's activities, advertising effectiveness, distribution methods and pricing research. Marketing research also plays a vital role in the development of new products and new advertising and promotion strategies. It can also monitor performance following implementation of those strategies.

The techniques used in the collection of marketing information depend largely on the nature of the research problem, but will vary from the well-known street interview carried out by the 'ladies with clipboards' to more sophisticated techniques such as projective techniques used in such areas as motivation research.

4.2.5 Types of research

Although marketing research techniques can be applied to all areas of marketing, not all techniques are appropriate to every situation. Broadly speaking, there are two types of research: qualitative and quantitative.

Qualitative research uses techniques such as group discussions, individual depth interviews, projective techniques and observation. The information obtained attempts to find out the 'how' and 'why' of a situation, rather than 'how many'. Analysis may be difficult owing to the depth and complexity of the data collected and so it should be carried out by experienced and trained researchers. Qualitative research is invaluable for basic exploratory studies, new product development and creative development studies.

Quantitative research provides information to which numbers can be applied. Quantitative research is the best-known face of marketing research and its main survey method is what most people recognize as marketing research.

4.3 An overview of the marketing research process

The collection of information is a process that must be planned. There are many different areas in which planning decisions need to be made, so good organization is vital.

4.3.1 Stages in the research process

Research procedures will vary depending on the nature of the research problem, but in general, the process of marketing research can be seen to be made up of a number of stages. They are:

1. Define the research problem and set the research objectives.
2. Design the research. This includes:
   (a) data sources;
   (b) select the sampling method;
   (c) select the data collection method;
   (d) design the data collection form (questionnaire).
3. Test the research design (pilot).
4. Collect the data.
5. Analyse the data and interpret the results.
6. Present the findings.

4.4 Problem definition and setting research objectives

Defining the research problem is the most critical step in the research process. Unless the problem is accurately defined, the information collected will be of limited or no use. Careful thought and discussion about the problem, the information needed to address the problem and the relative value of the information collected should take place before anything else. A structured, systematic approach to decision-making will also enable management (or the commissioner of the research) to set the objectives of the research. In other words, what is the problem and what do we want to find out to try to solve it? This preliminary planning is important as it has implications for the design of the research and the quality of the information collected.

4.5 Research design

There are three types of research design: exploratory, descriptive and causal. The choice of research design will depend on the problem previously defined.

4.5.1 Exploratory research

This is most useful in the early stages of research, particularly if the researcher is not familiar with the subject area. There is no formal structure to exploratory research as the researcher needs to look at a wide range of information sources without being restricted. The aim of exploratory research is to uncover any variables that may be relevant to the research project as well as an investigation of the environment in which the research will take place.

4.5.2 Descriptive research

The purpose of descriptive research is to provide an accurate description of the variables uncovered by the exploratory stage. This could be used to investigate the market share of a company's products or the demographic characteristics of the target market (age, gender, income, etc.). Data are usually obtained from secondary data sources or from surveys.

4.5.3 Causal research

Causal research is used to determine the relationship between variables, e.g. the relationship between advertising and repeat purchases.

4.6 Data sources

Data come from two sources, primary and secondary. Secondary data sources consist of information that has already been collected for other purposes and primary sources of information are those used for the purpose of collecting information specifically for the current research project.

4.6.1 Secondary sources

These provide the researcher with a starting point for data collection. It may be possible to solve the research problem either wholly or in part by using secondary data. This reduces the cost of a research project as secondary data are cheaper than collecting primary data. Secondary sources of information, are in the main, fairly accessible, although some sources may remain confidential and others may be too expensive to acquire.

Secondary sources can be separated into the two types as shown in Figure 4.2. Internal sources are those that generate information within

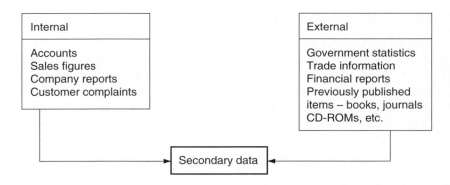

Figure 4.2 Sources of secondary data.

a company or an organization, e.g. sales figures and accounts information. External sources are those that generate information outside a company or an organization. These are by far the more numerous, and some examples of external sources are listed below:

- ◆ *Government statistics*: Census data, family expenditure surveys, trade and manufacturing trends.
- ◆ *Trade information*: Trade press, e.g. Fashion Weekly, Drapers Record; trade associations, e.g. CBI, trade surveys, company reports and competitors' accounts.
- ◆ *Financial institutions*: Many major banks publish reports on regional and national industries.
- ◆ *Commercial research*: Many market research companies undertake continuous research and omnibus surveys covering an extremely broad range of topics, including consumer, media and retail (e.g. Taylor Nelson Sofres, NOP, Ipsos-RSL). Various market reports are available, from, Mintel, Keynote and Retail Intelligence, for example.

The use of secondary data sources, also called desk research, can be very time consuming because there is such a lot of information available, including CD-ROM and 'online' data. Keeping the objectives of the research in mind will help to ensure that time is spent efficiently.

4.6.2 Primary sources

Most marketing research projects will involve the collection of more up-to-date information than is available from secondary sources. Primary sources of information may include consumers, designers, buyers, manufacturers, retailers, and so on, depending upon the research problem.

4.7 Practical sampling methods

In designing research a major decision that the researcher must make concerns the selection of a sampling method. Sampling is a very important tool in marketing research. It involves selecting a small number of people from the larger survey population whose characteristics, attitudes and behaviour are representative of the larger group.

Before selecting the sample, however, the researcher must first define the research population from which to draw the sample. Exploratory research can help to define the population to include all the players and variables that are relevant to the survey.

For some surveys, particularly if the survey population is small or concentrated in one geographical area, it may be possible to take a census, which is a useful method in some business surveys. More commonly a representative sample is interviewed as this reduces both the time and the cost of the research.

4.7.1 Deciding sample size

Deciding how many people to include in your sample is as important a decision as how they should be selected. Factors such as cost, time and staff availability, level of accuracy required, data collection method and location of the population all play a part in deciding sample size. In reality, cost-effectiveness is the most important factor in deciding how many should be contacted in the research, followed by time and staff availability. If it is decided to select a large number for the sample, there may be insufficient staff available to contact the respondents within the time constraints of the survey, so a smaller sample size may be accepted as a compromise.

When selecting a sample it is important that there is a high level of confidence that the sample is representative of the research population as a whole. The sample must be large enough to provide accurate results, without being so large as to increase research costs unnecessarily. It is possible to calculate confidence levels for different sample sizes and there are several texts that cover this adequately (see Further reading at the end of this chapter).

4.7.2 Choice of a sampling method

The two main types of sampling method – probability methods and non-probability methods – are shown in Figure 4.3.

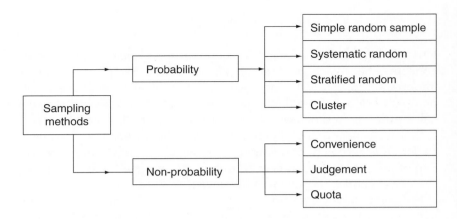

Figure 4.3 Types of sampling method.

Probability methods

Statistically speaking, these are the best types of sampling method as each respondent has a known chance of being selected, so bias is minimized. They also allow the accuracy of the results to be estimated statistically. Sometimes probability sampling methods are referred to generically as 'random sampling' methods. In fact, this refers to a specific type of very precise probability sample. There is often some confusion over the use of the term 'random'. Selecting people in the street at random is not technically random sampling, but more often refers to selection of respondents by interviewers for quota sampling.

The main types of probability sample are simple random sampling, systematic random sampling, stratified random sampling and cluster sampling.

Simple random sampling   Items can be selected from the sampling frame by using the lottery method, e.g. taking numbers out of a hat. In the UK, ERNIE the computer selects Premium Bond winners, and does so by using simple random sampling. Random number tables are generated by computer and often used in marketing research.

Systematic random sampling   With larger samples it is more convenient to divide the population by the sample size to calculate the sampling interval (n). A random starting point is selected using random number tables and every nth time after that is selected.

Example   If the sample size is 50, and the population size is 3000, then the sampling interval is calculated as:

$$n = \frac{3000}{50} = 60$$

If the random number picked from the tables was 35, for example, then the first item selected from the sampling frame would be 35. Every 60th number after that would be selected until a sample size of 50 was achieved.

As the first number was selected randomly, this method is sometimes called a 'quasi-random' method.

The advantage of these methods is that they are relatively simple to carry out and sampling error and confidence levels can be calculated statistically. The main disadvantage is that samples may be produced that do not reflect the characteristics of the survey population. For example, if a sample of students were drawn from a list of all students at a university, it is possible that all the students in the sample might be design students. This is clearly not representative of the student population as a whole.

Stratified random sampling   One way to try to overcome this type of sampling error is to use stratified random sampling. This is used when it is felt that different groups within the population have characteristics that are likely to lead to different types of answers. The population is divided into distinguishable groups (strata) who have similar characteristics. Stratification factors should be as relevant as possible to the survey (e.g. consumer surveys are often stratified by age, gender, socio-economic group, and so on). A random sample is then taken from each stratum.

There are two main methods used to stratify samples. First, with a uniform sampling fraction (proportionate sampling), or secondly, with a variable sampling fraction (disproportionate sampling).

Proportionate and disproportionate sampling   If all the strata are equally important to the survey, a proportionate sample would be taken, i.e. the same number selected from each stratum. Frequently, some strata are more important to the research than others. For example, if you were conducting a survey into the purchase of outsize garments (size 18+), it would be reasonable to assume that most of these items would be purchased by those who were larger than size 16 rather than those who were not. It is logical that more of these people should be included in the sample. In other words, a disproportionate sample would be taken. If a proportionate sample were taken, too few of the people who took larger sized clothes would be included in the survey and it would be difficult to extrapolate the results to the general population with any degree of accuracy.

Cluster sampling   Cluster sampling is a variation of stratified random sampling and may be used when the survey population is concentrated in a relatively small number of groups (clusters) that are considered typical of the market in question. A random sample of these clusters is then taken. A random sample of units from within these clusters is then taken. If the number of units within a cluster is small, a census may be carried out. In a national survey of specialist bridal wear retailers, for example, sales areas could be identified by geographical region and a random sample of these taken. Within each selected sales area, all or a sample of the store managers would be interviewed.

There is a problem with cluster sampling that occurs if the clusters are not sufficiently representative of the survey population. For example, in a small geographical area, it is likely that it will consist of people with similar housing, incomes and lifestyle. Although cluster sampling can be more cost-effective than some other methods of probability sampling, there is a danger that sampling error will increase if the clusters are not carefully defined before the first stage of sampling.

Sampling frames When using probability sampling methods it is necessary to use a sampling frame. This is a list of every element in the survey population. The sample is drawn from this list. A sampling frame is essential for probability-based techniques, as each element must have a known chance of selection, and so must be included in the sampling frame. According to Webb (1999), a sampling frame must have the following characteristics:

- Each element should be included only once.
- No element should be excluded.
- The frame should cover the whole of the population.
- The information used to construct the frame should be up-to-date and accurate.
- The frame should be convenient to use.

Examples of sampling frames include electoral rolls, the telephone book, the Royal Mail's lists of postcodes and other similar databases.

In practice, most sampling frames are not perfect. Not everyone with a telephone is in the phone book, for example. Finding a sampling frame that is suitable for your research can occasionally prove difficult.

Non-probability methods

With non-probability sampling methods, some element of judgement enters the selection process. The extent to which judgement is used, and therefore the element of bias introduced, varies in these methods. Non-probability methods do not require a sampling frame and the chance of each unit being selected is unknown. Statistical estimates of the size of the sampling error cannot therefore be made.

The methods are convenience sampling, judgement sampling and quota sampling.

Convenience sampling Items are selected that are close or easily available. This is useful in the exploratory stage of research, giving the researcher a 'feel' for the subject. Despite being very cheap and quick to carry out, the level of error and bias with this method is likely to be very high and so it should be used with caution.

Judgement sampling Items are selected by the researcher that are felt to be representative of the survey population. This method attempts to be more representative than convenience sampling. Experts also may be consulted for advice on which items are likely to be more appropriate for the survey. For example, in a survey of textile manufacturers, a staff specialist such as a product developer may provide useful advice on which manufacturers would be suitable for selection.

Quota sampling This is the most likely non-probability method to produce a representative sample as items selected are based on known characteristics of the population.

Example Assume that your survey population has the following characteristics:

    Age: 16–29 = 26%; 30–64 = 58%; 65+ = 16%
    Gender: Male = 48%; Female = 52%

If we wanted to interview 150 people who were representative of the above population in terms of the two quota controls (age and gender), we would calculate the quotas as shown in Table 4.1.

This is more conveniently represented as shown in Table 4.2.

A survey's accuracy of representation can be increased by narrowing the bands and including more characteristics, e.g. social class. Interviewers are then allocated a number of interviews (quotas) with specific types of respondent.

The advantages of quota sampling are that it is relatively quick to carry out and easy to administer from a fieldwork point of view. It is also cheaper to use than probability sampling methods. The disadvantages of quota sampling involve problems of bias and sampling errors. The responsibility for selection of respondents lies with the interviewer, which may introduce bias. There is the added problem that there is no probability mechanism with quota sampling, so the sampling error cannot easily be calculated.

Table 4.1 Quota sampling frame (A)

	16–29	30–64	65+	Total
M	16–29 = 26%	30–64 = 58%	65+ = 16%	
A	Male = 48%	Male = 47%	Male = 48%	
L				
E	26% of 48%	58% of 48%	16% of 48%	
	of 150 = 19	of 150 = 42	of 150 = 12	
	Quota = 19	Quota = 42	Quota = 12	73
F	16–29 = 26%	30–64 = 58%	65+ = 16%	
E	Female = 52%	Female = 52%	Female = 52%	
M				
A	26% of 53%	58% of 52%	16% of 52%	
L	of 150 = 20	of 150 = 45	of 150 = 12	
E				
	Quota = 20	Quota = 45	Quota = 12	77
TOTAL	39	87	24	150

Table 4.2 Quota sampling frame (B)

Age	Male	Female	Total
16–29	19	20	39
30–64	42	45	87
65+	12	12	24
Total	73	77	150

Quota samples are often used in surveys where fine degrees of accuracy are not required, for instance in product testing for preference between products.

Although many companies who provide continuous research services use probability sampling, the majority of *ad hoc* marketing research is conducted using quota samples. If this method gave consistently biased or misleading conclusions, it would not be used.

4.8 Primary data collection methods

The researcher should not rely on the use of secondary data alone to answer the research problems. Not all secondary data are available to the researcher as some may be unavailable, for example in confidential reports, and other data may simply be too costly to acquire. The information that is available may be out-of-date or not sufficiently

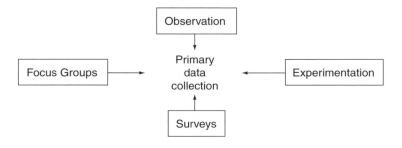

Figure 4.4 Approaches to primary data collection.

detailed to solve the research problem. Usually, primary data need to be collected.

The four main approaches to primary data collection – observation, focus groups, experimentation and surveys – are shown in Figure 4.4.

4.8.1 Observation

There are occasions when it is more useful to observe behaviour than to interview the respondent about it. Observation is usually used to complement other research methods in marketing research, rather than being used alone, as this method can identify patterns of behaviour, but cannot provide information on the reasons behind that behaviour. There are a number of methods available for the observation of behaviour, as follows.

Personal observation

The researcher observes behaviour and records it as it occurs. The skill and the objectivity of the researcher play a key role in the collection of unbiased data. The audit data are collected by taking an inventory of certain products or brands at the premises (at home or office) of the respondent.

This type of ethnographic research (observing respondents in natural settings, e.g. observing fashion buyers at trade fairs) is particularly useful in fashion marketing research. Methods such as accompanied shopping can provide insight into the processes by which decisions are made. Using this method the researcher would accompany the respondent on a shopping trip, often following a prior discussion of the process in the respondent's home, observe the respondent and often use direct questioning to gain insight into underlying reasons for certain behaviour, e.g. why certain products attracted the respondent's attention. This is a useful tool for store layout research and evaluation of point-of-sale displays. Wardrobe analysis is another observational method employed by many image consultants. Here existing garments and accessories that constitute a respondent's wardrobe are examined. This is combined with information on work and lifestyle needs to provide advice on how best to build on existing outfits and to expand the wardrobe to obtain a desired image. Some companies also offer this service online.

Mechanical observation

Recording devices may be used either in laboratory settings or in natural settings. In the laboratory, devices such as the psychogalvanometer are used to measure the respondent's level of perspiration (and so the level of arousal) following exposure to an advertisement or other stimuli. Other devices include the eye-movement camera that detects the movement of the eye over an advertisement, identifying the visual aspects of the advertisement that gain attention. In natural settings, in-store video cameras may be used to record behaviour, with the film being used later for analysis such as researching store layout.

4.8.2 Focus groups

The focus group (also known as the group discussion) is a form of qualitative research. The group usually consists of between 6 and 12 respondents who discuss products, services, attitudes or other aspects of the marketing process. The discussion is led by a skilled researcher called a group moderator, who guides the discussion, following a checklist of topics. The group usually meets in an informal setting, often someone's home, and the group members are paid a small sum for attending. These discussions can take several hours to complete and are often used as a preliminary to survey research. It is also possible to conduct online focus groups via the Internet (see Section 4.14).

4.8.3 Experimentation

According to Kotler (1994), this is the most scientifically valid type of research. Here, matched groups of respondents are subjected to different treatments and the difference in the responses is observed. All variables outside the scope of the research are controlled and as such, the observed responses are taken to be as a result of the difference in treatment of the group. Experimental research seeks to identify cause-and-effect relationships that are central to marketing work.

4.8.4 Surveys

Survey research is the most well known of the research approaches and is widely used for descriptive research. Surveys collect information from a representative sample of the survey population on such topics as consumer behaviour, attitudes and beliefs, as well as buying intentions. The strengths of these beliefs, attitudes and intentions are measured and the results extrapolated to the population as a whole.

4.9 Data collection methods

If a survey is to be conducted, there are a number of methods available for the collection of data and each has its relative advantages and disadvantages. The three main traditional methods are by personal interview, telephone interview and mail questionnaire. Online data collection methods will be discussed later in the chapter.

4.9.1 Personal interview

Face-to-face interviewing is still the most widely used method of primary data collection in the UK, although telephone interviewing is becoming increasingly popular. This method is labour-intensive and costly, but is more likely to result in a satisfactorily completed questionnaire than any of the other methods. This is particularly true if the questionnaire is long or complicated or covers sensitive subjects. Respondents have the opportunity to build a rapport with the interviewer, who can elicit full and accurate answers to questions without biasing the responses.

In a personal interview there is the opportunity to show supporting material, such as examples of a product or still photographs from advertisements. Open-ended questions can also be included in the questionnaire design as the interviewer is present to record the answers verbatim.

The interviewer or fieldworker also plays a vital role in the selection of respondents for interview when using quota sampling. This, however, may introduce bias into the survey.

There is another type of personal interview, the depth interview, which belongs to the realm of qualitative research. Typically, these interviews can last for over an hour. The interviewer does not have a questionnaire as such, but uses a less structured interview schedule. This may consist of either a series of open questions that must be asked as they are written or a checklist of topics for discussion, as with the focus group. The interviewer must be very highly trained in the art of asking unbiased questions, and usually, the interviews are recorded for transcription and analysis later. This method is particularly useful and is a rich source of information if the subject of the survey is of a personal or embarrassing nature.

Increasingly technology has made data capture easier for fieldworkers. CAPI (Computer Assisted Personal Interviewing) using laptops has meant that the large amounts of paper questionnaires no longer have to be carried by interviewers. Progress in wireless technology has allowed some market research companies to equip their fieldworkers with XDAs (small hand-held devices, similar to palmtops) for the administration of short face-to-face questionnaires. The questionnaires are sent directly to the XDA and allow for fast data capture and subsequently, fast turnaround of data to the client.

4.9.2 Telephone interviewing

The development of CATI (Computer Aided Telephone Interviewing) has greatly increased the extent to which telephone interviewing is undertaken. Interviewing is done from a central location, cutting the costs of fieldwork considerably, providing the sample size is large. It is not a cost-effective method for small samples. With the increased demand for immediate information, particularly for commercial omnibus surveys, CATI is ideally suited for the provision of a very fast turnaround of data as the results are recorded and processed as the questions are answered. The sample also can be drawn from a wide geographical spread, as the fieldworkers do not have to travel.

There are disadvantages to this method of data collection. It is difficult to establish a rapport with the respondent by telephone, which is partly why this method is not successful for the researching of personal or embarrassing topics. Many respondents are fearful of 'sugging', selling under the guise of marketing research, and expect the interviewer to try to sell them double glazing and the like. With a disembodied voice it is also easier for a respondent to refuse or end an interview prematurely. The telephone interview demands the use of very structured, precoded questionnaires that may be completed quickly without having to rely on examples of supporting material. An ideal telephone interview will last no longer than 15 minutes, on average.

4.9.3 Mail (postal) questionnaire

If the survey population is widely dispersed, it may be more useful to send the questionnaire by mail than to have an interviewer call on the respondent. Mail surveys also have the advantage of a reduction in field staff, and if there is a high response rate, the cost per questionnaire is low. A high response rate is more likely if the survey population consists of members of a special interest group (e.g. keep-fit enthusiasts) and the questionnaire relates to their area of interest. Otherwise, a response rate of 30–40% is not uncommon. The advantage over the telephone interview with this method is that the questionnaire can be lengthy and ask for detailed information.

The disadvantages (apart from the low response rate) are several. A mail questionnaire has to compete with the increasing amounts of junk mail that pour through our letterboxes. If there is a high non-response rate then the cost per questionnaire is high, particularly if a reply-paid envelope is included. There is no guarantee that the selected respondent will actually complete the questionnaire, and in spite of careful design, the control of the question sequence is removed. If the respondent does not understand any of the questions, there is no interviewer present to clarify the problem. There also may be a long time lag between sending out the questionnaires and receiving completed forms.

4.10 Questionnaire design

Questionnaire design is an aspect of research in which many people automatically assume expertise, even those without prior research experience. The questionnaire is a vital part of most surveys and great care must be taken with its design. To the novice, the problems inherent in designing a questionnaire tend not to become apparent until the pilot stage of the survey.

Many factors will affect the design of the questionnaire, such as the nature of the data required (qualitative or quantitative) and how the questionnaire is to be administered (by personal interview, telephone, mail or other self-completion, or whether electronic instruments will be used). However, most questionnaires tend to lie between two extremes: first, the highly structured questionnaire used, for example, in telephone interviewing, where the question wording is fixed and responses are limited; and secondly, an unstructured interview schedule used in qualitative research, which consists of a list of topics to be covered, with the actual wording of the questions left to the trained interviewer.

A well-designed questionnaire will provide the researcher with complete, accurate and unbiased information using the minimum number of questions and allowing the maximum number of successfully completed interviews.

4.10.1 The decision areas

Questionnaires are notoriously difficult to construct, but Tull and Hawkins (1997) suggest that a convenient way of tackling the design is by breaking up the task into a number of decision areas, namely:

- preliminary decisions;
- question content;
- question wording;
- response format;
- question sequence;
- questionnaire layout;
- pretest and revise.

Preliminary decisions

These include decisions on what information is required, who will be included in the survey and how they will be contacted.

Question content

This section is concerned with the content of individual questions: what to include, rather than how to phrase the question. Points to consider include the following:

Is the question necessary? The first decision to be made here is whether or not the question is actually necessary. If the question is not necessary for the purposes of meeting the survey objectives, then leave it out.

How many questions are needed? If the question is necessary, one must take care that the information you elicit will answer the question without ambiguity. For example, if you asked a respondent: 'Do you think woollen trousers are comfortable and warm to wear?' and the response was 'No', would that mean woollen trousers were uncomfortable or did not keep the respondent warm? Rather than ask double-barrelled questions, it is better to use one question for each point of information required, so you would ask: 'Do you think that woollen trousers are comfortable to wear?' and 'Do you think that woollen trousers are warm to wear?'

Has the respondent the information to answer the question? Sometimes respondents are asked questions on subjects about which they are not informed. A husband may not have the necessary information if asked how much his wife spends a month on clothing, for example. Some respondents will attempt to answer questions without being adequately informed, which will affect the validity of the results.

Is the respondent able to articulate the response? Even if the respondent has the necessary information to answer a question, they may not always be able to articulate their responses successfully. If asked to describe the type of person who might wear a particular fragrance, many respondents would find difficulty in phrasing their answers. It is easier for the respondent if they are presented with a set of alternatives from which they can choose the response that they feel to be the most appropriate. Using aids such as descriptions and pictures makes it easier for the respondent to answer the questions, and so complete the interview.

Asking questions beyond the memory span of the respondent   Asking questions about behaviour over a long time span may not produce accurate information. For example, asking the respondent how much they spent on tights in the last year would result in an answer that was pure guesswork. Asking how much they spent on tights in the last fortnight would be more likely to provide accurate information.

Question wording

Great care must be taken with the wording of questions. This is of particular importance when conducting cross-cultural or international marketing research. Decisions about question wording include:

◆ Does the word mean the same to all respondents?
◆ Some words such as 'dinner' and 'tea' mean different things in different parts of the country. Words should be chosen to mean the same to all respondents.
◆ The use of vague or ambiguous words also should be avoided. For example, 'Are you a regular purchaser of nylon tights?' is not specific enough. How often is 'regular'? This may mean different things to different respondents.

Are the questions loaded?   Some words or phrases should not be used in questionnaire design as they are likely to result in bias. Emotive words or phrases invite particular responses; for example, 'Are you in favour of sending money to help the poor, starving people in Africa?'

Response format

There are a number of types of response format that may be used. The most commonly used are dichotomous, multiple-choice and open-ended formats. Most questionnaires contain a mixture of these.

Dichotomous   Only two responses are allowed, such as 'yes' or 'no', 'male' or 'female'. A neutral 'don't know' category is sometimes included. The advantages are that these questions are quick to ask and the responses are easy to record and analyse. The disadvantages are that they do not allow for any shades of meaning to be included in the responses, and many questions would have to be asked to derive information of any detail by using this format alone.

Multiple-choice   Here the respondent is presented with a choice of several possible answers to the question. Frequently, the list of choices is shown to the respondent on a card. The order of the alternative answers should be rotated to avoid bias. Again, the questions are quick to ask and the responses are easy to record and analyse. This format also allows for more shades of meaning and the respondent has more freedom of choice in the response. The difficulty of this format is that it is difficult to ensure that the list of possible responses is complete.

Open ended   The respondent has complete freedom of choice in the response given with this format. This format is often used where little information exists to construct a multiple choice list, or when great detail is required. The advantage is that the information produced is extensive and is free from any bias of suggested answers. The main disadvantage is that the responses are slow to record as they must be recorded verbatim. This can lead to interviewers selecting what they think are the most important points, resulting in bias. These responses are also difficult to analyse as coding frames must be constructed for each question after the fieldwork has taken place. Coding of responses at a later stage requires grouping of responses, which can lose some shades of meaning.

Question sequence

The questions need to be organized logically to avoid introducing error or bias. Generally, you should move from general questions that the respondent finds easy to answer, to more specific or difficult questions about attitudes or behaviour.

In some surveys it is possible to ask classification questions, which may appear personal or embarrassing, at the end of the interview. If a quota sample is being used, some of these questions will need to be asked at the start of the interview, as they may form part of the

```
(A)  15–24          (A)   under £5000 p.a.
(B)  25–34          (B)   £5000–£9999 p.a.
(C)  35–44          (C)   £10 000–£14 999 p.a.
(D)  45–54          (D)   £15 000–£20 000 p.a.
(E)  55+            (E)   £20 000+ p.a.
```

Figure 4.5   Sample showcards.

quota control. To overcome this, showcards may be used, e.g. with age or income bands (Figure 4.5).

Questionnaire layout

The overall aim is clarity. There are some procedures that can aid clarity. These include ensuring that all questions are numbered; filter questions (ones that may be omitted in certain situations) should be clearly marked; instructions to the interviewer should be in block capitals; arrows or visual aids may be used.

Pretesting (pilot) and revision

The questionnaire must be thoroughly tested, using respondents similar to those who will take part in the final survey. This is known as the pilot stage and is vitally important to the reliability and validity of your survey results. Once this has been done, any modifications needed can be made, and the questionnaire tested again.

4.11 Attitude measurement and rating scales

These are used to quantify the strength of a response. The two scales most commonly used in attitude measurement are Osgood's semantic differential scale and the Likert summated rating scale.

4.11.1 Types of attitude scale

Attitudes are measured in scales. The main types of scale are as follows.

Nominal scales

These classify individuals into two or more groups, e.g. male/female, agree/disagree.

Favourable ⌐ | | | | | | ⌐ Unfavourable

Figure 4.6   Interval scale.

Ordinal scales

These rank individuals according to certain characteristics, e.g. Yves St. Laurent fragrances according to preference:

◆   Opium
◆   Paris
◆   Rive Gauche, etc.

Interval scales

These scales have regular calibrations, for example see Figure 4.6.

The advantage of this scale is that it can be used to measure the strength of a particular attitude. It also allows the use of statistical measures such as standard deviation, correlation coefficients and significance testing.

Ratio scales

These scales have a fixed origin or zero point, which permits the use of all arithmetical functions, e.g. measurement of length or weight. Measurements of market size, market share and number of consumers are also examples of ratio scales.

As previously mentioned, the most widely used attitude scaling techniques are the Likert and semantic differential scales.

4.11.2 The Likert scale

Respondents are asked to indicate their level of agreement or disagreement with a series of statements about a subject or an object. The statements used are identified as either positive or negative, and scores are allocated for particular responses. The list of possible responses is usually:

◆   strongly agree;
◆   agree;
◆   don't know/neutral;
◆   disagree;
◆   strongly disagree.

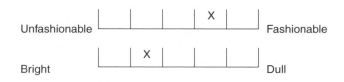

Figure 4.7 An example of the semantic differential scale.

The Likert scale is not an interval scale, so it is not possible to infer that 'strongly agree' is twice as strong an attitude as 'agree'. The scores achieved by individual respondents are only relative to those achieved by other respondents. Likert scales are popular as they are easy to construct and give reliable information about the degree of respondents' feelings.

4.11.3 The semantic differential scale

This is another widely used technique in marketing research. A series of bipolar (opposite) adjectives of descriptive phrases are presented to the respondent at opposite ends of a five or seven point scale. Respondents are asked to indicate where on the scale best describes their feelings towards the subject or object. An example is shown in Figure 4.7.

Semantic differential scales have been successfully used for such investigations as corporate image, brand image and product image. It is often difficult for consumers to articulate their feelings in these areas, and the semantic differential scale offers them an easy way of expressing themselves. These scales are widely used in marketing research as they obtain information about consumer behaviour that may not be obtained with the same degree of success by direct questioning.

4.12 The role of marketing research in new product development

Marketing research has a vital role to play in ensuring that new products launched onto the market are successful ventures, rather than dismal failures. The main input that marketing research makes into the new product development process is in the areas of:

- idea generation;
- evaluating and developing new product concepts;
- evaluating and developing new products;
- pricing new products.

These inputs are similar in the development of fashion.

Since the late 1970s, there has been an increase in the number of stores developing their own product lines. Specialists called product developers create products and test them on customers. There may be numerous reasons why a product is developed or modified to be sold in a particular market; new government legislation, changes in culture, the economy or even the climate may be responsible.

The creation of a marketing strategy for the development of a fashion product involves four stages. Each of the stages (discussed below) involves marketing research with the ultimate aim of testing a product for feasibility prior to its production, and to produce a plan for its production and marketing.

4.12.1 Creation of a customer profile

By identifying potential target markets for the proposed product, it is possible to prepare a customer profile for each one. Profiling characteristics such as age, gender, occupation and geographical location are considered, together with lifestyle characteristics as used in market segmentation.

Once these target markets have been identified, the attitudes and perceptions of potential consumers may be researched. Different groups of consumers have different needs, and by addressing the variables associated with buyer behaviour, it is possible to identify the product attributes that will appeal to each target group.

The information necessary to write a customer profile is available from several sources, both primary and secondary. For example, trade press, reports from fashion shows, sales staff, industry analysis and buyers can all be called upon to supply information.

The identification of specialized target markets is as important to the area of fashion retailing as it is to fashion design. Many fashion retailers (Next and GAP, for example) have deliberately targeted very specific niche markets, in an attempt to differentiate themselves from the competition. Emphasis has been placed on the development and acquisition of appropriate merchandise to satisfy particular market segments.

4.12.2 Preparing a profile of the competitors

Information about competitors' market size, market share, product range, consumers and marketing strategies comes under the scope of marketing research. With this information it is possible to analyse the relative strengths and weaknesses of the competition, and decide how much of a threat they pose.

Some of this information can be found from secondary data sources such as company reports, trade press, brochures and other promotional materials. Online sources also provide useful information for competitor research. It may also be possible for sales representatives to gather primary data from customers regarding competitors. Buyers, for example, will usually be contacted by a range of alternative suppliers and may be able to provide insight into competitors marketing intentions.

4.12.3 Preparation of a marketing strategy report

Once the target market has been identified and a profile prepared for both the consumer and the competition, a marketing strategy must be prepared. The report will include general information about the market (size, structure, etc.) as well as particular information about the proposed target market. It will also contain information about the product, including the product's differential advantage and pricing policy. An evaluation of potential retail outlets will also be included, and an assessment of the resources will be needed to produce and market the new or modified product.

4.12.4 The merchandise plan

This stage involves product testing, i.e. exposing prototypes of the product to fashion buyers. Any further developments suggested by these 'experts' will be considered, and the prototypes modified, as is the usual practice with product testing.

These are the main steps in developing and evaluating a new fashion product. The steps are slightly different from those involved in the development of more conventional consumer products, but the information necessary for a successful launch (such as an evaluation of the concept, its acceptability, consumer attitudes and preferences, information on the market in general and testing the product) is very similar.

4.13 Forecasting fashion

Estimating future demand for goods or services is extremely difficult in any market, but particularly so in fashion. Anticipating what buyers are likely to do under a given set of conditions is made more difficult by the eclectic nature of fashions, so any predictions about the future should be flexible and open to modification as the seasons change.

There is a problem with the use of formalized techniques for prediction in that many fashion professionals mistakenly believe that their creativity will be inhibited or that their fashion acumen and flair will be trivialized by this process. This is clearly not the case, and these methods should be used to assist the decision maker.

4.13.1 Uses of information

The basis on which forecasts can be made is one of sound information. Past and present consumer purchases are analysed for trend data. The target market for your products must be clearly identified and described by using marketing research techniques. The use of geodemographic systems such as ACORN (A Classification Of Residential Neighbourhoods) can be used to identify and contact your target market, and collect information about attitudes, preferences and future buying intentions such as 'Are you likely to buy a new coat in the next three months?'

Millers and tanners who often work years ahead of the market can be contacted for primary data on future developments, as can fashion editors and buyers, who are in the forefront of current consumer behaviour. Secondary sources such as trade magazines and newspapers provide information which is readily accessible. Range plans covering such variables as material, product type, colour and price are also an important source of data.

4.13.2 Further techniques

Information gained from the above sources will provide an analytical base for more specialized forecasting techniques. These include the use of ordinal scales to rank product alternatives as well as panels of up to eight people, who are asked to provide a consensus view of forecasts. A consensus is sought to avoid the bias introduced if the opinion of a single person regarding future sales potential was taken. Computer forecasting software has been specially developed for use in the fashion industry, which has facilitated the use of complex statistical techniques.

A form of product testing, called style testing, is used to involve the consumer in the forecasting process. A representative sample of target consumers is shown several provisional styles and ranges for future seasons. The consumers are then asked to state which they believe will be 'winners' and which are likely to be 'losers' in terms of customer appeal.

Test marketing of new styles, colours or silhouettes often takes place using a 'sample, test, re-order' system. Small quantities of garments are made up and placed in selected retail outlets. Customer reactions may be monitored without incurring the costs of full production. Similarly marketing research is used to monitor sales performance at the start of each season to identify any variations away from the forecast that may occur.

Fashion forecasting methods involve much organization and planning, and are not easy to establish in the first instance. All fashion businesses are involved in forecasting to some degree, and an increasing number of companies are being set up solely to provide specialist prediction services.

Fashion buying will always rely on a high degree of intuition and gut feeling about the market. When this is combined with a structured approach to planning and the use of research, more accurate forecasting is possible.

4.14 The Internet as a research tool

Rather than go into specific details of web page design (on which there are numerous available sources), this section will concentrate on the usefulness of the Internet as part of research methodology. Rapid developments in technology and corresponding reductions in costs have meant that the use of the Internet for both business and social use has proliferated in the past few years. Businesses all over the world are considering whether e-commerce can improve profitability. Consumers are increasingly embracing online shopping, with the choice of goods available broadening all the time, particularly with regard to apparel. Designers and retailers alike have websites that can be found easily on the Internet (e.g. Next, Paul Smith, La Redoute).

The increased use of the Internet as part of the marketing process has similarly had a great impact on the marketing research industry. The number of marketing research companies that now provide specialist Internet research services ('e-research') has also grown considerably.

It is easy to be very enthusiastic about the use of the Internet for research, but as with all available research tools, care must be taken to ensure that it is appropriate to the particular study. As with the more traditional research methods, there are advantages and disadvantages. Conducting research via the Internet may increase the speed of research from design to results and reduce costs, as well as appearing to facilitate research on an international level. Problems related to research via the Internet include using samples that are not representative of the target population and rapid obsolescence of information, such as e-mail addresses. In spite of the problems, the Internet is increasingly being used in marketing research for both primary and secondary data collection, and is proving to be a very useful addition to the researcher's 'tool kit'.

4.14.1 Online secondary data sources

Online commercial databases have been available to researchers for many years (e.g. www.FT.com – *The Financial Times*' website), providing access to news sources, trade publications and market reports. (It is useful to note that as with conventional sources, access to online secondary data is not always free.) The Internet contains a wealth of information but it may be time consuming to find as there is no single index of information available, rather a range of search engines (e.g. AltaVista, Yahoo!, Google), and sources may not necessarily be logically linked. Although online databases and search engines may be searched using keywords, the selection of appropriate keywords may be problematic. It is not always the most obvious keywords that will provide the best information. Searches using short phrases in quotation marks may provide more relevant results. The speed of searching and the breadth, if not always depth, of information available does make the Internet a useful tool for secondary data searches, however, particularly in exploratory research.

The Internet can be a particular useful resource for business-to-business research. It is possible to visit companies' websites which contain much useful information about products or services offered, financial information and an indication of the target market.

It is also possible to gain access to a whole range of market reports and articles online. Not all of these reports are free, which may limit access for some researchers. A useful source for market research information is www.marketresearch.com which offers more than 110 000 market research reports from over 550 publishers. Other online sources include:

www.companieshouse.gov.uk	Provides free information on more than 2 million companies.
www.londonstockexchange.com	Provides a free annual reports service, giving information on the performance of over 1300 listed companies.

For the fashion industry, there are a number of websites providing access to a range of industry information. These include:

www.fashionweb.co.uk	A dedicated web portal for the fashion industry. Also offers a website design and hosting service.
www.fashion.net	Provides links for agencies, news, services and employment in the fashion industry.
www.fashioninformation.com	A mainly subscription-only service providing information on trend forecasting for fashion industry professionals.
www.wmd.com	Womens Wear Daily website – giving current information on all aspects of the fashion industry plus access to archived reports available by subscription.

4.14.2 Primary data collection online

The main methods of collecting primary data via the Internet are by e-mail or website-based surveys or by online discussion groups.

With e-mail surveys, questionnaires are sent to respondents at their e-mail address. The questionnaires are then completed and returned online. The advantages of speed of both delivery and return are clear, as are cost savings over mail surveys. Disadvantages of this method are that e-mail is not completely confidential and that respondents selected as having e-mail addresses may not be representative of the research population. There may also be a time lag for replies as not everyone reads their e-mail regularly! It should also be noted that with the increase in use of the Internet, the amount of e-mail and therefore 'junk' e-mail has increased. The response rate to e-surveys, although often lower, can be compared to mail surveys as similar problems with unsolicited mail exist. Now most e-mail surveys are completed following an e-mail invitation to participate and is a useful means of conducting business-to-business research. The usual problems associated with questionnaire design are still relevant when designing e-mail surveys.

Web-based surveys consist of questionnaires posted on a particular website which are then completed by respondents who 'hit' that given site. Website surveys allow for more complex presentation, using both graphics and sound. This method relies on convenience sampling of users who access the website. These self-selected respondents may not be at all representative of the target population and as such this method should be used with care. It should also be noted that the costs of setting up a website of this complexity mean that it is more frequently employed by commercial research organizations.

Online discussion groups are frequently used for qualitative research in a similar way to focus groups, for new product development, product testing and evaluation. One key advantage of this method is the fact that results are available immediately and a transcript of the discussion can be taken easily. Research costs are also reduced as travelling expenses, venue hire, etc. are not incurred. The fact that respondents are able to participate from their place of work, however geographically dispersed they may be, has meant that this method is increasingly being used in business-to-business research. An incentive may be paid to the respondents, however, as the costs of connection will be borne by them. Visuals and sound files may also be included within the discussion site, but as respondents cannot touch the items, this method may not be suitable for certain products, e.g. where softness of fabric is important.

4.14.3 Using the Internet for research

The rapid developments in technology have meant that access to information via the Internet is becoming faster and easier for an increasing number of people. There is currently a great deal of enthusiasm about the Internet as a medium for both leisure and business activities, but this should be tempered with caution when considering the Internet as a means for conducting research. Problems associated with access, sampling response rate and quality of information, etc. all need to be considered against economies of time and cost. As with all tools available to the researcher, each must be considered for its appropriateness to the study and selected accordingly.

4.15 International marketing research

International marketing research generally refers to marketing research undertaken in countries other than that in which the research was commissioned. The challenge for the researcher here is to provide information from a culturally diverse, rapidly changing world. Each country in which research is conducted will have its own unique characteristics and mores with which the researcher may not be familiar. At the outset certain factors need to be taken into account in the research design. These include:

Conceptual equivalence	Do concepts such as 'brand loyalty' have the same meaning and significance in each country selected?
Functional equivalence	Does a product have the same or similar function in the selected countries?
Scalar equivalence	Do scale measurements taken in selected countries produce the same or similar results?
Linguistic equivalence	Does language used when translated provide the same meaning for respondents, whether verbally or in written form?

4.15.1 Cultural influences

Researchers must also understand the culture in which the research will be conducted. Some subjects will be easier to study in some cultures but not in others, depending upon the research population selected. It should not be assumed that a 'one size fits all' approach will be successful. Research design may have to be modified between countries and cultures to ensure comparability of data. For example, in Arabic countries it is generally harder to obtain samples of women respondents. Issues regarding access and culture have to be carefully addressed. In many instances, international marketing research may be designed in one country but administered by local agencies because of their knowledge of local custom and practice.

4.16 Summary

This chapter has covered the nature and scope of marketing research, starting with the survey research process:

- ◆ definition of the research required;
- ◆ decisions about the survey population;
- ◆ sampling methods;
- ◆ questionnaire design;
- ◆ data collection.

The chapter has also covered types of research design and approach, and the sources of data available to the fashion marketer. The application of marketing research to the development of new products and fashion prediction has been discussed, as well as a consideration of some of the issues around international marketing research design and the impact of the Internet on research methodology.

Further reading

Collins, M. (1986), Sampling, in Worcester, R.M. and Downham, J. (eds), *Consumer Market Research Handbook*, 3rd Edition, Esomar, McGraw-Hill, Maidenhead.

Entwistle, J. and Rocamora, A. (2006), The field of fashion materialized: a study of London Fashion Week, *Sociology*, Vol. 40, No. 4, pp. 735–751, BSA Publications Ltd., London. DOI: 10.1177/0038038506065158.

Hague, P. (2003), *Marketing Research: A Guide to Planning, Methodology and Evaluation*, 3rd Edition, Kogan-Page Limited, London.

Journal of the Market Research Society, Special issue: Research on the Internet, Vol. 41, No. 4, October 1999.

Kent, R. (1999), *Marketing Research: Measurement, Method and Application*, International Thomson Business, London.

Kotler, P. (2000), *Marketing Management: The Millennium Edition*, Prentice Hall, Englewood Cliffs, NJ.

Mouthino, L. and Evans, M. (1992), *Applied Marketing Research*, Addison-Wesley, Wokingham.

Proctor, T. (2000), *Essentials of Marketing Research*, Pearson Education Limited, Harlow.

Richards, E. and Rachman, D. (eds) (1978), *Marketing Information and Research in Fashion Management*, American Marketing Association, Chicagos, IL.

Tull, D.S. and Hawkins, D.I. (1997), *Marketing Research: Measurement and Method*, Macmillan Publishing Company, New York.

Webb, J.R. (ed.) (1999), *Understanding and Designing Marketing Research*, Academic Press, London.

Part C
Target Marketing and Managing the Fashion Marketing Mix

Chapter Five
Segmentation and the Marketing Mix

5.1 Introduction and overview

This chapter will discuss the nature of market segmentation and the related strategies that are open to the fashion marketer. The preceding three chapters have concentrated on customers, in the context of the marketing environment in Chapter Two, as buyers with differing needs and social characteristics in Chapter Three and as a focus of research efforts in Chapter Four. This chapter attempts to draw together several themes to look at how to decide which market or markets to aim at, namely the target market(s).

Having determined the target market or markets, the next consideration is the positioning of the fashion marketing organization and its marketing efforts towards the target, and this will be covered later.

The chapter also forms an important link with the rest of the book by introducing the concept of the marketing mix. Having shown how an organization can position itself within a market, the next task is the planning and organization of controllable variables to meet the requirements of the market profitably. The particular combination of marketing variables offered to specific markets is known as the marketing mix, and this is described shortly.

5.2 Mass marketing and market segmentation

5.2.1 What is a market?

To constitute a market a number of conditions have to be met. There should be a genuine need, the customer(s) should be willing and able to buy the product, and the aggregate demand should be sufficient to enable a supplier to operate profitably.

5.2.2 Mass marketing

Fashion marketers who assume that all customers in the market are the same are adopting a mass marketing or undifferentiated marketing approach. The assumption is based on the idea that customer needs do not vary and that the company can offer a standardized marketing mix that meets the needs of everyone. The standard marketing mix means the same product, method of distribution, prices and promotional effort aimed at everyone. The best example of this is China during the cultural revolution of the 1960s where the whole nation was offered the Mao outfit of dark blue jacket and trousers.

In Chapter Two, when considering the development of markets, it was noted that the aristocracy and wealthy classes were able to obtain products that met their precise needs. Most people in the pre-industrial revolution period dressed in a variety of styles which were greatly influenced by local skills and raw materials. Mass production methods, coupled with the experience of producing clothing for large armies, led to the possibility of mass markets for clothing. Indeed the practice of mass marketing linked to the military can be illustrated by the existence of the 'demob' suit issued to servicemen upon demobilization from national service.

Where a product can be standardized, perhaps because of the pre-dominance of function over style, then it could be argued that a mass market exists. Also, when mass production methods enable consider-able economies of scale, some items may be produced so efficiently that the product becomes a low-priced commodity. Certain items of underwear such as white Y-Fronts or one-size tights are certainly capable of consideration as products suitable for mass marketing. The reality, however, is that although the possibility of mass market-ing of clothing remains, it has never been a major feature of fashion markets in any advanced economy.

Given choice and the diversity of suppliers, consumers have amply demonstrated the desire for individuality that clothing can give them and they have rendered elusive the idea of a mass market for clothing. This is not to argue that homogeneity is absent in the clothing market or that there is not just one mass market, but many different clothing markets. One of the big success stories of the last decade has been Zara who have targeted younger customers with fast fashion as com-petitive prices (Figure 5.1).

Recognizing that the existence of many markets reflects the needs and purchasing capacity of clothing buyers leads to the idea of seg-menting markets. Markets may be segmented or divided where, for instance, a group of consumers has a set of homogeneous needs that is different to other groups.

Figure 5.1   Zara, an example of successful market segmentation.

5.2.3 Heterogeneous markets

The extreme form of market segmentation is where everyone has different needs and purchasing capability, and this is described as market heterogeneity. An example of this would be if everyone had bespoke tailoring, which, given the economics of the prospect, is an unlikely scenario. The nearest example is the market for corporate clothing. Here large organizations may require custom-made uniforms or limited ranges of clothing for their staff to enable the achievement of corporate image and personnel goals. However, even within the corporate clothing market, there will be some homogeneity, with for example smaller regional and local non-competing organizations such as restaurants who are willing to accept similar garments for their staff. Security staff and cleaning personnel from many organizations may be provided with the same garments.

5.2.4 Market segmentation

Market segmentation is where the larger market is heterogeneous and can be broken down into smaller units that are similar in character.

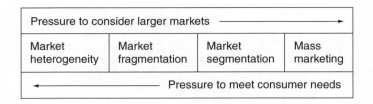

Figure 5.2 Factors influencing segmentation strategies.

In practice there is always the problem of balancing the similarity of needs with the desire for substantial numbers of potential buyers.

Pressure to target more closely can lead to greater fragmentation of a market so that the overheads of promotional support and information overload for consumers can become associated with lower levels of market efficiency. An acceptable balance has been found by many firms in what is known as niche marketing, where a clearly defined segment is targeted with a narrow product range. Wolford, Tie Rack and Thomas Pink are examples of this approach. Niche marketing is just another form of market segmentation. The extreme form of meeting customers' needs along this continuum has already been described as market heterogeneity, where each customer is treated as being unique.

There are other pressures to aggregate consumers with needs that are 'similar enough', but this can lead to a situation where the resultant marketing mix is a compromise that satisfies no one. The desire for larger markets is understandable as large markets enable economies of scale in production and marketing, and can command higher profits. The compromise solution of aggregating those who are 'similar enough' is vulnerable to competing businesses, who can demonstrate that they are better able to satisfy more closely targeted segments. These two pressures are shown in Figure 5.2.

5.3 Segmentation: rationale, bases and strategy

5.3.1 The advantages of market segmentation

By segmenting markets, fashion marketers gain several strategic advantages. Analysis of markets necessarily means consideration of competitors and their relative strengths and weaknesses in relation to customer needs. Such knowledge enables fashion marketers to decide whether to compete directly, if a strategic advantage is evident, or to position the company to exploit strengths and avoid retaliation from a stronger competitor.

The marketing research necessary to describe and segment a market usually leads to a deeper understanding of the customer that enables the most effective design of a marketing mix and the ability to respond to changes in the market.

Market segmentation enhances marketing planning in that it forces management to consider the relative costs, efficiency and effectiveness of the alternatives that segmentation reveals. Marketing planning is considered in detail in Chapter Ten.

5.3.2 Segmentation bases

Segments have been described above as groups of customers with similar characteristics. This section deals with ways of describing and analysing those characteristics. A larger market, say the womenswear market, may be divided or segmented into many different ways. There is no standard or preferred way to divide a market; however, it is important that the base(s) selected should relate to customers' needs.

Indeed it is not uncommon to find that fashion marketers use different methods for analysing the same market. What follows is an examination of some bases or dimensions that may be used to help categorize customers into meaningful and profitable segments.

5.3.3 Segmentation based on descriptors

One approach to segmenting markets is to describe the characteristics of potential customers. Such descriptions tend to look at demographic, geographical or personality characteristics of the buyer or a combination of the three measures. This approach is termed the descriptor perspective and has the merit that it is easily understandable and less costly owing to the availability of secondary data. An example would be to classify a market by age and income, thus for menswear we could show the market as shown in Table 5.1.

The next task using the table above is to quantify the various segments A to L and then analyse competitor activity within each segment. The fashion marketer can then make decisions about the positioning of the company within the market and in relation to competitors. The concept of positioning is described later in this chapter.

The prime weakness of the descriptor approach is the assumption that the dimensions selected relate directly to clothing purchase behaviour. Clearly gender, age and income are significant variables in many clothing markets, but there is a danger in assuming that they are the only, or even the most important, variables in every market. Some of the main descriptors used in segmenting markets are shown

Table 5.1 Market segmentation in the menswear market: an example based on simple descriptors

Age	Income		
	Low	Medium	High
16–25	A	B	C
26–35	D	E	F
36–55	G	H	I
56+	J	K	L

Table 5.2 Market segmentation descriptor variables

Variable	Potential categorization
Gender	Male/female
Age	<2, 2–5, 6–10, 11–15, 16–25, 26–35, 36–45, 46–64, 65+
Marital status	Single, with partner, divorced, widowed
Occupation	A, B, C1, C2, D, E
	Manual or non-manual
	Full- or part-time employment
Income	In decile bands, i.e. top 10%, next 10%, etc.
Net wealth	In decile bands or other bands, e.g. £0–4999, £5000–14 999
Education	Terminal age of education, e.g. <15, 16, 17, 18, 19, 20, 21–23, 24+
Customer size	In height, weight, dress/suit sizes, e.g. petite, large
Religion	Atheist, Christian, Muslim, Jewish, etc.
Youth	
Subcultures	Jazz, Goth, R&B, Rap, hip hop, punk, etc.
Family life cycle	Young single, young couple with no children, young couple with children, older couple with children, etc.
Type of neighbourhood	Urban/rural or, for example, ACORN
Housing/area	
Region/country	e.g. North East, Coastal, Central, UK, Italy,
Climate	Hours of sunshine, rainfall, extremes of temperature
Lifestyle	Groupings based on measurement of activities, interests and opinions

in Table 5.2. Notice that some descriptors contain more than one variable. The family life cycle, for example, refers to age of head of household, marital status, and the age and number of children, if any.

5.3.4 Segmentation based on benefits and customer behaviour

Another approach considers the behaviour of, and benefits for, consumers of fashion products and services as the main dimensions in segmentation. Here the concern is with monitoring how the consumer

Table 5.3 Market segmentation: behavioural and benefit variables

Variable	Potential categorization
Purchase loyalty	Brand loyal to non-committed
Purchasing mode	From comparison shopping to convenient outlets only
Usage rates	Heavy users, medium users, light users, occasional users, non-users
Expenditure	High spenders to low spenders in deciles
Usage situation	Working clothes, leisurewear, eveningwear, formal wear, e.g. weddings, and so on.
Price sensitivity	From very price aware and conscious to least price sensitive
Benefits	Easy-care garments, environmentally friendly fabrics and/or durability, etc.

behaves and the benefits she or he seeks from the product. Then and only then are descriptors considered. An obvious example may be the categorization of customers into those who are heavy spenders, moderate spenders or low spenders. For the fashion retailer operating a store card system the data should be readily available on a database along with other demographic information about customers, i.e. region, income, marital status, age, and so on (Table 5.3).

An important consideration is the number of variables that may be interlaced to provide a basis for segmentation. It would be unusual to use only one variable to divide a market, but it is wrong to assume that using more variables (multi-variable segmentation) is without difficulties. The use of more variables provides greater precision for the analyst. The cost of more variables, however, is the danger of greater market fragmentation as described above. Benefit and behavioural bases for segmentation are rarely sufficient on their own and so they are usually combined with demographic data to display a fuller profile of the segments. Knowing that some customers want easy-care garments is one thing, knowing how many customers and how to reach them via distribution outlets and promotional efforts is another matter.

5.3.5 Criteria for selecting segments

The bases for analysing market segments have just been described. Before developing a segmentation strategy one must select a segment or segments as a focus for marketing efforts. There are four main criteria that should be taken into account to achieve this.

◆ The segment should be measurable and easily identifiable. Before allocating marketing resources the target should be quantified. Producing garments to appeal to 'art lovers' may sound a good idea, but until it is known how to identify 'art lovers' and work out the market size little progress can be made.

- The chosen segment or segments should be relatively stable. Within the context of fashion this factor may seem ironic. However, fashion marketers invest considerable resources in building distribution networks and marketing information systems geared to particular groups or segments of customers and there must be the assurance that investment will yield long-term results. While styles may evolve over successive seasons, it is hoped that the core segment will remain loyal to the fashion marketer who leads and reflects their fashion tastes.
- The segment or segments chosen should be accessible. Accessibility refers to both distribution and promotional efforts. The role of demographic data in simplifying decisions about reaching the chosen segments has been described in the previous section.
- The segment should be large enough to be profitable for the scale of operations of the fashion marketer. Opening a boutique for women aged 35 plus in a small country town may be a sensible move for a small entrepreneur, but not for a large multiple retailer. It cannot be stressed enough that the long-term goal should be profitability rather than sales or market share. It is far better to have 7% of a high margin market earning £500 000 profit per week than 15% of a low margin market earning £196 000 profit per week.

Many companies describe their typical customers on websites, press releases or in advertisements, and this can give an indication of their target markets. However these statements can often be an aspiration rather than a reality as they are usually intended to flatter and attract consumers rather than defining the market segments in a way that informs marketing decision-makers. On their website, Warehouse describes their customers as 'Passionate about fashion, Knowledgeable about trends, Appreciates design and quality, Body confident, Independent and primarily 18–30, but Warehouse is about attitude not age!' This description is a nice complement to potential customers, but may not fully meet the criteria mentioned above for selecting a segment.

5.3.6 Segmentation strategies

Segmentation strategies can range from the choice of one target market or segment within the market to the selection of several segments in the market, each with a different marketing mix. The selection of only one segment is known as concentration strategy and the selection of two or more segments is called a multi-segment strategy.

The determinants of a segmentation strategy are the company resources, the nature of the competition and the nature of demand in the particular fashion market, for instance, whether it is stable or volatile. A concentration strategy can enable the company to become expert in satisfying one segment of customers and so to acquire enough prestige and goodwill to foster loyalty among customers, Herbert Johnson (Hats), established in 1889, being one such example. The risk of a concentration strategy is that a downturn in one market can expose the company to considerable financial risk.

A multi-segment strategy can provide a measure of stability in times of rapid market change by spreading risk across several segments. The same firm, while offering different marketing mixes, may find that the effort affords some economies of scale. For example, a company may target male and female segments via magazine advertising, and bulk purchasing of media space in magazines within the same publishing group may enable larger discounts to be earned.

Many companies have changed from a concentration segmentation strategy to a multi-segment strategy in a desire to expand or maintain growth rates. Both Jockey and Sloggi now produce underwear for males and females, having expanded from single-sex segments of the market. Sometimes the expansion into new segments can have a number of teething troubles, as with Jigsaw's first attempts to move into menswear and Marks and Spencer's recurrent attempts to target younger women.

The size of the customers is changing. Few people have the figure of a catwalk model and retailers recognizing this are offering more ranges in a wider variety of sizes. Taller consumers can buy from Long Tall Sally, a retailer who offers longer-length clothing. Evans Collection specializes in clothes for women of size 14 and over. Petite ranges for shorter women are now being offered alongside the usual ranges in many stores; Principles Petite is one example.

One leading clothing retailer, well known for floral designs, had tried to target a new market – that for boys between 8 and 11 – only to realize that particular age group often places great emphasis on distance from the feminine domain. Fortunately the lesson was learned after only a limited amount of experimentation with the new market segment and at small cost. Had the same retailer chosen a more masculine name and different outlets the outcome might have been very different.

5.3.7 Multi-segment strategies in practice

The idea of segmentation has been taken on board by most of the high street retailers. Several large groups try to cover the whole market by having a variety of stores catering for different groups of customers. The Arcadia Group plc (formerly the Burton Group) was formed in 1998 at the same time as the demerger of Debenhams. Under the Arcadia Group are Burton, Dorothy Perkins, Evans, Outfit, Bhs, Tammy, Top Shop, Top Man, Wallis and Miss Selfridge. Dorothy Perkins and Burton offer affordable mainstream clothing for women and men, respectively, and Evans is the UK market leader for larger size womenswear. The group has a significant online presence with an e-commerce and Internet service provider called Zoom. In total the group has over 2500 outlets, is the second largest clothing retailer in the UK and has over 2.7 million active store card customers. In international markets the Arcadia Group has over 420 stores and operates in over 30 countries. Total sales for the group exceeded £1.85 billion in 2007.

Labels offered at Top Man are aimed at fashion orientated 15- to 25-year-old men looking for keen pricing. Burton aims at 25–40 year olds who are primarily socio-economic groups BC1C2; in 2007 they launched a premium Black Label featuring classic designs and higher grade fabrics for the less price conscious customer. Miss Selfridge offers clubwear, Wallis concentrates on stylish well-cut clothes. Thus within the Arcadia Group as a whole there will be some crossover of appeal for each brand, but the current emphasis of the group is on building distinctive labels.

5.4 Positioning and perceptual mapping

Positioning is to do with the perception of the firm and its marketing mix by the target market. Positioning is how customers see the market, although that perception may have been influenced by marketing action. The customers' perceptions include the role of the competition and may embrace some notion of an ideal offering.

The main method of determining a market position is the use of marketing research to construct a perceptual map of the market. A perceptual map is the consumers' view of the market, where consumers provide the main dimensions or criteria for making judgements. Ideally, these criteria will be the same ones identified when the firm considered behavioural and benefit bases for segmentation. Perceptual mapping involves complex statistical procedures, but is often shown as two- or three-dimensional diagrams. A hypothetical example of a perceptual map for positioning within the women's shoe market is shown in Figure 5.3.

An important point to be made about the perceptual map is that it is hypothetical and may have little to do with the realities of style and pricing. If typical consumers believe things about shoe stores that are

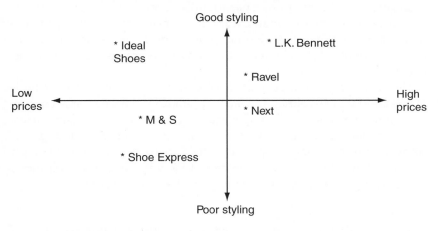

Figure 5.3 A market positioning example.

reflected in Figure 5.3, then they will behave in such a way to affirm those beliefs, as described in Chapter Three. Thus some customers may never even enter a Ravel store as they think it may be too expensive for them, while others do not consider Marks and Spencer shoes as their perception is that they are poor on styling.

The essence of positioning is to get the product right in terms of customer needs and expectations and then to tailor the image of the firm's marketing offering to meet the aspirations of the chosen market segment. Thus in the example above, if Ravel was trying to position itself to meet aspirations then the perceptions on pricing need to be addressed. If prices are too high in reality then the purchasing policy should be reviewed. However, if the prices are in fact lower than shown by the perceptual map, then promotion efforts could emphasize, for example, the value for money aspect of Ravel shoes.

5.5 The fashion marketing mix

The marketing mix is the range of variables that can be controlled by the fashion marketer to meet the needs of buyers profitably. Simply put, the marketing mix is getting the right product to the chosen market segment at the correct time, in the right place and for the right price.

Conventional descriptions of the marketing mix concentrate on what is known as the four Ps of marketing, namely Product, Price, Place and Promotion. This book does not deviate from that view but prefers the phrase Distribution decisions instead of Place decisions, as a synonym. Other approaches identify several other ways of dividing up the mix with between 2 and 12 components. The 4P approach is still the most popular among practitioners and academics, and has the merit of facilitating, the understanding about marketing activities.

The last section ended with a discussion of positioning within a market and that should be the starting point for the development of a marketing mix. The positioning statement is a strategic decision taken by a company and the marketing mix is concerned with turning that decision into a reality via specific activities. To devise a combination of marketing elements, i.e. the mix, to meet customer aspirations while having a competitive advantage is the route to profitability.

5.5.1 The planning and co-ordination of the marketing mix

All fashion firms have a marketing mix whether they consciously design one or not. The mix, as seen by the customer, works in varying degrees. Over-concentration on promotion to the neglect of adequate and timely distribution is a common feature of a flawed approach, as described in Chapter One. There is little point in advertising in magazines about the new range for a new autumn season in early September if retailers do not have the product in stock. Similarly, a public relations campaign to create an upmarket quality image can be easily undermined by a policy of almost continual discount sales.

All elements of the marketing mix should be co-ordinated towards the positioning objective. Thus a brand image may be reinforced by the pricing policy and the sales force should be sufficient to meet the needs of the distribution channels. Chapters Six to Ten deal in detail with the components of the marketing mix, and Chapter Ten will revisit planning and co-ordination, but the point should be noted now.

5.5.2 Alternative marketing mixes

Firms may pursue a multi-segmentation strategy and offer different marketing mixes to different market segments. Therefore a designer dress offered at a higher price in department stores to an upmarket customer may be accompanied by a diffusion range with less design content and lower-quality fabrics at lower prices through chain stores to another segment by the same company. Different marketing mixes from the same company can coexist easily and are often unknown to consumers through the use of different company names and brands.

Table 5.4 Different marketing mixes aimed at similar menswear markets

	H&M	River Island
Segment	20–35 Male Mid-market	15–35 Male Mid-market
Product	Extensive range Staples, Active lifestyle L.O.G.G. Sports Casual/leisure Well-dressed formal wear	Casual/leisure Broad range Different fibres and fabrics
Price	Mid-range From tops at £4 to suits at £250+	Slight premium over mid-range Tops from £25 to suits around £200
Distribution	Online shopping not available in UK in 2008 100+ high street stores	Online shopping available in UK 200+ high street stores
Promotion	Direct marketing, brochures, press advertising Billboards	Press advertisements Strong visual merchandising

An important principle to note in relation to the marketing mix is the principle of equi-finality. This means that there may be more than one way to reach a goal, and that alternative routes or mixes may be equally effective in achieving marketing objectives. Table 5.4 gives a brief example of alternative marketing mixes to illustrate, in part, the principle of equi-finality.

5.6 Summary

This chapter has introduced the concepts of segmentation and the marketing mix. Segmentation was discussed in terms of:

- ways of segmenting a market;
- criteria for selecting target markets;
- descriptor, behavioural and benefit dimension of segments;
- concentrated and multi-segment strategies, and their benefits and risks;
- examples from real fashion markets.

The chapter then went on to discuss market positioning and the relevance of the marketing mix to this, covering:

- building a strategy;
- co-ordinating the mix elements;
- alternative marketing mixes;
- customer perceptions of the marketing mix.

Further reading

Cahill, D.J. (2006), *Lifestyle Market Segmentation* (Haworth Series in Segmented, Targeted, and Customized Market), Haworth Press Inc., New York.

Cova, B. *et al.* (eds) (2007), *Consumer Tribes*, Butterworth-Heinemann, London.

Dibb, S. and Simkin, L. (2007), *Market Segmentation Success: Making It Happen*, Haworth Press Inc., New York. International Thomson Business Press, London.

Hooley, G. *et al.* (2008), *Marketing Strategy and Competitive Positioning*, 4th Edition, Financial Times/Prentice-Hall, Harlow.

McDonald, M. and Dunbar, I. (2004), *Market Segmentation: How to Do It, How to Profit from It*, Elsevier Butterworth-Heinemann, Oxford.

Wedel, M. and Kamakura, W.A. (2000), *Market Segmentation: Conceptual and Methodological Foundations* (International Series in Quantitative Marketing), 2nd Revised Edition, Kluwer Academic Publishers, Boston.

Chapter Six
Designing and Marketing Fashion Products

6.1 Introduction

This chapter will examine the product element of the marketing mix and its pivotal role in the success or failure of businesses within the fashion industry. First it addresses the concept of fashion and its economic and social importance, followed by an analysis of the nature and attributes of fashion products. Then there is a description of how the industry is organized for the diffusion of new trends and an examination of the process of new fashion product development. Concepts are then applied by examining a retail buying sequence.

Later there is an assessment of the concept of fashion and other life cycles and the implications for marketing decision-makers. Finally the relevance and use of the concept when determining seasonal product mixes and planning and controlling the introduction of new ranges are examined.

In this chapter, the definition of fashion as a current mode of consumption behaviour has been applied specifically to clothing products. However, it is acknowledged that in its broadest sense the term can be used to describe any product or service consumed as part of a particular way of living. More specifically the contents of the chapter could equally apply to other clothing-related aspects of fashion, such as shoes, cosmetics, accessories or hairstyles, as outlined in Chapter One.

6.2 The importance of fashion products

6.2.1 The concept of fashion

The product element of the marketing mix is fundamental to the fashion design industry. The continual process of new product development and resulting change drives the whole industry and answers the demand from consumers for a constant stream of new ideas and offerings. Indeed it could be argued that without this constant generation and introduction of new ideas into the marketplace, the concept of 'fashion' would not exist.

Axiomatically, if consumers were not constantly engaged in the process of looking for new products or services to satisfy their emerging needs (and once having consumed them, allowing a set of new and different needs to emerge), the fashion process could not function.

Thus the industry revolves around a time-based, i.e. seasonal, process in which new fashions are introduced into the marketplace and are adopted by enough consumers to warrant the description of 'fashion' in its proper context in the first place (as a current mode of consumption behaviour), only to wane eventually in terms of popularity, thus rendering them 'unfashionable'. While some product offerings will remain popular over several or even many seasons, others will fade very quickly; these differences are discussed further in the chapter. The important point to stress here, however, is that this regenerative process is intrinsic to the fashion industry and is very necessary for its continued survival.

6.2.2 The economic importance of fashion

In 2006 the UK clothing market was valued at £13.9 billion at manufacturers selling prices and had been growing steadily for the previous few years. However, also in 2006, the number of UK clothing manufacturers reached an all-time low with large job losses to overseas suppliers of underwear and lower-priced garments. Many UK designers and fashion companies have been successfully exporting their ranges for many years; indeed the ratio of exports to imports has been rising steadily (in value terms) over the past few years. Nonetheless the UK remains a net importer of clothing.

Although the percentage of household expenditure on clothing and footwear in the UK has slightly declined during the past decade, it still amounts to nearly 6% of the total of all consumer expenditure at current prices. Due to intense competition at the retail level and low-priced overseas sourcing and a strong pound, UK consumers have seen real reductions in clothing prices since 2000. While historically not as fashion conscious as their European counterparts, many UK consumers have become much more fashion aware and consequently much more discerning when it comes to appearance.

To remain competitive many UK clothing manufacturers have chosen to follow an upmarket, high-cost route embracing high quality rather than competing with manufacturers elsewhere in the world who are able to maintain very low labour costs (and therefore offer volume-produced garments at very low prices). Others, however, have developed purchasing strategies that involve subcontracting work into low-cost countries while still maintaining a high design 'edge' over competitors.

Clothing is now a global activity with China and the EU having 30.6% and 33.8% of world trade in clothing exports in 2006, respectively. Hong Kong with clothing exports of US$28.4 billion is much more active in this market than the USA with clothing exports of US$4.9 billion.

6.2.3 The social role of fashion

It has often been suggested that fashion plays an important societal role in terms of individual wellbeing. This, it is maintained, comes through enhanced self-esteem and acceptance by peers and various other social groups through the 'correct' choice of clothing and use of other image-developing accessories. Therefore it could be argued that the primary objective in gaining greater understanding of the nature of fashion products and the process of new product development is to become more effective in targeting specific market segments and thereby satisfy some of the most basic needs within a society.

Commercially this will lead to increased customer loyalty resulting in trust in what is being offered by the organization or the designer in question, resulting in improved sales performance and profitability. In the UK in particular, improved marketing capabilities have led to the maximization of design and manufacturing potential; British manufacturers cannot compete with low-cost producing countries on price and so have used their design and marketing talent as a basis to distinguish the UK in the marketplace.

6.3 The nature of fashion products

6.3.1 Product definition and classifications

Quite literally a product can be defined as anything that might satisfy a need that can be offered in the marketplace. Classifying products in terms of their characteristics and how consumers purchase them assists marketers in determining the appropriate blend of other marketing variables, i.e. promotion, pricing and distribution for the product in question.

Traditionally three categories have been used to define tangible product offerings, namely convenience, shopping and specialty, as shown in Figure 6.1.

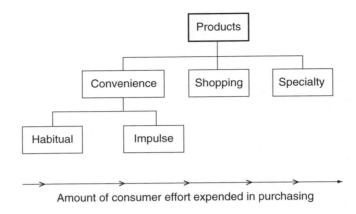

Figure 6.1 Classification of products.

Convenience goods

Convenience goods are frequently purchased with little thought, effort or attempt to undertake comparisons with similar products. Convenience goods can be further subdivided into staple goods, purchased habitually and where brand loyalty is probably very strong, and impulse goods, purchased without any pre-planning or searching. It could be advocated that certain basic items of clothing such as hosiery and underwear are often purchased as convenience goods, perhaps along with the family's regular one-stop shopping from the supermarket. Indeed many food retailers have capitalized on this approach by stocking such ranges alongside other non-food ranges.

Shopping goods

Shopping goods are where consumers compare product attributes such as price, quality and design by shopping around. Products in this category will constitute high-volume markets similar to those of high street fashions. However, they will lack the seasonal variations intrinsic to the fashion industry and are likely to be purchased less frequently than most clothing items.

Specialty goods

Specialty goods are products with characteristics that differentiate them from the other two classifications, usually based on high-quality and higher-perceived value. Brand image is very important here; often customers will make the effort to seek out the exact product they require. It may be that they will also expect some degree of exclusivity in the product offering and will go out of their way to find it. More upmarket, branded fashion items obviously fall neatly into this category. However, over the past decade the demand for brand names in most garment categories and price ranges (triggered specifically by the mass market growth in sports and leisurewear) has dramatically risen. Therefore it could be argued that all except the most basic of clothing items could be described as specialty. As a result the high street has seen the development in recent years of what has come to be known as the 'capricious consumer'. By this we mean one who shops on a whim with little or no degree of store or brand loyalty but who has a keen eye for value for money with all the necessary design and brand name requisites. As a result, at the lower end of the market discount fashion chains such as Primark, H&M and Matalan find themselves the current 'value champions' on the high street through having low operating margins and still being able to offer viable customer propositions. At the premium end, brand-builders such as Gap and Next are still able to command premium prices despite having substantial operating costs, while companies such as Alexon with less brand strength found it difficult to sustain profitable operations.

6.3.2 Classifying products with a fashion element

Although the categories above do apply to certain items of clothing in the fashion industry, they are slightly limited in use when one is trying to analyse buying motives and methods. It is probably more accurate therefore to classify tangible fashion products slightly differently, categorizing them as classics, fashions or fads.

Classics

It is possible to use the term classic in several contexts. In terms of 'bundles of utilities', classics can usually be seen as the midpoint compromise of any style, i.e. total look or composite effect. Indeed, the term 'style' is often used to describe the classic in this context, complying with the basic laws of harmony in proportion, aesthetic sense and incorporation of balanced design features. Colour and pattern may vary but the classic customer does not seek the satisfaction of a new seasonal experience in the way that his or her fashion and fad counterparts do. However, it is likely that some satisfaction will be sought at the core of the product's tangible attributes, e.g. good quality, good fit and durability. Aquascutum is such an example as shown in Figure 6.2.

In a product sense a classic is never out of style for its market segment and will rarely appeal to the majority. Design changes will be

Figure 6.2 An example of a fashion classic.

minimal; these changeless and always acceptable garments are found in all recognizable areas of fashion, e.g. the women's tailored suit with knee- or just above knee-length skirt or for men the City pin-stripe, the double-breasted trench coat, the blazer; even denim jeans have their classic in the five-pocket Western style.

Classic garments, sharing the quality of 'timelessness', will collectively make up the classic styles described above. At any given time, however, it will be possible to identify dominant and secondary styles. What should be added here is that although often described as timeless, classics also evolve gradually over many years according to the style of the age.

Certain designers have also been described as classic, producing fashions that are seen by many as timeless and therefore can be worn despite the season and current high fashions. Barbour, Pringle and Nike provide good examples of brand names, while Paul Smith and Donna Karan are two examples of contemporary classic designers.

Classic products may occasionally become fashionable, e.g. the ongoing revival of the Chanel suit, albeit with more up-to-date styling detail. However, it is more likely that the classic will form the basis for the annual slow, continuous change that forms fashion. There is a skill in combining the appropriate variations on the appropriate classics for any given moment in time to create an appropriate contemporary style.

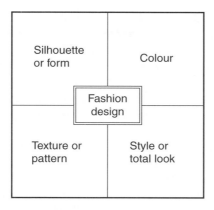

Figure 6.3 Four basics of fashion design.

Fashions and fads

The distinction between a fashion and a fad is usually defined on the basis of their acceptance cycle. Fashions usually have a slower rise to popularity, reach a plateau with continuing popularity and then decline gradually; often this cycle relates to a season, whether autumn/winter or spring/summer. Mid-season modifications to the original fashions may be introduced with the specific intention of maintaining buying interest and encouraging further purchases from early as well as later adopters (see Chapter Three).

Fads, in contrast, will rise meteorically in popularity only to suffer an abrupt decline as they become adopted. As a fad becomes fashionable it also becomes unfashionable. Adoption of a fad is based solely on the desire by the individual for a new experience that is not likely to become popular on a large scale. For this reason a fad tends to be viewed as non-viable in the commercial sense and usually eccentric in nature.

Retailers like Zara, who operate a system of fast fashion where catwalk ideas can become translated into lower-priced fashionable items made available in stores within weeks, have contributed to the erosion between fashion and fad in some market segments.

6.3.3 Product attributes

In designing and developing new products, it is essential to understand what is being offered and therefore to appreciate the customer's perception of the product. As shown in Figure 6.3, there are four basics in terms of fashion design, namely silhouette or form, colour, texture or pattern and style or total look. However, the fashion consumer will tend to view the garment as a series of attributes. Some of these will relate more closely to the social or psychological needs of the consumer and therefore will not always be recognized by the individual. However, it is essential that the fashion marketer is aware of both the subconscious and the conscious aspects of the product to offer the best combination of need-satisfying benefits to the customer.

Thus the product offering can be analysed at three levels. First, the *core* product that satisfies the most fundamental needs. Secondly, the *tangible* product can be seen as the physical interpretation and presentation of the four design basics to create the most appropriate fashion for the market in question. Thirdly, there is the *intangible* product, i.e. the additional services and benefits that supplement the previous two levels and create the total product offering.

Core attributes

The core of the product's attributes will revolve around the three basic tenets of clothing: protection, modesty and adornment. Since every garment will offer combinations of these functions to a greater or lesser degree, the consumer must decide how well the combination matches his or her basic criteria for purchase. Buyers will always look for those products that satisfy the maximum set of needs simultaneously. In practice, offerings will seldom satisfy all of them simultaneously and so each purchase decision will result in a compromise. The extent to which the customer has to make these compromises indicates the extent to which there are apparent gaps in the marketplace and therefore the need for more differentiation. This in turn helps to perpetuate fashion change.

Tangible attributes

Tangible product attributes, or the interpretation and presentation of the four design basics to provide an overall style, will revolve around in the first place the set of design features which make up the actual product. For example, a basic ladies' blouse may offer variety in terms of shape (loose, fitted, etc.), sleeve type (set-in, raglan, dolman, etc.), type of collar and shape (one piece, two piece, pointed, round, etc.), any decoration or trimmings, etc. In addition, the designer must have regard to the appropriate use of fabric, texture, pattern and colour for any given season. These are set in the context of both overall style and, for instance, co-ordination with other garments and accessories to form a 'total look'.

For example, it could be claimed that a hypothetical range of garments designed for the executive working woman offered high performance (durability, washability, etc.), an acceptable level of fashion for the given season, suitable styling for the executive role and versatility in wear. However, although the consumer may purchase specific items in the range at different times, it is highly likely that she would still expect co-ordination within the range to provide a suitable total look with whatever combination of garments she had purchased.

A designer and manufacturer should also strive to maintain standards of quality appropriate to the market which they have chosen to target. Quality control is becoming more and more important, although garment manufacturing does not have to comply with any British or European Standard in the way that product and engineering designs do. Therefore there is a variety of qualities of make and sizing specifications in clothing. Many consumers are quick to point out that a size 12 from one manufacturer or retailer may vary considerably from that of another. In 2006 the European Clothing Size Standard will aim to gradually replace national dress sizes and is based on body measurements. Metric sizing, anthropometric data, is derived from a major European study of sizing and benchmarking with similar international (ISO 3635) standards. If the European standard is widely accepted it will give the adopters of the standard a competitive advantage in world markets as both consumers and retail buyers will have greater confidence in the sizing information they use to make decisions. However, retail dominance since the 1980s has resulted in the introduction of more stringent quality control procedures. More discerning consumers now require quality of service and choice as well as product, and there are significant marketing implications in this.

Most retailers now employ teams of garment technologists whose remit is to work with in-house buyers and manufacturers to establish and maintain standards of make in line with given company policy. Quality manuals are used to provide guidelines on general standards such as fabric performance and size specification through to specifics such as the number of stitches per inch on seams which suppliers to use for component parts of the garment, such as trimmings.

The quality procedure in one large UK retail organization is as follows: retailers will require that buying samples (sample garments made to relevant quality standards) are approved before volume production. Once they have been checked by the technologist and buyer against established standards, two sample garments will be 'sealed', one to be kept by the manufacturer and one by the retailer. These samples will become the yardstick against which the quality of volume production will be measured. When volume garments begin to come off the production line a technologist will usually approve

Figure 6.4 Branding strategies: a continuum of approaches.

and seal a further three samples, confirming that quality standards are being met and that the goods can be delivered into a central warehouse or direct to the store.

A further tangible attribute is seen in use of suitable packaging and branding. This is important in image creation, leading to differentiation in the marketplace which can be achieved very effectively through the use of labelling. Branding can be in the form of brand names, logos, trade marks, etc. Certain brand names have become so powerful that they are synonymous with the product. Consumers may talk of their Nike's instead of their training shoes, or of a Burberry instead of a raincoat. In the same way, suitable packaging is as important in the fashion industry as any other.

Brand names are a very important vehicle for providing the customer with assurances regarding quality and consistency of standard, the brand name of Marks and Spencer is a case in point. They can also provide assurances as to the suitability of fashion content for the season in question. Strong brand names can be very advantageous when establishing overseas markets. Young Japanese consumers with very high levels of disposable income are dedicated followers of British fashion. Traditional labels such as Burberry have established strong links in Japan, as have designers such as Paul Smith, Mulberry and Vivienne Westwood.

As shown in Figure 6.4, companies can employ various strategies as regards the use of brand names, such as:

◆ A variety of names can be used with no obvious link, the caveat here being that substantial promotional budgets will be needed to establish each one in the mind of the consumer. The Arcadia group have Topshop, TopMan, Wallis, Miss Selfridge, Dorothy Perkins, Outfit, Evans and Burton as separate brands (Figure 6.4).

◆ Specific ranges may be given individual brand names; in this way some common link can be emphasized such as range co-ordination across several garment categories, or ranges that have been designed with a specific theme or purpose in mind.

For example, Max Mara uses Max and Co as an affordable brand name for their younger market, Pianoforte for more expensive eveningwear and Marina Rinaldi for larger sizes.

♦ Use of only one brand name across the entire organization and its offerings can create a powerful image in the mind of the consumer. In time, use of well-established brand names can be stretched to introduce new products into different markets. This policy of brand stretching goes beyond brand extension, where new products are introduced into the same category. Use of this approach can increase the survival chances of new products and reduce launch costs. Indeed, brands that are too closely associated with particular types of products and do not use the power of relationship (in the consumer's mind) to extend and evolve into new formats and markets are likely to have very short lives. Towards the end of the 1990s the claim was that a new kind of brand was emerging – one capable of expressing a certain kind of attitude to life and somewhat reminiscent of the 'lifestyle' concept in the 1980s. Major brands are now becoming more 'elastic' in the sense that companies are increasingly defining them as a way of life and stretching them into new areas. Virgin now uses its name for airlines, music, broadcasting, broadband, trains, finance, soft drinks, mobile phones, health care, cosmetics, holidays, bridal wear and cinemas and an online car buying service. At a time where many companies are making similar types of products within similar price bands, functionality does not often succeed as a means of differentiation. Therefore it is essential that companies emphasize the emotional aspects of their brands in the hope that consumers will identify with sets of values that the brand is meant to represent. Even here, however, brands that stress highly intangible, emotional qualities must provide merchandise that is consistent with the brand promise.

The role that packaging plays within the tangible product offering will depend very much upon the nature of the product's image and the importance of branding and packaging within that. Although the main function of packaging is that of protection, it has often become intrinsic to the overall offering and its status, as exemplified by labels such as Monsoon or Shanghai Tang, where the brand name and corporate colour scheme of fashion stores are reflected in the packaging design. The packaging may even have a functional use in its own right; continued use will help to reinforce brand and image with the customer.

Intangible attributes

Intangible attributes, the additional services and benefits that supplement the core and tangible attributes, include services intrinsic to
the purchase such as credit facilities, delivery arrangements, and after
sales service such as alterations and money-back guarantees. Several
UK fashion retailers such as, Selfridges and John Lewis, are beginning
to follow the example of their American counterparts in providing
customers with consultation as to personal image. This may include
advice on the most appropriate garment styles for different body
shapes and height, as well as colours most suited to the individual's
complexion and hair colour.

Image and reputation of the seller, possibly because of an effective promotional campaign, constitute further intangible attributes.
However, word-of-mouth recommendation, appealing shop interiors
and exteriors and even satisfaction with previous purchases can all
be contributory factors to the build up of longer-term loyalty. Lastly,
there are consumers' quality and value perceptions, which are closely
related to image and reputation but more often linked to customers'
attitude towards price levels.

6.3.4 Licensing

The 1980s spending boom encouraged many big name fashion
houses to expand their commercial activities through retailing and
licensing. For many large investors, the appeal of high fashion lies
not so much in their collections, but rather in the lucrative licences
for perfumes and other products bearing the designer's name. Under
a licensing agreement the designer will lend his or her name to products made by mainstream manufacturers. In spite of changing economic circumstances and problems associated with a strong pound
and weak yen, the demand for British goods continues to grow in
Japan. As a result, leading edge designers such as Paul Smith now
have a high percentage of their business in Japan as licensing since
the first licensing agreement was signed with C. Itoh in 1986; the
company had sales of over £300 million in 2006. Burberry has signed
a licensing agreement with Luxottica a world leader in premium eyewear developer and distributor to produce its first premium eyewear
collection in 2007. Around £86 million, comprising 11% of Burberry's
sales turnover, was derived from licensing in 2007.

In licensing, fashion houses such as Lauren and Dior must maintain a delicate balance between profiting from the prestige of their
name and not simultaneously jeopardizing their exclusivity and high
fashion image and reputation. Ralph Lauren concerns himself with

every detail, from the quality of the product to how it is delivered and presented in the shops. Licensing royalties for Ralph Lauren were US$236 million in 2007.

Cardin, in contrast, has more than 8400 licences for items ranging from scuba diving equipment to sunglasses and while it is now one of the highest turnover fashion companies with estimated sales of over US$1 billion in 2006, it has foregone its status as a high fashion house to become so.

6.4 The fashion industry and new product development

6.4.1 The role of the designer

The role of designer in the fashion industry is crucial to its success. The task is specifically one of interpreting society's current and antici-pated mood into desirable, wearable, garments for every type and level of market. To do this effectively, designers must be in tune with the wider social, cultural, economic and political environment within which human beings conduct their daily lives; only then will their ideas truly reflect current prevailing conditions and the impact they are likely to have on future consumer needs. Thus the designer will draw on a wealth of ideas; the media and entertainment, other cul-tures, social attitudes and mores, historical and contemporary events all provide important sources of inspiration.

The skill in any good design really lies in maximizing the value that can be added to a set of basic raw materials. It is therefore dependent on the quality of the original design, its suitability for the market and the way it is made to meet customer requirements. Any designer should be skilled in striking the right balance between new product develop-ment and other marketing costs and the life expectancy and therefore anticipated sales and profit contribution of the product. However, ser-ious concern is being expressed within the industry that the increased speed of the whole fashion cycle is beginning to stunt the growth of young designers and that the demand for new ideas and collections is so strong that the chance to develop ideas properly does not arise.

6.4.2 The influence of haute couture

In terms of influence the industry continues to operate in a hierarch-ical sense. The more renowned and internationally accepted designers (historically the haute couturiers, although this section of the industry is now in something of a downturn) continue to be a very significant source of new ideas regarding fashion direction. At the same time, however, influences from elsewhere will pervade. From the late in the 1980s the influence of 'street fashion' has been felt throughout the industry. The skill for many designers, and particularly those who are trying to appeal to the wider, mass market, will be to interpret the wealth of ideas and sources of inspiration into garments that are appropriate for high street consumption.

The point should be made here that haute couture and mass production are quite different. The former evolved from the desire for luxury and conspicuous consumption from the elite strata of society; the latter developed in response to the growing post-war affluence of the majority and the desire for an improvement in living standard and lifestyle. Thus it has historically been the function of mass production to select and adapt appropriate couture design to meet the needs of the public at large. While the recognized leading designers in Europe, America, Japan and elsewhere continue to act as sources of inspiration, their supremacy and unattainability for the masses is maintained by employing the best in fabric, make, embellishment, etc. and producing fashions that can only be afforded and worn by a select, fashion conscious and extravert few. However, even the leading designers are vulnerable; if their sense of direction and development is not consistently strong they will fail to develop a progressive adaptability. The stereotypical style that may result could leave the way open for new designers who have a better understanding of the way fashion develops.

6.4.3 Organization of the fashion industry

In recent years the haute couturiers have, along with established designers, tended to move towards greater brand differentiation to capitalize on their names and some have also decentralized their manufacturing operations to cut costs. Some manufacturers now produce and distribute designer collections, enabling haute couture or designer names to be made available to a larger market at more accessible prices through ready-to-wear ranges. The announcement by the French government in the early 1990s that it was planning to encourage new designers into haute couture indicated the fact that the couture market was in decline. Younger customers are being tempted away from the idea of luxury for its own sake and are now demanding clothes by the newer designers that are indisputably contemporary in their direction and approach.

Production capacity of the manufacturing sector in the industry will be split into different ways. Some will devote their entire production to retail own-label ranges, while others may run own-label (i.e. manufacturer) ranges alongside. The third possibility is to allocate certain capacity to manufacturing garments under licence (see earlier). Similarly, retail strategies may be based on 100% own-label ranges in store, or mixing retail label with manufacturer- and/or licensee-labelled merchandise.

Thus within the industry chain the process of converting basic raw materials into finished marketable goods will involve teams of people working together at each level. Yarn and textile producers will employ designers and technologists and may employ the services of colour consultants and fabric forecasters in their work. Teams comprising in-house designers, pattern cutters and sample machinists, production and sales personnel will work together in manufacturing organizations on the development of own label and licensed ranges.

At the same time their designers and production personnel will be working with buyers and merchandisers in retail organizations on the development of retail own-label merchandise; retail buyers and merchandisers will, in turn, be working with teams of their own in-house designers, quality controllers, garment technologists and possibly even store personnel during their planning cycle. Retail dominance as described earlier has also led to retail buying and merchandising personnel working closely with yarn and textile producers in a bid to differentiate ranges at an even earlier stage in the chain. Fabric will be dyed or woven according to retail specification and subsequently ordered for the garment manufacturers.

6.4.4 The sequence of events

There are four major stages of influence in the new product development and fashion diffusion and adoption process. These are, chronologically:

- ◆ 'The Colour Meeting' in Paris known as the *Concertation* where approximately 40 leading fashion industrialists representing major yarn, textile and garment manufacturers, top designers, stylists, colour consultants and fashion forecasters gather. Together they will establish the major colour trends (based on around 30 colours) that will dominate the fashion scene two years from the time of their meeting. The trends will usually be based on themes of darks, brights, pastels and neutrals. Work will then begin by various sections of the industry on interpreting and adapting the basic story to suit their own particular requirements. For example, the International Wool Secretariat and Cotton Institute will work on appropriate interpretations for their respective yarn and textile industries.

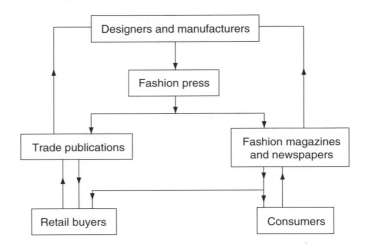

Figure 6.5 The two-way flow of fashion information.

- The biannual yarn and fabric fairs where the new colours, textures and patterns will be presented as trends for 12 months ahead. These fairs are now held in most of the major cities of Europe.
- The biannual international fashion fairs in Paris, Milan, Tokyo, Shanghai, Moscow, New York and London where leading designers will present their latest collection ideas six months ahead of the season in question. Representation by the media is very strong at the international collections, showing the enormous influence the media now have on fashion awareness and acceptance.
- Reportage in the trade and commercial press of the designer collections is described above. The power and extent of modern-day mass communication systems are such that the media are instrumental in shaping and influencing the fashions that are ultimately accepted. This process is shown in Figure 6.5. Simultaneously, journalists now provide a two-way flow of information, reporting 'upwards' on street styles that have been a significant influence on top designers over the past few years (and often creating their own fashions and fads in the process), as well as 'downwards' on developments in the collections to the public.

6.4.5 The process for developing new products

Change in the form of new product development is an intrinsic part of the culture of all organizations associated with the fashion industry whether directly in manufacturing or retailing or indirectly in the media or public relations. While product strategies will invariably be linked closely to corporate objectives, continual new product development will also enhance and strengthen image, brand name, etc.

Traditional models used to describe the new product development process will describe many stages from concept through to actual launch. However, the timescale to which the fashion industry works is such that several of these stages will function simultaneously. To demonstrate this, the example chosen to work through is that of a high street multiple retailer. Whether textile or garment manufacturer or retailer the principles and procedures described are very much the same since all are involved in the process of buying, sampling and selling. Obviously the timescales will vary according to how far back in the chain they go.

6.5 Retail buying sequence: autumn and winter season

6.5.1 Early September

Analysis and development of new concepts take place, along with analysis of last year's range, to identify good and bad sellers based on performance and average weeks' cover. This is an indication of the rate at which a style is selling and the number of weeks it would take to sell out completely at the current rate. Lines which have averaged 10 weeks' cover, or less, will be seen as good sellers, anything above this will not have been such a success and is not likely to be repeated. If a line has averaged over 20 it will be deleted. The analysis will be by style, fabric, colour and price point and will form the basis for the range going forward. Supplier performance also will be examined, by line (rate of sale, prices and profitability) and by quality and reliability, for instance, in delivery.

At the same time an analysis of forward trends is conducted (working here with in-house design studio staff and colour and fashion forecasters if relevant). This is to gather new ideas, colours, fabrics, etc. that can be applied to the range.

The actual plan will be built up around improvements or revisions to existing products, additions to existing product lines and the incorporation of new products into the range.

6.5.2 Late September

First stage screening, further development of concepts and initial product development are all now able to proceed. Initial presentations of range plan ideas for basic approval take place and the alteration cycle begins. Further research is now needed for concept development and is conducted by, among other ways, shopping trips to Europe and America. Initial buyer and supplier meetings take place to exchange ideas and give direction, while sampling and the alteration process also take place at this time.

6.5.3 Early to mid-October

Second stage screening is conducted, while product development continues. Visits are made to the fabric fairs. Supplier development continues. Once the concepts and styles have been approved by the controller, a presentation is made at director level.

6.5.4 November to the end of January

Product development is now finalized, and provision for test marketing within the proposed new ranges is planned. Sampling and negotiating with suppliers and agents is in full swing, culminating in agreement on prices. Range meetings take place with controller and directors at end of January for approval of final ranges. Sealed samples, as described, are taken and work now begins on accurate buying figures and phasing of deliveries.

Range plans at this stage will feature certain styles to be included as experiments or test lines at the beginning of the season. It may be that they have a higher element of fashion in them than the norm and are therefore seen as carrying more risk. However, flexibility will be built into the range to purchase more of the new ideas if they prove to be successful once launched.

6.5.5 Mid-February

Marketers begin to develop the other mix variables, and prices are finalized. Other marketing tasks include liaison on contract preparation, and the development of in-store and other promotional ideas.

6.5.6 April to May

Chasing production, quality checks and monitoring progress are the main pre-occupations now. Feedback from these is used in a continual review process.

6.5.7 July to August

The first phase of the range is launched in stores. Phasing of deliveries according to pre-planning is set at approximately every six to eight weeks.

6.6 The product mix and range planning

6.6.1 The nature of the product mix

The product mix or product range is the assortment of goods a company offers for sale at any time. Before each season the organization must not only consider how it might alter or modify its classic (i.e. more basic) lines, which are less liable to radical change, it also must undertake careful planning of its fashion ranges in terms of width, depth and fashion content (and simultaneously anticipate and plan for the risk involved). Decisions concerning the mix of products also will relate to changes in broader company objectives. These may range from sales and profit growth, via emphasis on increasing market share or targeting new markets to return on investment targets, etc.

6.6.2 The planning cycle

The frequency of the planning cycle is probably greater in the fashion industry than any other because of its seasonal nature. Changing customer preferences ensures a perpetual drive for change. Volatility in terms of the seasonal variety of products offered and the speeds of change in fashions require skill, creativity, a propensity for risk taking and in-depth knowledge of end-user requirements in order for companies to plan effectively, and implement and control what is being offered in any given season.

Traditionally companies have planned for two seasons, autumn/winter and spring/summer. However, many are now moving towards the incorporation of mid-season ranges. For some this will mean a totally new set of garments, accessories, etc. and for others it will merely involve adding top-up variety to the major lines that were introduced at the beginning of the season.

At every stage in the planning cycle the team, which may comprise any combination of textile and/or fashion designers, production managers, sales-people, buyers, merchandisers and store personnel, will focus on the permutation of fashions being offered. The following terms are used in the example below which highlights the two major stages.

Garment category

This refers to types of garments in a generic sense, i.e. as a whole class or group. This could be such terms as market being served, context of wear, fashion look or statement. For example, a manufacturer of men's and women's jackets may offer ranges that appeal to the same target market in terms of age, income, interest in fashion and other segment characteristics. Alternatively, the ranges may be functionally based on, for example, rugged outdoor use, and appeal to a wide age range.

As another possibility, the ranges may comprise a mixture of classic through to high fashion garments that have been manufactured using similar production methods and materials. However, owing to their fashion content their appeal lies at either end of the fashion spectrum. In such a situation it is highly likely that the manufacturer would differentiate the ranges by distinct promotional, distribution and pricing strategies.

Product line

This is a breakdown of garment categories into fashions that are related in more specific, identifiable ways. Here an established variety of words or terms will probably be used to describe the breakdown into product types. Thus a casual jacket might be described as an anorak, a parka, blouson, yachting, donkey, etc.

Style

Each product line can be broken down into a variety of specific designs appropriate for the given season.

Width and depth

The dimensions in terms of number and variety in each stage of the planning process are shown in Figures 6.5 and 6.6.

Figure 6.6 shows how a hypothetical range of womenswear might be broken down into the following garment categories: tailored separates, blouses, casual tops and bottoms, and accessories. Casual tops have then been further broken down into specific product lines as follows: casual jackets, cardigans, sweaters and T-shirts. At the same time, the figure shows a possible percentage breakdown of total sales revenue and profits for the range by garment category. A further breakdown has been given within casual tops showing the percentage contributions of each to their own garment category and to the overall range.

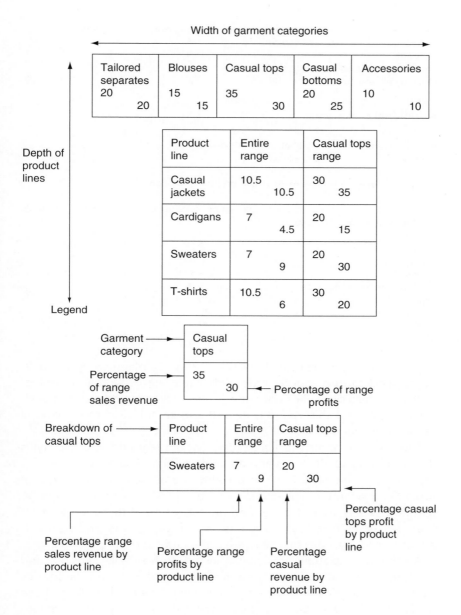

Figure 6.6 Stage 1 range planning: hypothetical womenswear range analysis.

Range plan detail for style 1:

Design detail   Round neck, long sleeve, single cotton jersey T-shirt.
                                              Single rib collar with top stitching, straight edge cuff.
Pattern   Printed triple stripe.

Colourways	Navy with white stripe, ivory with navy stripe.			
Size range	S	M	L	XL
Pack size	2	4	4	2
Total quantity (units)	720			
Quantity per size (units)	120	240	240	120

Additional comments:

If manufacturer:	Own label, to all UK licensees
If retailer:	Basic, all-store line

Analysis of percentage sales revenue and profit contribution:

	Percentage sales revenue	Percentage profit
Contribution to casual tops range:		
Style 1	12.25	9.0
Style 2	12.25	9.0
Style 3	7.00	7.5
Style 4	3.50	4.5
Contribution to T-shirt range:		
Style 1	35	30
Style 2	35	30
Style 3	20	25
Style 4	10	15

Figure 6.7 demonstrates how stage 2 in the planning cycle could be applied to one specific style within the line of women's T-shirts. The figure also quantifies percentage sales revenue and profit of each style within the T-shirt range itself and as a contribution to the overall casual tops range.

Thus in retail terms the T-shirt range would feature two basic styles that would go to all stores and amount to 70% of sales revenue. The more fashionable style 3 might be sent to specific branches, e.g. the top 50%. Style 4, the highest risk in terms of fashion content, might be featured in only 10% of stores and probably only at those stores most likely to sell high fashion garments. At the same time profit expectations would vary: *pro rata* style 4 has the highest profit potential.

As the organization grows, it may be strategically sensible and profitable for it to diversify its ranges into non-garment categories such as accessories, luggage and home furnishings. However, these decisions will usually be taken at board level since they will relate fundamentally to the nature of the company's business.

The retail examples of Next plc, Ted Baker and Ralph Lauren demonstrate how it is possible over time to move into broader clothing and non-clothing areas from an established base. From its original target group of 25- to 40-year-old women, Next plc has established itself with appeal to a much wider age range. Success eventually led to the development of several differentiated womenswear

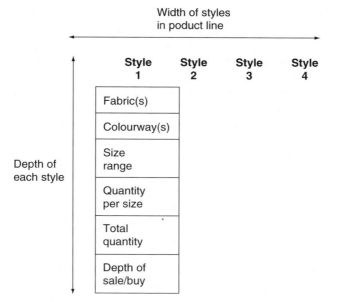

Figure 6.7 Stage 2 range planning: women's T-shirts. Hypothetical breakdown of specific product line.

ranges, menswear and childrenswear, footwear, jewellery, watches and giftware.

6.6.3 Range planning checklists

Improved technology means that planning teams are now better informed regarding sales histories for previous seasons. At any one time there are many dimensions of historical information available, e.g. seasonal best and worst selling styles, colours and sizes; customer sales patterns; geographical variations; specific rates of sale for garment styles; most popular price levels. The first essential stage in any planning cycle is to analyse what has happened in previous seasons to enable more informed decision-making so the firm can ultimately capitalize on previous success.

Pre-planning checklists

The following pre-planning checklist indicates where the analysis should focus:

- ◆ Sales history: Good and bad sellers; most popular designs and why? Best/worst customers in relation to best/worst stores. Specific styles and why?

- Rates of sale of styles offered, reasons for variations. Although certain styles may appear to be faster sellers there may have been problems regarding others, e.g. availability.
- Colour/fabric/pattern trends. For example, were best sellers limited to only certain colours, fabrics, etc. and if so, which ones?
- *Emerging trends*: Are there any new trends emerging from sales of high fashion lines, e.g. colours, styles, fabrics? Which are applicable to the range in question, i.e. which will suit the intended target market? To what depth should risk be taken?
- *Pricing*: Were the price levels appropriate?
- Did the styles offered represent good value for money?
- Was the balance of price levels right?
- Was it similar to that of competitors?
- Were target profit margins achieved overall by various styles?
- If not, how can profit margins be improved?
- *Competitors*: How successful in the previous season in question? Regular analysis of competitors should have been carried out during the season via comparative shopping surveys, information from other manufacturers or retailers, trade press articles, publicly available financial information, etc. Have there been instances of successful practice that can be followed?

Balance, cohesion and synchronization

Once ranges have been determined, the following will serve as a useful checklist to ensure balance, cohesion and synchronization:

- *Garment categories*: Is the percentage breakdown appropriate? Is the balance correct for customer requirements, and are there enough options to meet a variety of preferences and tastes?
- *Product lines*: Are the styles within each appropriate for the target market in terms of design content, style, fabric, colour, pattern and texture? The tension here will be between offering width or depth of range – where should the balance lie between offering safe lines and high fashions with more risk? Decisions regarding which new fashion directions should be incorporated are crucial; today's riskier lines could very easily become tomorrow's best sellers, as they become more widely accepted and therefore safer over time.
- Do the above two items fit the company image we are trying to portray? For example, the garment label or company name may be well established in a high fashion context.
- Is each range balanced? Is there cohesion in what is being offered or might there be too much emphasis on certain

styles and not enough on others? If there seems to have been a tendency to favour one or two styles, might competitors be doing the same? If this is a possibility the market will be flooded when the ranges are launched. Are the proposed size ranges balanced?

◆ Is the range profile balanced over time? This is particularly important when styles are phased in over a season rather than launched simultaneously. Does the phasing ensure availability of interest in the range at all times?

◆ Are the design proportions synchronized? For example, when considering a range of men's outerwear, if jacket lapels are narrow, are shirt collar point lengths also small? Are ties slim enough to provide a small enough knot? Are widths of trouser bottoms and other design features in proportion to those of the jackets?

◆ Is there balance across the pricing structure? Are the price levels right? Is there a relative balance of prices across lines and garment categories?

6.7 Fashion and related life cycles

6.7.1 The risks inherent in fashion

The cycle of marketing activity begins and ends with consumer needs; as the most urgent set of needs is satisfied in the form of appropriate products, others emerge. In turn, these new needs become of prime importance and create the driving force leading to a desire for further new products. Nowhere is this process more apparent than in the fashion industry; the continual development and introduction of new products into the marketplace are axiomatic to its very existence.

Paradoxically, while an essential undertaking, no aspect of the marketing mix is as uncertain as the introduction and acceptance of new products, particularly when they have a fashion element in them. Implicit in the pluralist nature of today's fashions is the existence of several typical looks or styles in any given season, and the incorporation of many modifications and variations according to the market requirements. The result is that all levels of fashion conscious consumers are able to distinguish between styles that are currently popular and others that belong to previous seasons and are therefore deemed out-of-date. The ability of the individual to observe and react to these phenomena in a negative way ensures the perpetuation of the fashion cycle.

Implicit in the above is that at any moment in time a style considered unfashionable by some may yet be deemed fashionable by others. The net effect of this is that the product's profile will vary over time in terms of sales revenue, profits generated and the target market it appeals to as the fashion becomes more widely accepted and therefore less fashionable. To avoid or at least minimize the risk of failure of new fashions, a method of forecasting the onset of popularity with the rate and extent of possible adoption and diffusion patterns would be invaluable to marketers. Furthermore, the ability to recognize symptoms of decline or failure at an early stage or perceive changes in the nature of the target market during the season could lead to appropriate changes being made to promotion, pricing and distribution policies to maximize sales and profit potential.

6.7.2 Limitations of theoretical models

Although it has been argued that fashion is the synthetic creation of the seller, particularly with the growth of retail concentration in the last decade, the existence in terms of diversity of direction offered in the marketplace at any one time and the numbers of 'dictated' designs that fail every season are evidence enough that fashions are decided by the majority. Taken collectively the public is closer to the *zeitgeist* or 'spirit of the age' than any individual designer, manufacturer or retailer; it is the consumer who has the last word in what will or will not become fashionable. At the same time the majority of tastes do not swing from one extreme to another every season; in the main changes are gradual and incremental. The implication here is that historical data relating to sales patterns of previous seasonal successes and failures can, to a certain extent, be used as the basis for planning anticipated success rates for new styles (or at least estimating the degree of risk involved). However, the real skill lies in being able to identify the most appropriate seasonal fashion directions for the target market in question, while using historical data to plot the likely success rate of the new selections in an effective way.

While the concept of the product life cycle described below provides a useful framework for analysing sales revenue and profit patterns over time, such analysis will always be retrospective. Thus the model is not able to answer important questions relating to the why and how of product acceptance or failure, or why different rates of acceptance and success exist. However, if the seasonal performances of incremental product changes are analysed in the context of variations in the rest of the mix during the cycle, and their performance is compared over time, it is feasible that acceptance and diffusion trends can be identified on the basis of product attributes or bundles of utilities. The caveat here is that relying solely on this information and using it too literally can very quickly lead to boredom on part of the consumer, ultimately leading to purchase decisions being made elsewhere in the pursuit of fashion.

Therefore, the real value of the product life cycle concept lies in its use as a tool for planning and controlling anticipated as opposed to actual rates of sale, at the same time understanding how varying the emphasis of other mix variables can impact on product performance at different stages in the cycle. In the longer term, greater understanding of interrelationships will result in more effective planning for appropriate changes according to emerging sales and profit performance.

6.7.3 The fashion product life cycle

The concept of the product life cycle is based on the proposal that all products have a finite 'life cycle' that can be plotted over a given period using the biological analogy of growth, development and decline. It proposes that all products will go through four major stages, namely introduction into the marketplace, growth, maturity and decline. However, it has already been pointed out that the nature of products in the fashion industry varies according to the rate, extent and timescale of acceptance of any new offering. Thus while fashion and fads do make up successful new product introductions, garments that are more classic in nature will never actually go 'out of fashion', nor will they rarely be 'in fashion', rather they will continue to meet established target market requirements. Thus the concept should be modified when analysing various fashion product classifications.

The life cycle of a fashion garment, extending over one or several seasons, probably comes nearest to the bell-shaped curve normally used to depict the product life cycle model (Figure 6.8).

The sales and profitability patterns and marketing implications of the model are described below.

Introduction

New fashions take time to gain acceptance. Some consumers will be more innovative than the majority and, while they are willing to pay higher prices, unit costs could potentially still be high due to low sales. However, to counterbalance this, the high fashion element (and therefore exclusive nature) of the style at this stage may mean that customers are willing to pay very high prices, leading to generation of high profits. Selected promotion will emphasize image and high fashion nature; the main aim will be to educate and inform the customer as quickly as possible. The size of the market will, however, be limited. Distribution will tend to remain exclusive.

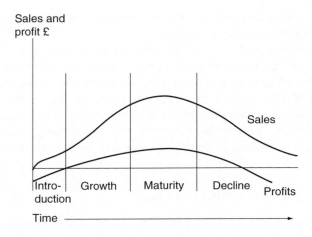

Figure 6.8   The fashion product life cycle.

Growth

Competition increases as the fashion gains exposure and begins to have wider appeal. Products will be modified to reduce costs and be offered at lower price levels. Sales will begin to rise sharply; new price bands will be established quite quickly. Distribution, still select-ive at this stage, will be wider as the fashion is diffused. Promotional emphasis will be on broadening exposure to gain acceptance of the fashion by the opinion forming element of the mass market.

Maturity

At this stage the fashion will have mass appeal; this period will be the longest in its life cycle. Competition will be intense, and prices will begin to fall to appeal to a very large market. Products will be further modified to achieve the ensuing lower price levels and profit poten-tial will be falling. Distribution will be wide; promotional emphasis will be on reinforcement of what has by now become an established fashion.

Decline

The style is rapidly going out of fashion. Competitors are gradually eliminated as sales and profits are falling drastically and the pros-pect of being left with obsolete stock is near. Those left in the market may try to extend the product's life by intensive advertising, extend-ing distribution or searching for new segments. The alternative seg-ments are likely to balance concerns about the likely success of the

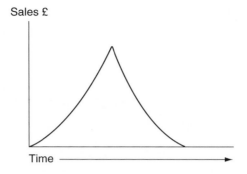

Sales £

Time

Figure 6.9   Sales of a fashion fad.

product against others such as price levels and the remaining life of the product.

6.7.4 The fad life cycle

The life cycle of the fad will tend to be very short, peaking quite sharply and declining almost as quickly as it rose in popularity (Figure 6.9).

The sales and profitability patterns and marketing implications of the cycle are described below.

Introduction and growth

In the case of a fad there is no introductory period coupled with rapid growth; the objective will be to capitalize on popularity as quickly as possible. However, the ability to do this will be restricted to a great extent by its 'fad-like' nature. Thus sales are pitched at a price the market will bear, probably higher than the fashion item it has been derived from, if this is applicable. Pricing strategy will aim to maximize profits even at launch stage, and the general emphasis will be on offering the new and different to a very specific type of consumer.

Maturity and decline

As maturity is reached, decline will begin very rapidly. Sales and profits will also decline; the emphasis here will be on getting rid of any remaining stocks as quickly as possible, either by reducing prices or by varying distribution channels. Promotional costs may be incurred in persuading new segments of the fad's dying appeal.

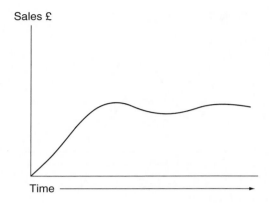

Sales £

Time

Figure 6.10 Sales of a fashion classic.

6.7.5 The classic life cycle

The style will have established itself over a time and, once established, will maintain its popularity with its target markets. Periodically the style will become fashionable; the shape of its curve, therefore, will tend to undulate gently (Figure 6.10).

Sales and profitability patterns and marketing implications of the cycle

Classics will already be established in the mature stage of the cycle (although they will occasionally be revived as fashion). Distribution channels, price and profitability levels will rise relative to what the established market will bear. Promotional policies for classics will tend to be based on reinforcement of well-established, accepted styles. Over time the market for classics could increase as demographic shifts in the population lead to larger numbers in mature age brackets (classics tend to be bought by older, more mature consumers). Earlier in this section the point was made that the life cycle concept would be most useful where analysis of decisions regarding product and other mix variables could be made regarding sales and profit patterns, and where analyses could then be compared over time.

A second dimension in terms of the concept's utility as a planning tool is where comparison can be made over time between the performance of specific styles of brands and broader market and sector trends. Analysis of life cycles here can be made at three related levels (as shown in Figure 6.11), from a general product classification or garment category through to specific product lines within each category and then to various garment styles or brand names (see Section 6.6).

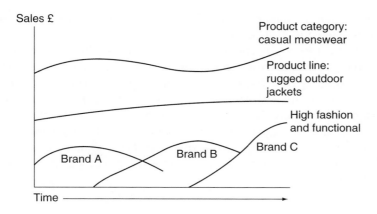

Figure 6.11 Hypothetical example of a three-level analysis within the general menswear sector.

6.7.6 Fashion oscillations

Some empirical evidence exists to substantiate the proposition that fashions will oscillate over time from one extreme or opposite to the other. These extremes may be in the form of silhouette or shape, colour, fabric texture or pattern and overall style/total look; in other words the four basic design dimensions mentioned earlier.

The driving force behind these oscillatory trends is the continual search by the individual to satisfy a variety of needs, ideally within one purchase decision, and the inherent inability of any one garment to satisfy all of them simultaneously. The net result is that a compromise has to be made between the ideal set of satisfactions sought and the reality of the product's potential set of satisfactions. This will ultimately open up possibilities for many different offerings, the spread of which will depend upon the extent to which compromise has had to be made.

However, every satisfactory purchase made will initiate new drives. These drives will be based on the perpetual need to search for different offerings to satisfy new needs. Paradoxically, therefore, as one design satisfies a combination of needs it extinguishes the very needs that produced it, simultaneously encouraging those needs least fulfilled by the design to come to the fore. The human drive for social approval results in the tendency for oscillations to reach extremes that are still universally adopted within market segments, e.g. miniskirts which are worn by a variety of body shapes and sizes within the youth market.

Neglect of some essential design element or embellishment over a long period also can lead to a vigorous revival. The sudden upsurge of many fashions can be explained from such frustrations, the classic example being Dior's post-war 'New Look' or Alexander McQueen's famous 'Bumster' Trousers in the 1990s.

Sophisticated mass communications have resulted in consumers becoming more fashion conscious and fashion aware. The trend now is towards the desire for considerably more diverse ranges of products in the marketplace and the need for more personalized, or customized, fashion. The general result of this is that fashion swings or oscillations are becoming shorter in a time-based sense, often leading to confusion in the marketplace. Here again, however, historical analysis of trends can help when trying to determine future developments.

6.8 Summary

At the end of this chapter readers should be able to:

- understand the role and importance of the product element of the marketing mix in the fashion industry;
- analyse and describe the perceived attributes of fashion items by the intended target market;
- describe the fashion diffusion process within the industry and its bearing on the process of new product development;
- understand how product mixes and ranges are planned and controlled.

Further reading

Baker, M.J. and Hart, S. (2007), *Product Strategy and Management*, 2nd Edition, FT Prentice Hall, London.

Barclay, I. *et al.* (2000), *New Product Development*, Butterworth-Heinemann, Oxford.

Elliot, R. and Percy, L. (2006), *Strategic Brand Management*, Oxford University Press, Oxford.

Goworek, H. (2007), *Fashion Buying*, 2nd Edition, Blackwell Publishing, Oxford.

Jackson, T. and Shaw, D. (2000), *Mastering Fashion Buying and Merchandising Management*, Palgrave Macmillan, London.

Pendergast, L. and Pendergast, T. (2003), *Fashion, Fad and Style*, UXL, MI.

Trott, P. (2004), *Innovation Management and New Product Development*, 3rd Edition, FT/Prentice Hall, Englewood Cliffs, NJ.

Chapter Seven
Pricing Garments and Fashion Services

7.1 Introduction

This chapter begins by considering price first as a concept and then in relation to other elements of the fashion marketing mix. External and internal factors affecting price are examined. The principal methods of setting prices used in the fashion industry are outlined and an explanation of discounts and the concept of break-even are given. The chapter concludes with a discussion of pricing strategies and the administration and nature of price changes.

7.2 Different views of price

According to economists, price is the point at which exchange between buyer and seller takes place, where supply and demand are equal. Anyone who has witnessed sales of out-of-season garments or clothing that have not enjoyed the popularity hoped for will notice that reductions occur to a point at which the stock is bought. However, price as an element of the marketing mix involves much more than the perspective of the economist.

The accountant tends to concentrate on the relationship between costs of production and the need to provide a certain return on capital invested with the final price that is to be charged. Cash flow is a major concern of all accountants and as such, price decisions can influence the volume of an item that is sold over time. For example, pricing bikinis at £8.99 each may mean that the entire stock is sold within four weeks of launch within a retail outlet. A higher price of £12.99 may mean that the same goal of selling all the stock takes eight weeks. Admittedly, in the latter case an extra £4.00 profit per pair has been earned, but at the cost of holding the stock for a longer period. An additional risk of charging £12.99 is having to reduce prices to shift stock that is particularly susceptible to changes in the climate.

Marketing personnel are interested in price decisions for many reasons. Prices that are set can determine the rate and extent to which marketing objectives are achieved. A company with a goal of achieving a 10% increase in market share will conclude that lower prices may give a competitive advantage that encourages purchases. Similarly, the goal of building a reputation for good quality may well lead to higher prices that follow from the higher costs of using better quality fabrics and imposing more quality checks in manufacture. Marketing managers are also interested in the price perceptions of buyers. As noted in Chapter Three, perception flows from an inner reality that may not be an accurate representation of true price levels. A company's products may be the cheapest on the market, but the advertising or the stores that sell the product may contribute towards an image that contradicts one of low prices. In such a case, opportunities may be missed as consumers do not even bother to check the accuracy of their perceptions. At the level of organizational buyers, from the manufacturer selecting fabric to the retailer acquiring stock, the awareness of price levels is usually a professional imperative. However, consumers vary considerably in their levels of awareness of prices. With branded products it is easier for consumers to make judgements, therefore comparison shopping is likely to be a common practice for many shoppers. Products from different manufacturers, even if within the same product category such as blue boot-cut denim jeans, present consumers with challenges to make direct comparisons due to differences in styling, quality of construction, quality of materials used and image.

The above perspectives and salience of pricing decisions for companies mean that many people within a company may have direct and legitimate interests in price decisions. The locus of influence and control will vary according to the organization of particular firms and to the relative importance given to financial and marketing matters. This is not an argument for the supremacy of marketing over other functional considerations, but a recognition that many disciplines should be involved in price decisions.

7.3 The role of price decisions within marketing strategy

The price levels for a product range selected by an organization can, along with other elements of the marketing mix, decide the success or otherwise in attracting certain target markets. Setting price levels too low may send confused messages and alienate some buyers who feel that the product may be poorly made. Excessive prices may inhibit other people who may feel other products, while not similar, offer better value for money. Others may feel that high prices are solely a premium for immediate ownership and that waiting for a short period may yield price reductions. Therefore price decisions help to determine who buys and how much they buy.

In relation to decisions about place matters, pricing decisions can secure access to certain outlets. To give retailers opportunities to achieve their profit margins, manufacturers must recognize the needs of the retailer's target market and the margins that are expected. If a retailer expects that an item will be a fast seller then a lower margin may be accepted. Similarly, higher margins are expected on slow moving items or risky new fashion products that may or may not be quickly accepted by the consumer.

Product matters are related to price decisions in many ways. The nature and extent of the product line may limit the flexibility possible in setting prices. For example, a co-ordinated range of skirts, jackets, blouses and accessories may be so priced as to encourage the purchase of several items by the consumer. Rigidly sticking to a fixed profit margin on each product in the range could undermine a policy that would otherwise lead to higher sales and profits by varying margins of items within and between the co-ordinated product lines. If the prices of products were left as a sum of their costs of manufacture plus a fixed markup, then variations in prices of different sizes of the same garment would be the obvious outcome. A size 18 overcoat may use nearly twice as much material as a size 8, yet few retailers would contemplate charging more for the larger one. In this sense, smaller customers subsidize larger customers, but in practice most manufacturers, retailers and consumers accept the notion of averaging costs and prices across different sizes.

Promotion and pricing decisions most closely relate with regard to the image that is being put forward to consumers. Most people perceive a relationship between price levels and quality, though not always a linear one. Usually, the expectation is that, high quality goes with high prices and low prices reflect low quality or possibly out-of-date or out-of-season clothing. The selection of a particular medium to reach a certain target market may mean that prices are not even mentioned in promotional messages. An accessory from Gucci, advertised in *The Times* with no mention of price, is such an example. At the other extreme a store selling garments aimed at low-income groups may make price a prominent feature of its window displays and advertising. Marks and Spencer originally began promoting itself as a store where everything was priced at one penny, but strategic repositioning and greater competition in the particular market segment have changed the company's practice since then.

The above discussion shows the interrelationship between price, target markets and other elements of the marketing mix. There is one particular area where pricing does differ from other elements of the marketing mix. All other elements of the marketing mix entail costs which it is hoped will lead to increased sales and profit. Pricing, while also affecting sales, will be a direct determinant of revenue out of which marketing and other costs are met.

7.4 External factors influencing price decisions

7.4.1 The nature of competition in the particular market

At a broad level it should be noted that competition comes not just from other garment suppliers, but also from other products and services that compete for consumers' discretionary income. High prices for garments may encourage consumers to spend more money on other consumer durables such as high-definition televisions or on leisure activities such as holidays. The unattractiveness of the prices of garments in relation to other competing products and services should be kept in mind. The relative sales and trends of various sectors of industry, plus the inflation rates by sector, are indicators of how well or otherwise this inter-sector competition is being met.

The more homogeneous the product the greater the price competition. The fashion industry tries to encourage non-price competition by the branding and creation of unique designs and images for ranges. At the designer level of the market, such garments are in limited supply through exclusive outlets and, the creators hope, for limited periods. The ability of competitors to produce similar products is restricted by some legislative protection of the design. Consumer confidence in garment quality and the ability to purchase an up-to-date design immediately enable higher prices to be charged. For other products such as socks the latitude to command exclusivity or any special design point that can be reflected in a higher price is more restricted.

7.4.2 Joint or related demand for products

This may arise where the increase in demand for one product is accompanied by an increase in demand for another. Good weather may well spur demand for swimwear, sun hats and sunglasses, whilst

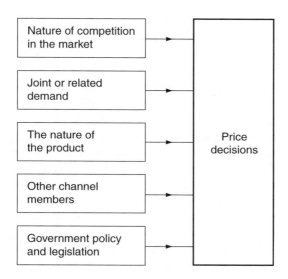

Figure 7.1 External factors influencing price decisions.

poor weather may lead to an increase in demand for rainwear, hats and scarves. Retailers, well aware of these linkages, may design the layout of the store and adjust prices accordingly to make the most of complementary demand. Other examples include the purchase of a new tie that may stimulate the purchase of a new shirt. New colour themes for a season, if adopted, may stimulate a whole range of purchases. Thus a new evening dress may be accompanied by the purchase of new hosiery, underwear, coat, cosmetics, hairstyling, shoes and handbag. Such outcomes are the aspiration of many department stores. It is the relative pricing, besides the selection and co-ordination of appropriate items in the above list, that is crucial in deciding the successful sale. Manufacturers who produce such complementary items independently need to anticipate the needs of intermediaries and the ultimate customer when setting prices (Figure 7.1).

7.4.3 The nature of the product

Whether the product is seen as an essential or not is a factor that influences the power of the seller in setting prices. Target markets differ considerably in what is seen as essential. A dinner jacket may be seen as a luxury by some, but as an essential item by a manager who has to attend many formal functions.

Some items of clothing and footwear are essential for protection and warmth. The rate of replacement of garments and the ability of consumers to defer purchase, obtain repairs, make clothes themselves or buy second-hand goods remain within the consumers' discretion. One related factor that influences the pricing of fashion products is the perceived life of the product. If a garment is seen as a 'classic' that will last for many seasons or years, such as a Barbour jacket or Burberry raincoat, then premium prices are more easily tolerated. In relation to other markets such as power supply, the fashion industry does not enjoy the privilege of producing items whose demand is insensitive to price changes. The nearest that the fashion industry comes to such demand is when there is only a limited supply of a unique design that is eagerly sought by buyers.

The speed with which some firms in the industry are able to produce garments that are similarly styled and made from comparable fabrics or fibres means such uniqueness does not go unchallenged for long. The issue here is not one of counterfeits, although that is a serious problem for some firms. The intrinsic difficulty of ensuring full protection for fashion designs is where the slightest difference in styling can be used as a basis for contesting a claim for breach of copyright. Inelasticity of demand is therefore limited in the fashion industry by the ease with which comparable alternatives can be quickly supplied.

7.4.4 Other members of the distribution channel

If one member of the distribution channel is able to charge higher prices this may tempt those earlier in the chain of distribution to increase prices and share in the profit potential. The ability of manufacturers to change retail outlets and the willingness of other outlets to stock a profitable product range are key variables that influence the setting of prices at the retail level.

Within certain sections of the retail clothing sector there are traditional margins that must be accounted for when setting prices. One large retail group, for instance, is known to have a company policy of multiplying supplier prices by 2.3 to arrive at a retail price. Such practices must be anticipated by manufacturers as, depending on the balance of power with the retailer, these traditional margins may be used as a mechanism to force down the manufacturer's selling price.

Changes in the costs of raw materials, labour or manufacturing at earlier stages in the distribution chain are factors that can influence the ultimate price to the consumer. With the growing internationalization of the clothing industry, the ability of retailers to procure stock from sources in different countries is greater than ever before. The power of suppliers to pass on price increases unchallenged is diminished except where the supply of a fabric or design is either unique or very well known, such as Gore-Tex or Lycra.

7.4.5 Government policy and legislation

As has been noted in an earlier chapter on the market environment, governments can influence the readiness of consumers to pay particular prices via policy related to inflation, investment and employment.

Government policy on taxation, in particular value added tax (VAT) and corporation tax, might be said to provide extra 'costs' that must be borne by the fashion consumer. The change of emphasis in taxation from earnings to expenditure in recent years has, at the macro-level, influenced demand for fashion products. The Office of Fair Trading, the UK Competition Commission and the European Commission are all charged to defend the public and business against various price fixing methods, as described later in this chapter.

7.5 Internal factors influencing price decisions

7.5.1 The ability to control costs

The ability of the company to minimize costs is a major determinant on the price levels that can be set. As costs can be decreased so either profitability can be enhanced or the ability to compete at low prices can be strengthened.

7.5.2 Other elements of the marketing mix

The relative importance of other elements of the marketing mix of the company is a factor influencing pricing decisions. The company competing directly on price to achieve high-volume distribution at low margins is in a very different position from the company setting out to create an image of high quality at premium prices.

7.5.3 The product range

The breadth and depth of product lines and the price relationships between items in those lines are factors that must be considered when setting prices. A warm lining for a raincoat sold separately will need to be assessed not only in terms of individual cost, but also for the impact it has upon the total demand and profitability of the rain-coat and lining together.

7.6 Main methods of setting prices

There are many ways of setting prices, but most are variants of the two principal methods, namely cost-plus pricing and market-based pricing. Cost-plus pricing is simply calculating the cost of raw materials, labour and overheads such as administration and adding an amount to cover profit to arrive at the selling price. Market-based pricing is founded on market research to find the optimum selling price which then acts as the main driving force on cost containment via design and quality control effort.

7.6.1 Cost-plus pricing methods

A cost-based method aims to ensure that no product is sold at a loss. The practice is common where the product is non-standard, such as designer wedding gowns, or where there are many small independent retailers supplying the market. Cost-plus pricing is also used with tender proposals, for instance, when a clothing manufacturer makes a proposal to supply uniforms to a large corporate client. A simple example is given below based upon a manufacturer supplying a retailer with zip-up tops made of cotton jersey.

The concept of the markup is explained in more detail below. In the example in Table 7.1, the profit margin per item is fairly low, but this may be deemed appropriate for an item that faces much competition and is expected to sell in very large quantities. The markups for the manufacturer and retailer have been set at 25% and 65%, respectively, as the minimum rates of return needed to service the capital required for each business, namely shareholder dividends or the cost of loans.

The example assumes that all of the zip-up tops will be sold at the full price. If the retailer is determined to clear stock, but not to sell below the cost of any item, then the lowest 'sale' price will be £6.70 plus VAT. If the retailer sells at VAT exclusive prices of between £6.70 and below £11.06 then the technique of contribution analysis is being applied. Contribution analysis is a variant of cost-plus pricing and works on the idea that any excess of price over cost enables a contribution to be made to the cost of capital to run the business – simply put, some profit is better than no profit. Clearly the whole of a company's pricing cannot be based on covering costs alone, as fashion companies need to do more in order to survive and grow. More

Table 7.1 An example of cost-plus pricing

Item	Details	Quantity	Unit cost	Total cost
Cotton	Jersey	1.5 m	£2.22/m	£3.33
Trim	Polyfil thread	1	£0.09	£0.09
	Metal zip	1 @ 20 cm	£0.27	£0.27
	Knitted collar	1	£0.21	£0.21
Label	With logo and care instructions	1	£0.06	£0.06
Labour to cut, make and trim @ 15 minutes				£1.40
Cost of production				£5.36
Manufacturer's markup @ 25%				£1.34
Manufacturer's selling price (excluding VAT)				£6.70
Retailer's markup @ 65%				£4.36
Retail price excluding VAT				£11.06
VAT @ 17.5%				£1.94
Retail price including VAT				£13.00

Table 7.2 Calculation of target buying prices

Cotton jersey hooded top including VAT at 17.5%	£12.99
Less VAT at 17.5%	£1.93
Retail price excluding VAT	£11.06
Less retailer's markup at 65% of buying price	£7.19
Retailer buying price or manufacturer selling price	£3.87

sophisticated variants of contribution analysis can be used to link price setting to several financial ratios.

7.6.2 Market-based pricing methods

These methods rely on a good knowledge of consumer price sensitivity and awareness levels. For example, market research may indicate that buyers in a certain target market may respond very favourably to a hooded top made of cotton jersey, if the item is priced at £12.99 (including VAT). If the retailer enjoys considerable purchasing power then the retail price of £12.99 can be used as a base to determine target buying prices for the retailer. The example in Table 7.2 shows how with a starting price of £12.99 the target retailer buying price or manufacturer selling price is determined.

Similarly, the manufacturer may then use the selling price of £3.87 as a target to challenge designers, pattern cutters and production staff achieve certain economies. In practice, many large UK retailers work very closely with manufacturers to decide prices that attempt to match consumer expectations.

7.6.3 A comparison of markups and markdowns

A markup is where profit is expressed as a percentage of costs and it is shown by the following formula:

$$\frac{\text{(Price} - \text{Cost)}}{\text{Cost}} \times 100$$

Thus a selling price of £30 with a cost of £20 gives a markup of 50%.

A markdown is where profit is expressed as a percentage of the sale price and it is shown by the following formula:

$$\frac{\text{(Price} - \text{Cost)}}{\text{Price}} \times 100$$

Thus a selling price of £60 with a cost of £24 gives a markdown of 60%.

Different firms use different approaches to calculate profit and selling price. However, all are variants of either a markup or a markdown. Indeed, knowing one it is easy to express profit in terms of the other. The formulae showing the interrelationship of the two main measures of profit margin are shown in Figure 7.2.

$$\% \text{ markdown on selling price} = \frac{\% \text{ markup on cost}}{100\% + \text{markup on cost}} \times 100$$

$$\% \text{ markup on cost} = \frac{\% \text{ markdown on selling price}}{100\% - \% \text{ markdown on selling price}} \times 100$$

Figure 7.2 Markup and markdown formulae.

Using the above formulae we can see that, for example, a markup on cost of 25% is the same as a markdown on selling price of 20%. Similarly a markdown on selling price of 66.7% is equivalent to a markup on cost of 200%.

Sometimes fashion retailers use a simple formula to calculate a retail selling price, including VAT, given a particular quotation from a manufacturer. The retailer wanting a markup of 120% and knowing that VAT is charged at 17.5% may simply multiply the quoted cost price, excluding VAT, by 1.375 to arrive at a tax inclusive retail selling price.

7.6.4 Discounts

The issue of margins leads naturally into a discussion of the purpose and types of discounts that are offered. The principle of economies of scale applies by which both buyer and seller recognize that larger quantities enjoy larger discounts. For the manufacturer, selling large quantities to fewer buyers means lower delivery and other overhead costs. Retailers naturally appreciate such advantages for both manufacturers and wholesalers and will press within negotiations for the largest quantity discounts possible.

Variations on the simple quantity discount are the cumulative and non-cumulative discounts available. Some negotiations may result in extra discounts becoming available should the buyer purchase certain minimum quantities over a fixed period, say one year. This extra discount may then become available as a rebate or credit against future purchases. The main aim of cumulative discounts is for the seller to encourage loyalty to the supplier and to induce small buyers to purchase more.

At the consumer level the retailer may encourage a customer to buy a jacket and a skirt, for example, by offering 10% off one item if both are purchased simultaneously. This type of discounting at the retail level operates erratically and is usually offered by the small outlets to tempt those potential consumers who are vacillating about a purchase.

Another common form of discount is the cash discount. Business to business discounts of this form usually take the form of a percentage reduction if payment is made within a fixed, usually short period. For example, 1.5% discount may be offered if payment is received within 30 days. Changes in legislation in the UK now allow retailers to charge different prices to consumers depending on the method of payment, be it cash or cheque versus a credit card payment. The obvious benefit for the retailer of a cash payment is improved cash flow and the avoidance of a payment of between 2% and 5% to the credit card company. The incidence of differential prices has yet to become widespread and, owing to the different charges levied by the credit card companies, is most likely only to be favoured by the small retailers.

7.6.5 Break-even calculations

A central concern of marketing personnel in the fashion industry is balancing the relationship between price and volume. For example, a clothing manufacturer may manufacture 20 000 skirts and wish to know how many must be sold to cover costs. In other words, at what point will the manufacturer break even and begin to earn profits? The first example assumes the manufacturer is in a relationship where prices are fixed by fierce competitive pressures and tough negotiating from retail buyers.

Alternatively, a designer who owns a retail outlet may have considerable discretion over price levels, but wonder about the profitability of the different volumes that could be sold at different prices. Break-even analysis is a technique that can help decision-making needs in the two examples just given.

Break-even analysis is an aid that can show the relationship between fixed costs, variable or marginal costs, total costs, sales revenue and output or volume. Fixed costs are those costs incurred by the fashion company that do not change as the volume of purchases or production changes. Some examples of fixed costs include business rates, purchase of a computer for wages and salaries for security staff. In practice, many fixed costs are variable in the long term, such as costs of plant for manufacturing. If these variations can be set aside, then a simple technique that can give a fairly sound guide to setting price level can be found in break-even analysis.

Variable costs are those costs that are directly affected by the level of output; some examples are the amount of material used, the direct labour costs in pattern cutting, making up and tailoring, and packaging costs. Total costs are the sum of fixed costs plus variable cost per unit multiplied by the output or volume. Sales revenue is simply price multiplied by volume sold. In practice, the price taken for the calculations is one that is exclusive of VAT.

The formula that shows the relationship between the above variables is as follows:

$$\text{Revenue} = \text{Price} \times \text{Volume} = \text{Total costs} + \text{Profit} \qquad (7.1)$$

When revenue is less than total costs, a loss (or negative profit) will result.

Where

$$\text{Total costs} = \text{Fixed costs} + (\text{Variable cost per unit} \times \text{Volume})$$

and

$$\text{Profit} = \text{Profit per unit} \times \text{Volume}$$

At the break-even point, no profit is earned and all costs are covered by sales revenue. Hence

$$\text{Revenue} = \text{Fixed costs} + (\text{Variable cost per unit} \times \text{Volume})$$

or

$$\text{Price} \times \text{Volume} = \text{Fixed costs} + (\text{Variable cost per unit} \times \text{Volume})$$

To determine the break-even point we can do some simple simultaneous equations where

$$FC = \text{Fixed costs}$$
$$VC = \text{Variable cost per unit}$$
$$V = \text{Volume}$$
$$P = \text{Price}$$

Thus we know that at the break-even point:

$$(P \times V) = FC + (VC \times V)$$

By taking (VC × V) from each side of the equation we get:

$$(P \times V) - (VC \times V) = FC$$

which, when simplified is:

$$V \times (P - VC) = FC$$

Next divide both sides of the equation by (P − VC):

$$V = \frac{FC}{(P - VC)} \qquad (7.2)$$

Of course (P − VC) is really the gross profit per unit.

To calculate the break-even volume, we divide the fixed costs by the difference between the price and the variable cost per unit.

If we wished to know the minimum price at which all the output was sold and covered all costs, i.e. the break-even price point, the formula is calculated as follows:

We know that at the break-even point:

$$(P \times V) = FC + (VC \times V)$$

If we divide each side by V we get:

$$P = \frac{FC}{V} + VC \qquad (7.3)$$

The value given here for price is the minimum that must be charged if the entire volume is sold and no profit is earned. In practice, a seller would wish to charge higher prices and earn some profit. The formula does at least help to establish a baseline for making pricing decisions.

7.6.6 Break-even analysis: an example

A small retailer of knitwear in a franchise operation may have rental and other fixed costs amounting to £45 000 per annum. If 3000 items of stock for resale are purchased per year at say £16 each (excluding VAT), then the total variable cost is £48 000. Assume here that the sales assistants are paid a fixed wage of £45 000 that is included in the fixed costs. If sales assistants were paid a commission for each item of knitwear sold, then this would be a variable cost and would have to be added to the purchase cost per item. Thus the total costs for the knitwear retailer are £45000 fixed costs plus £48000 variable costs, giving £93000 per annum.

If the knitwear retailer wishes to calculate the minimum price that must be charged to cover costs and sell all the garments then formula (7.3) must be used:

$$P = \frac{FC}{V} + VC$$

Substituting we get:

$$P = \frac{45\,000}{3000} + 16$$

Therefore, if a price of £31 (plus VAT) per unit was charged the business would break even.

If the retailer, after undertaking market research into competitors' prices, wishes to charge £39.95 (including VAT) per item, the question is now to determine the minimum number that must be sold to break even. A price of £39.95, including VAT at 17.5%, gives a VAT exclusive price of £34.00.

Formula (7.2) is used to calculate the break-even volume, thus:

$$V = \frac{FC}{(P - VC)}$$

Substituting values we get:

$$V = \frac{45\,000}{(34 - 16)}$$

which gives a volume of 2500 units to break even.

If the retailer sells all 3000 garments then if the original formula (7.1) is used:

$$\text{Revenue} = \text{Price} \times \text{Volume} = \text{Total costs} + \text{Profit} \qquad (7.1)$$
$$34 \times 3000 = 45000 + (16 \times 3000) + \text{Profit}$$
$$102000 = 45000 + 48000 + \text{Profit}$$

Thus the profit earned is £9000 or 8.82% of sales revenue.

7.7 Pricing strategies in relation to new products

The pricing objectives derived from a marketing strategy in relation to new products are to achieve growth, maximize profitability or generate cash flow. The crucial decisions to be made prior to selecting a pricing strategy are the identification of the target market(s) and careful consideration of the other elements of the marketing mix.

7.7.1 Market skimming

This strategy is to charge high initial prices and then only reduce them gradually, if at all. A skimming price policy is a form of price discrimination over time and for it to be effective several conditions must be met.

First, the demand for the garments must be relatively inelastic. Inelastic demand only really exists for essential items that are in short supply or items that have a degree of exclusivity and a significant number of buyers who are relatively unconcerned about price. A limited edition luxury handbag by Furla would be an example of such an item. For the supplier the unit costs of producing a small volume must not be too high. Finally, the high-profit margins on each item in a skimming policy will attract competitors unless the seller can protect the garments from being copied. Such a situation usually applies to haute couture and to a lesser degree to designer ready-to-wear ranges.

7.7.2 Market penetration

This strategy is the opposite of market skimming and aims to try to capture a large market share by charging low prices. The low prices charged stimulate purchases and can discourage competitors from entering the market as the profit margins per item are low. To be effective this policy relies upon considerable economies of scale in either manufacture or retailing or both. It also depends upon potential customers being price sensitive about the particular item and perhaps not perceiving much difference between brands. An example of this sort of policy may be seen in the plain 15 denier tights sold in supermarkets.

7.8 Pricing strategies to match the competition

Pricing objectives in relation to the competition include, as both active and reactive positions, an attempt to maintain price leadership, to stabilize prices or to discourage others from entering the particular market. Such strategies may also be linked to objectives concerned with building and maintaining the loyalty of other parts of the distribution chain. Aiming for stable prices while recognizing the traditional margins in the channels of distribution are the characteristics of the marketing activities of many fashion marketing companies.

7.8.1 Price leaders and followers

In the case of the follower, the firm identifies a target market and sets prices in line with competitors who are serving the same market. A firm with limited marketing resources may simply shadow a competitor. Within fashion retailing it is quite common for sales assistants to visit other stores to monitor the price points for garments and accessories. Monitoring the competition is an essential part of any market research, but slavishly aping one's rivals' actions without a clear long-term goal is another matter. The leader in such a situation is usually the firm with the lowest costs and best profit margins. Followers hope to avoid a price war by stressing non-price aspects of competition such as a higher customer service level.

Market research may indicate, for example, that a certain income group targeted by the firm is willing to pay between £25 and £35 for a blouse. The same research also may find that the main competitor is pricing similar garments at £29.95. The conclusion may be to charge at the same price or marginally lower, say £29.50. Such a policy of price matching can avoid a price war while maintaining profit margins. The policy of matching the competition is particularly vulnerable to enterprising newcomers to the market who may be able to upset the cosy reassurance that sometimes emerges in some sectors. An economic downturn with pressures on margins or the slow sales on some product lines can easily render this policy susceptible to change.

The large retail groups may incorporate an element of matching the competition within an overall pricing strategy, by allowing local managers some discretion in meeting local competition by adjusting prices where necessary.

7.8.2 Price fixing

Overt or covert price fixing by sellers is illegal in the European Union (EU) and most western nations unless a defence can be made that such action is not against the public interest. Manufacturers are, in the main, prohibited from imposing retail prices upon retailers in the UK, and this is known as retail price maintenance. Manufacturers are sometimes able to use pressure relating to the supply or withholding of products or financial incentives to exert influence over retail prices and effectively inhibit competition. The EU has an aim of free movement of goods within and between the member states and the intense competition within the fashion market works strongly against price fixing tendencies. However, in 1993, the French perfume industry was able to claim a victory in the European Court by winning the right to exclusive distribution of perfumes, thereby protecting the margins of outlets against the so-called grey imports. In 2001, the battle over exclusivity and free competition in the setting of prices continued with a legal case between Tesco, the supermarket group, and Levis Strauss over the distribution and pricing of jeans in the UK with Levi Strauss winning the case for exclusive distribution. However, there are strong pressures with the EU to review legislation in line with WTO principles of free trade. The role of online purchasing in international trade is another factor that is undermining the ability of retailers to control prices via exclusive distribution.

7.9 Price changes

Prices for clothing may need to change for a variety of reasons, but the administration and communication of those changes are important matters that can affect profits greatly. An overview of price changes is given in Figure 7.3. Prices can increase because of higher costs, rising inflation, excess demand for the product or simply a misjudgement of prior price levels.

Decreases in price can be attempts to drive out or meet competitors, to take advantage of lower costs or to generate more demand. As fashion is about change, garment prices usually fall over time. The only exceptions seem to be rare items previously owned by celebrities or clothing in short supply that is identified with a fast emerging cult.

Whatever the cause of the price change, it will affect customers, competitors and other members of the distribution channel. The uncertainty that accompanies the potential effect of any price change means that research and planning are essential. Buyer responses to price changes can be varied. For reductions, many may perceive the items to be end-of-season, unpopular, faulty or of lower quality. It also may be that buyers resist initial price reductions in anticipation

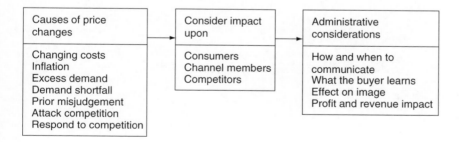

Figure 7.3 Price changes.

of further falls. Price increases are only popular with those who bought at a lower price. Increases can signal that the product may soon be unavailable or that it represented good value for money with very low margins at the old price.

All price changes, when clearly marked, can attract attention and raise buyers' price awareness levels so that purchase values may then be reconsidered. As noted in Chapter Three, the concept of learning is important as price changes 'teach' consumers what to expect. Thus, if a store always marks items down by 20% after eight weeks, then a further 20% after another two weeks, some consumers will learn not to pay higher prices. The cycle of price reductions can therefore become reinforced as more people in the target market learn to avoid paying the premium prices.

The communication to consumers of price changes requires particular consideration. Changes promoted as 'massive reductions' can alienate those customers who paid higher initial prices, while simultaneously attracting the bargain hunters the supplier is seeking. How price changes are communicated depends upon the marketing objectives of the firm and the target markets being served. Indeed some target markets are defined by bargaining pricing as shown in Figure 7.4; the drawback of this for the fashion marketer is that

Figure 7.4 Example of retail discounts.

loyalty is hard to engender with this type of customer. Announcing large clearance discounts in a sale in an outlet catering for higher income groups may be inconsistent with other aspects of the image. However, when the change is announced, it is imperative that the sales staff and customers are in no doubt what price is to be charged and when the change takes effect. Much damage to customer good-will can be done by lack of care in announcing price changes. Given the practices of a minority of unscrupulous retailers, many consumers approach sales with a healthy degree of scepticism. Thus care is needed to avoid a small oversight being construed as a deliberate attempt to mislead.

7.10 Summary

This chapter has considered price, both as a concept and in the context of the marketplace in relation to the other elements of the fashion marketing mix.

Pricing decisions are:

◆ subject to a wide variety of influencing factors, internal and external;
◆ a strategic matter, and not to be approached in a short-term reactive way;
◆ to be made within the wider framework of a clear understanding of the target market, the firm's overall marketing strategy and the competition.

Further reading

Baker, R.J. (2006), *Pricing on Purpose: Creating and Capturing Value*, John Wiley and Sons, NJ.

Cram, T. (2006), *Smarter Pricing: How to Capture More Value in Your Market*, Pearson Education Ltd, Harlow.

Cravens, D.W. and Piercy, N. (2005), *Strategic Marketing*, 9th Edition, McGraw-Hill, London.

Nagle, T.T. and Hogan, J.E. (2007), *The Strategy and Tactics of Pricing: A Guide to Growing More Profitably*, 4th Edition, Pearson Education, London.

Ruskin-Brown, I. (2007), *Practical Pricing for Results*, Thorogood, London.

Chapter Eight
Fashion Distribution

8.1 Introduction

This chapter examines the retail sector which for many people is the 'face of fashion', describing the structure of the industry and its constituent parts, and includes an outline of recent developments. It concludes with a brief examination of criteria against which retail marketing effectiveness can be judged. The large-scale retailers are all involved in marketing activities and most have specialist marketing departments.

8.2 The importance of fashion retailing

The retail industry is important to the marketing of fashion clothing in a number of ways. First, and most obviously, it is the mechanism through which the clothes reach the consumer.

Secondly, with the growth in applying information technology, it is also able to provide, within hours at most, detailed feedback of what the consumer is buying. This allows changes in the marketplace to be quickly assessed, thus helping range renewal, particularly in such areas as replacement sizes and colours. Benetton has the tills of all its shops linked directly to its marketing and design departments as well as to its dyeing facilities so that changes in demand can be quickly observed and production changed accordingly.

Thirdly, it facilitates the application of target marketing (see Chapter Five).

Fourthly, it has been active in the promotion of design awareness to the shopping public, two well-known examples being Habitat and Next, in terms of product design and store layout and equipment.

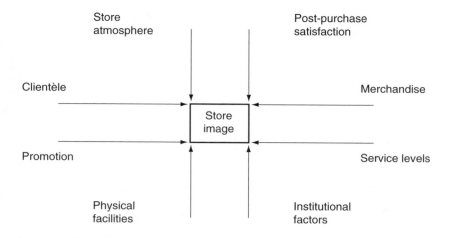

Figure 8.1 Components of store image.

Design also serves to promote market segmentation and to improve sales and productivity ratios in relation to increasingly expensive selling space.

Fifthly, manufacturers and designers can achieve stability by owning their own retail units. As Paul Smith has said of his retail side, 'it is a regular earner for us' (*Independent*, 9 August 1993, p. 19).

Finally, the retail outlet through its store image can create loyal customers who may provide a measure of stability in sales income and profits. A 1999 Verdict Clothing Report indicated that 86% of main users prefer their current main store, and that loyalty was highest in the south of England.

What goes into creating a store image? Various writers have offered suggestions, and Lindquist reviewed many studies and synthesized the following from them – merchandise, service, store atmosphere, promotion, clientèle, physical facilities, institutional factors and post-purchase satisfaction. Physical environment is an important influence on image, as Mary Jo Bitner (1992) outlines in a journal article. The main components of store image are shown in Figure 8.1.

Another factor in building store loyalty has been the introduction of store-based credit cards, which in addition to encouraging sales afford opportunities for database marketing. The Bhs Gold Card is one example and the Recognition FraserCard with more than 1 million cardholders is another.

Such is the importance of store image that some manufacturers and designers actively strive to be represented in certain stores. This, alongside other issues such as reliability, cost, stockholding capabilities and coverage of the market sought, is a major consideration in channel management.

8.3 Structural issues

8.3.1 Basic structure

The industry has traditionally been divided into three distinct segments, which have over the years performed differently.

Womenswear, the largest segment, has traditionally shown most growth, and was worth an estimated £31 billion in 2003.

Menswear has shown greater growth than womenswear in recent years as men become more fashion conscious. The men's outerwear market was worth an estimated £6.6 billion in 2004. However, just as it seems to do relatively better than womenswear when the economy is booming, so it seems to suffer greater decline in recessionary times.

Childrenswear is the smallest of the three retail markets, at an estimated £5.0 billion in 2004. In retail fashion terms it is a difficult market to cater for, but in recent years it has seen a growth in specialist retail chains such as Adams and the introduction of continental retail brands such as Chipie and Oilily. As children become more fashion conscious at a younger age, this affords new opportunities at all levels in the retail clothing industry.

8.3.2 Concentration

In common with other sectors of the retail trade, concentration in the fashion retail market has increased over the years. All three market segments described above are dominated by variety chains and multiples except at the designer level. Clothing retailing in the UK is perhaps most concentrated in the world. The top five companies in both womenswear and menswear account for over 40% of total sales. In the childrenswear market the top five retailers account for over 40% of sales. This has been achieved through economies of scale, e.g. buying power, promotional spending and managerial expertise.

It has been suggested that customers who want something other than the mass produced and marketed clothes provided by the major retailers will enable a considerable independent sector to thrive. Others point to entrepreneurial flair and ability to cater to local needs as reasons for their continued survival.

In this context those retailers who try to combine an element of exclusivity and the benefits of scale by trading from a limited number of outlets, such as Jigsaw, seem to have done relatively well in recent years.

Multiple clothing retailers (with 10 or more branches) have over 25% of the market, variety chains slightly less and independents about 15%. Department stores, the last major grouping, have approximately a 7% market share.

8.3.3 Numbers of outlets

The Department of Trade and Industry's (DTI) periodic retail enquiry shows a gradual decline in the number of outlets. Though most closures are small retailers, they nonetheless continue to make up the bulk of the specialist outlets. This to some extent is offset by an influx of European and American clothing companies setting up retail outlets in the UK, two examples of which would be Ouiset and The Gap.

The 1996 retail enquiry figures put the number of outlets specializing in one or other of the three markets at 33 000.

The retail boom of the 1980s also resulted in a large increase in the amount of selling space, particularly in out-of-town locations. It also created greater demand for sites in town centres with Next, for example, taking over Combined English Stores so as to acquire additional prime selling space. There is now an argument for saying that the nation has too many shops, and some reduction in numbers is necessary. The development of non-shop outlets such as the Internet is likely to encourage this trend.

8.3.4 Outlet size

To the extent that clothing retailers and particularly those who serve the upper market levels continue to trade from established city centre sites, there is limited scope for increasing the size of outlet, though Marks and Spencer did build a fifth floor onto its Marble Arch store.

Moving to out-of-town locations offers the potential for increasing store size but can affect the image of the store. Out-of-town supermarkets with their larger selling areas are offering an increasing range of clothing, much of it is fashion based. Marks and Spencer now has over 40 stores of over 100 000 ft^2 (10 000 m^2).

8.3.5 Import and export

In common with other UK industries there is a considerable amount of overseas trade and as in sectors of UK industry the degree of import penetration is high and rising. The value of exports is a small and decreasing fraction of UK imports of clothing.

The reasons for this state of affairs are many and complex and often apply equally to other sectors such as the exchange rate, comparative labour and other costs, together with tariffs and other barriers to trade such as subsidies and quotas. Free trade, that is countries being allowed to buy and sell goods and services worldwide without any restrictions, is theoretically desirable but the international textiles trade, like others, is regulated though less so with the ending of the Multi-Fibre Agreement in 2004, which resulted in a surge of imports from China. A subsequent attempt by the EU to reintroduce quotas in 2005 resulted in many millions of garments being temporarily stuck in European warehouses and many retailers fearing gaps in their product ranges.

8.3.6 Exports

Exports are mainly restricted to high value and traditional sectors such as knitwear, where cost is less important as retail customers appreciate and are willing to pay for quality and style.

Much of the UK trade in textiles is with the other members of the EU, though the USA and the Far East are important markets. British retailers that expand overseas may provide useful export markets for the manufacturers who supply their UK stores.

8.3.7 The future for UK clothing firms

Under increased pressure from low-cost producers, the British textile industry has steadily declined over the years as retailers have increasingly sought to import their merchandise from low-cost countries, originally in the Far East, particularly China.

However, there is some hope: improvements in technology and manufacturing techniques hold out the possibility of UK manufacturers being able to meet the demands for small-scale production runs. Retailers' increasing reluctance to hold large stocks and consumer pressure towards more diversity and exclusivity encourage the need for small runs and put a premium on a fast flexible response that will tend to help UK-based manufacturers. Just-in-time (JIT) inventory control and a reluctance to commit budgets early in the season also offer the possibility of top-up orders even if the main order is initially placed overseas.

Pressure from the dominant retailers has resulted in UK manufacturers increasingly making use of subcontractors, many of which are overseas. An increased emphasis on design is also being placed on the manufacturers, many of whom now have an in-house design capability, though in recessionary times these may be cut back.

8.3.8 Relationships with manufacturers

One option for clothing firms is to operate as both a retailer and a manufacturer, though this is becoming increasingly less attractive. The major disadvantage of this form of vertically structured form of organization is that considerable capital is tied up in manufacturing assets that, because of changing market conditions and increased overseas competition, provide progressively lower rates of return.

The major advantages for retailers with their own manufacturing concern were total control of the manufacturing process and security of supply, these advantages have been retained by the major retailers in their dealings with their suppliers because of their dominant role in the marketplace. Often suppliers are almost totally dependent on a particular retailer, who can in return for regular and substantial orders, demand total control over the manufacturing process and enforce narrow profit margins on the manufacturer.

Many retailers are cutting the number of suppliers they deal with. Bhs is reducing this figure from some 750 in the early 1990s to about half that number. Those that remain must meet strict terms on price, quality, delivery times, etc. Arcadia is another example of a retailer concentrating on a limited number of suppliers; over 40% of its products come from just 20 suppliers.

At the same time, the reverse is occurring with some manufacturers who believe that the time taken to service small retailers would be better spent forging closer links with their major customers. An example of a supplier adopting this policy is Hardcore, the denim company.

8.3.9 Retail buying and selling

In all large-scale fashion clothing retailers central buying is now the norm. Experienced buyers visit trade and fashion shows, overseas and UK suppliers, and use prediction services to make decisions on what to buy for the coming seasons. Often the initial order will be for only part of the expected sales, the rest being confirmed later in the season as actual sales figures allow management to estimate likely demand more accurately.

Specification buying is becoming increasingly prevalent, whereby buyers place orders against rigorous predetermined standards of fabric quality, trim, etc. Many leading high street fashion retailers have extensive laboratory facilities to monitor the quality of the clothes they sell. Some retailers also employ staff to allocate stock to their various outlets to maximize likely sales – these staff apportion new stock to the outlets by using past sales figures to estimate potential

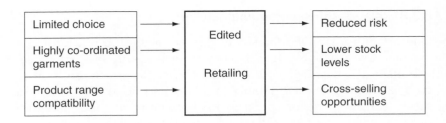

Figure 8.2 The edited retailing concept.

demand for new lines. Getting the allocations right maximizes sales and minimizes the likelihood of having excess stock in some branches which might, without a system of branch transfers to reduce it, result in this stock having to be cleared at a cost of heavy reductions. The biggest cost for all retailers is stock, so intelligent buying, good stock control and effective merchandising (see Chapter Six) are of paramount importance.

In this context several fashion retailers have adopted a concept known as 'edited retailing', whereby the customer is offered a limited though changing choice of merchandise that is highly co-ordinated, offering a high degree of product range compatibility. The concept of edited retailing is shown in Figure 8.2

Next is a good example of this approach. As well as reducing risk, stock holding, etc., it offers great scope for cross-selling, in effect buying the whole 'look'. As George Davies states in his book, *What Next?*, 'The exercise taught me one of the keys to success in retailing ... the trick is to give the illusion of choice.'

8.4 The industry's components

The retail fashion industry consists of many parts, the most important of which are outlined in this section.

8.4.1 Wholesalers

Market trends

The wholesale sector is in serious decline; the reasons for this are increased retail concentration and a more volatile fashion driven clothing market. Jaeger, perhaps anticipating these trends, withdrew in 1987, as did Jacques Vert in 1998.

The large multiples and department store groups deal directly with their suppliers, often overseas companies, through central buying departments. They are therefore able to avoid using wholesalers and the associated costs. Indeed Marks and Spencer, the market leader in many areas of the retail market, was one of the first, if not the first, to deal directly with a manufacturer (Corah) and so break the grip of the wholesalers. Besides financial savings and better control over product quality, dealing directly with suppliers allows retailers to satisfy their, or more correctly, customers' needs. A measure of exclusivity in terms of fabric, design content, etc., enables them to differentiate themselves from their competitors.

The extent to which customers see the retailer's own label as better value than other brands improves sales, especially in recessionary times when customers are even more value conscious.

Although they carry fewer overheads and staff than manufacturers or retailers, the number of wholesalers and their market share will continue to decline. No longer needed by the large retailers they find themselves catering to a diminishing number of small firms, many of whom find their services of little or no use.

Functions

The traditional functions of wholesalers are to:

- provide finance;
- break bulk;
- transport goods to the retailer;
- provide information or advice.

These may be attractive to small-scale retailers but are irrelevant to major retailers or small chains. Within the ranks of small retailers, those serving upper market levels will tend not to use them either.

Why is this the case? Each function will be examined in turn.

- *Provision of finance*: Financing stock is attractive, but even if this is less costly than other forms of finance it could be counterbalanced by possibly paying higher prices and being restricted in one's choice of stock.
- *Break bulk*: This is an attractive proposition if applied to large volume, homogeneous goods in constant demand. This to some extent applies to 'basics' such as T-shirts but for short-life fashionable clothing it is not appropriate.
- *Distribution of goods*: Numerous distribution companies exist that offer a high-quality, reliable and comparatively inexpensive service to suppliers and retailers alike.

◆ *Provision of information or advice*: A knowledgeable wholesaler may be able to offer this, but other arguably more relevant sources exist, e.g. trade shows, the trade press, prediction services and agents.

8.4.2 Mail order

Since the 1970s the mainstream mail order sector, providing large catalogues running to over 1000 pages, has declined in importance. Its two main advantages, easily available credit and a generous returns policy, are now offered by the high street stores. In addition, the agents who operated the catalogue were servicing on average fewer customers each year, and many catalogues are now promoted on the basis that no agency is necessary. The sector still tends to suffer from a residual downmarket image, though its image is improving. Another drawback is goods returned which can average 30%.

In recent years the more successful mail order operations have tended to be the smaller specialist newcomers catering to a specific target market, often with a higher socio-economic profile than the mainstream catalogues. These offer the convenience that is attractive to many with limited time to shop as well as an element of exclusivity and a more positive image. These specialist catalogues offer the opportunity to service niche markets profitably, sometimes where a store-based retail system would be much less successful. They are now facing increased competition from mainstream catalogues, which are featuring more designer merchandise, and of course the Internet.

8.4.3 Discount clothing retailers

As with other sectors of retailing, there exists a significant discount presence that caters almost exclusively for the lower end of the market. Sited in low-cost premises and offering keen prices on clothing of a lower quality than that available in many major multiples, they operate on very high levels of stock turnover. A second variety of discount store is the outlets run by the major retailers to dispose of excess stock from their normal branches.

Thirdly, the introduction of factory outlet centres such as the one in the Hornsea Freeport shopping village may affect sales in full-price outlets. However, it could be argued that they benefit both retailers and manufacturers since they provide outlets for out-of-date and substandard products that, if sold through normal retailers, could damage the brand's image. They also allow the retailers to dispose of surplus stock, so helping them to offer new lines to their customers.

8.4.4 Multiples and variety chain stores

The former are businesses with at least 10 outlets selling predominantly one merchandise group such as clothing or shoes. The latter, as the name suggests, sell a variety of merchandise, the three major variety chain stores with a significant clothing turnover being Bhs (part of Arcadia), Marks and Spencer, and to a lesser extent Woolworths.

Having a place in most of the nation's high streets and out of town developments, these shops represent the success story of British clothing retailing. Their sales and market share have increased year after year at the expense of other retailers. For many years the fashion element in their ranges was minimal, as mass market tastes were only gradually influenced by fashion and good profits could be earned by large volume orders placed with suppliers. Adopting a more fashion orientated range increased the degree of risk through entering a more volatile market that was difficult to monitor.

With a growing fashion awareness among their customers and increased competition from smaller, more fashion orientated retailers, they have moved to provide more fashionable ranges, often using established designers. In this they have been helped by advances in information technology such as Electronic Point of Sale (EPoS), and manufacturing techniques that make the supply and retailing of smaller quantities profitable. The adoption of segmentation policies, most notably by the Arcadia Group (see Chapter Five), has also allowed them to provide a more fashion-focused offering to their customers. Overemphasis on segmentation, though, has caused at least one failure, La Mama, where there were insufficient pregnant career women of means to justify its existence. One prerequisite of segmentation is that the market should be sufficiently large to justify catering to it.

These shops tend to have prime sites which guarantee high levels of customer exposure to their merchandise. Location is of prime importance to retailers, perhaps best summed up in the universal saying, 'There are three things of importance in retailing – location, location and location.' The enabling of consumer choice within a select shopping area is a key to success as shown in Figure 8.3. One charge levelled at these chains is that they have succeeded in creating a dreary uniformity in the high street, each one having its Bhs, Next, Miss Selfridge, etc., with the same corporate fascias and colour schemes and, more importantly, the same merchandise catering to the same middle market needs. This is a view the retailers naturally take issue with, though they are nonetheless trying to offer a more individualistic service, in which they are aided by systems such as ACORN, MOSAIC and Townprint (operated by Arcadia), which allows them to build up a picture of the market in their immediate catchment area.

8.4.5 Department stores

Though only small in number, only a few hundred, with some 7% of the overall retail clothing market, department stores have an important role to play in retailing fashion clothing. While catering to a wide market they are particularly attractive in terms of their strong AB customer profile and appeal to older customers. For mid- to upper-market labels they often provide the only suitable outlet, other than the designer opening his or her own store. This would not only demand a considerable capital investment, but also entail obtaining a suitable location for which, because of their relative scarcity, there is often great competition.

As those involved in purchasing fashion clothing are involved in an exercise in comparative shopping, department stores have the advantage that they have under one roof a wide variety of clothing

Figure 8.3   Example of the importance of location

from expensive designer labels to comparatively inexpensive basics. In addition, department stores have a growing range of own label merchandise, such as the Linea range in House of Fraser.

Having a variety of concessions enables them to offer a range of other labels in addition to own label and bought-in manufacturers' brands.

Many department stores have reduced the number of their departmental product groups but remain strongly committed to clothing. John Coleman the boss of House of Fraser thinks its upmarket, designer fashion-led offer successfully differentiates it from Debenhams.

Department stores often attract high concentrations of overseas visitors, many of whom spend considerable sums of money.

8.4.6 The independent sector

Independents have over a number of years been losing out to the multiples and variety chains, who have economies of scale. In addition many have succumbed to large increases in rents as leases came up for renewal, which has less of an effect on those others who often own the freehold of the site from which they trade. The introduction of a uniform business rate has also proved disadvantageous to many, resulting in massive increases in rates in areas until now favoured as low-rate areas. Some of these pressures are shown in Figure 8.4.

At the upper market levels independents are still strong and are positively encouraged in some locations such as Covent Garden. However, owners and developers tend to favour large retailers as they are better able to afford high rents and are more reliable in terms of meeting long lease commitments. Nonetheless in the late 1980s and early 1990s, when most major chains were registering declines in sales and or profits, as a category independents fared relatively better.

Figure 8.4 Pressures on the small fashion retailer.

A measure of exclusivity has provided some relief from these pressures through exclusivity of supply being granted to favoured independents. However, this may be subsequently lost to larger retailers.

8.4.7 Supermarket involvement

Historically the supermarket groups have not seen the fashion clothing market as particularly attractive, preferring to concentrate their own expertise and other resources on food, though competitive pressures are changing this.

Sainsburys became involved through the Savacentre operation which was originally a joint venture with Bhs. ASDA has the highest profile involvement through George, its in-store clothing operation set up by George Davies, the ex-Next chief executive. Tesco is developing an extensive and more fashionable clothing offering under its own label. Supermarkets are particularly strong in children's clothing having a 16% share in 2004.

8.5 Trends in retailing

The retail fashion market has seen considerable changes in recent years, as have other sectors of the retail trade. Some of the more important are outlined below.

8.5.1 Franchising

Franchising is defined by the International Franchise Association as a contractual relationship between franchiser and franchisee in which the franchiser offers or is obliged to maintain a continuing interest in the business of the franchisee in such areas as knowledge and training; wherein the franchisee operates under a common trade name, format or procedure owned by or controlled by the franchiser, and in which the franchisee has made or will make a considerable capital investment in his business from his own resources. The reasons for its success as a retail format are the advantages offered to both franchiser and franchisee as outlined below.

Advantages to franchisee

- ◆ Obtains the benefits of the name, reputation, brand image, etc. already established with the public.

- Less need for own capital as the franchiser helps to obtain capital; banks tend to be more sympathetic to requests for loans to the more established franchises than to those without the backing of a franchiser.
- Help in a number of areas, e.g. staff training, site selection and purchase of equipment and stock.
- Benefits of any national advertising, e.g. Benetton spends a multi-million pound budget to run the Benetton racing team.
- Exclusive sales territory granted for the duration of the franchise agreement.
- Less risk of business failure. A survey in 1986 undertaken for the *Financial Times* showed that after five years 80% of small businesses had ceased trading, while less than 20% of franchised businesses had failed – an example of the Pareto (80/20) rule.

Advantages to franchiser

- Rapid expansion is possible without causing cash-flow problems.
- 'Tied' outlets for products/service.
- Initial fee plus regular royalty payments.
- Less risk. The franchisee puts up the capital and as his or her own boss has a direct incentive to make a success of the venture.

Many niche retailers, so popular in the 1980s, were franchises. One of the earliest and most successful for many years was Tie Rack.

According to the British Franchise Association, any company offering a franchise to set ethical standards must have run its own outlets successfully for a minimum of one year.

8.5.2 Concessions

Also known as shops within shops, they can be defined as space leased by the host retailer to another retailer, wholesaler or manufacturer from which to sell its merchandise.

One of the earliest examples was Jaeger as concessionaire and Selfridges on Oxford Street as the host retailer. This concept expanded greatly in the 1970s and 1980s. Debenhams, before its takeover by Burton in 1985, had over one-third of its selling space and income from concessions. Since then Debenhams and many other retailers have reduced their dependency on this type of operation.

Examples of concessions are Moss Bros, which is both a host retailer and a concessionaire, CC formerly Country Casuals, Liz Claiborne and Jacques Vert. Many fashion clothing concessions operate in department stores, sometimes trading from a very small sales area.

Possible advantages to the host retailer provided by concessions include:

- flexibility through short-term contracts;
- benefit of specialist expertise in buying and merchandising;
- additional interest to customers;
- reduction of certain costs, such as fixtures and fittings, training and wages;
- reduced stockholding costs and risk;
- guaranteed income for the store.

Possible advantages to the concessionaire include:

- no high start-up costs for their own retail outlet;
- good exposure to host shop's high volume of customers;
- concessionaires can test market at a relatively low-cost new ideas that, if successful, could result in expansion and ultimately opening their own stores and, if not, still enable them to relinquish the concession.

There are of course disadvantages. In respect of the host retailer these revolve around the possibly adverse effect that poor concessions have on the store's image and the competitive threat to its own sales by the concession. One quoted acceptable industry figure is 8:2, eight sales to be generated from people to the store by the concessions for every two lost by the store to their concessions. The major disadvantage to the concessionaire is the high cost of the space leased, whether charged as rent per square foot or as a percentage of sales, which can be well over 25% of turnover.

8.5.3 Physical distribution

There are several transport companies who specialize in the clothing sector. This involves considerable investment in warehousing and equipment. In addition to moving and storing clothing, many customers are demanding additional services such as pressing garments.

Like others involved in the fashion industry the specialist carriers are having to change to meet new demands. Increasingly, their clients are looking for a complete supply chain with JIT supply at the end of it to allow better stock management. This situation is well developed in other parts of the retail industry, notably in the food sector. Deliveries of new seasonal lines are also taking place later and later, so allowing less response time. Some fashion retailers have already contracted out the distribution side of the business.

The physical delivery of goods is also important to the mail order sector. Next employed as one of its selling points a better system of getting clothing to its mail order customers, and Empire Stores now promises a 24-hour delivery service.

8.5.4 Supply chain management

Managing the whole supply chain is becoming increasingly important to industry in general but more so in the retail sector and especially fashion retailing where customers, demand is always changing and has given rise to the term 'fast fashion'. One example of this in practice is Next doubling the frequency of injections into its ranges to every six weeks rather than twelve, this requires enhanced supply chain management skills. Retailers are therefore encouraged to contract out most or all of this process to specialists such as TNT Fashion Group or Kewell.

Its importance in a fashion retailing context can perhaps be best summed up as follows:

'The whole industry will continue to move further towards having faster and more flexible supply chains, not just in order to get the latest looks onto the shelves quicker, but also because it de-risks your business'.

Source: M.D. Supermarket clothing retailer quoted in Mintel Womenswear retailing, April 2004.

8.5.5 Service provision

Many retailers in a variety of sectors now see the provision of a high level of service as a way of establishing a competitive advantage.

In the retail fashion sector high levels of personal service together with good product knowledge and knowing customers' likes and dislikes have traditionally been seen as a strength of the independent sector. Provision of a high level of service is likely to be seen as increasingly important in the more mature age market, which demographically and economically will become more important in the future. The growing tendency to promote shopping, and particularly clothes shopping, as a leisure activity is another reason for offering high levels of customer service.

Common areas of service include late night shopping, free parking (for out-of-town sites only), a liberal returns policy, pleasant decor, helpful staff and a variety of payment methods. For clothing retailers another important area is that of changing facilities, which in some stores are non-existent and in others range from poor to luxurious.

However, such provision is expensive and refurbishment costs are high, particularly so at higher market levels. The provision of high levels of personal service can conflict with a need to reduce operating costs in the form of staff levels, with many larger retailers moving towards employing part-time rather than full-time staff.

8.5.6 Internationalization

UK fashion retailers have been slow to expand overseas. Early examples such as M & S venturing into Canada and later Europe met with only limited success. Other UK fashion retailers with an overseas presence include Arcadia, Jigsaw and Paul Smith.

The successful retailers in this context tend to be those who establish their operation with a local partner, at least in the initial stages. Examples of such ventures are Arcadia entering the Spanish market through concessions in department stores, as has Laura Ashley in Japan. Marks and Spencer has an international franchise operation that enables it to recruit suitable local partners in markets where it feels the need to have one. The perceived high risk in relation to relatively low rates of return has in the past tended to discourage such expansion.

The retailers' overseas competitors have in the past few years been attracted to the UK in increasing numbers, particularly from continental Europe, with some building up a considerable branch network, such as the Spanish retailer Zara. Two of the major British mail order concerns, Grattan and Empire, are owned by Otto Verace, the German mail order house, and the French company La Redoute, respectively, and Renown (Japan) bought Aquascutum.

8.5.7 Teleshopping

Electronic ordering through the medium of a domestic television set and telephone can take place via a computer terminal. In America, the department store group Saks became the first upmarket retailer to enter the market in 1993. Its first one-hour show brought sales of $575000 of its own label casualwear range.

Teleshopping has the potential to effect major changes in shopping patterns. Its impact on the retail fashion market in the UK, in such areas as mail order, will develop over the coming years, influenced by consumer acceptance and its own cost effectiveness. Digital television will offer increased possibilities in this area, particularly in respect of those who lack the time or enthusiasm for more conventional shopping, though developments in this area are likely to be heavily influenced by the growth of internet shopping.

8.5.8 Retail branding

Branding as in other areas of retailing now plays a crucial role. It helps to differentiate one retailer from another and is both a consequence of retail concentration and a factor in its continued growth.

The attractiveness of brands or labels in terms of product has encourage some manufacturers to diversify into the clothing market and *vice versa*, often through the licensing of the brand name (see Chapter Six). Its importance to consumers is greater in the north than the south. Younger consumers also attach more importance to branding than do older age groups, as peer pressure to be seen with the 'right' label is not an issue with the latter.

Advertising (see Chapter Nine) plays an important part in building brand awareness and loyalty, and many major retailers spend heavily in this area.

8.6 The Internet

8.6.1 Growing importance

As a distribution channel the Internet is becoming ever more important as the factors that previously limited its development, as detailed below, have declined.

- Limited access – now widespread, available in most homes, also thorough laptops or mobile phones, it can even be accessed from the local library.
- Security of payment – advances in encryption have allayed fears in this area, even though such fears appear as somewhat irrational given many people's willingness to give credit card details over the phone, which is arguably a less secure medium.
- Cost of access – now largely limited to a small separate monthly fee though increasingly included in a bundle of other computer/communications services.
- Need physically to examine the merchandise – as customers come increasingly to trust retail and other labels this, coupled with a liberal returns policy, is less of a deterrent.

Various predictions exist for Internet usage with virtually all suggesting very strong growth in general and as a retail channel. Those who have adopted a so-called 'clicks and bricks' approach, i.e. having both an actual shop presence and Internet site, have tended to be more successful; the classic site's only failure being Bo.Com, which launched amid much hype in 1999 only to crash the following year.

8.6.2 Limits on growth

In general, the Internet as a medium of distribution shares many of the problems of mail order and teleshopping, namely returned goods, delivery costs and other logistical problems.

Clothes shopping is often seen, particularly by the young, as a 'social experience' and as such will continue to take place in a physical environment, be it high street, shopping mall or other venue.

Another issue is that of cannabalization, which also applies to other forms of home-based shopping: Internet sales may take place at the expense of other company outlets.

8.6.3 Retailers' use of the Internet

This revolves around the following potential advantages:

- Cost savings – a physical presence on the high street or other location can involve considerable costs which can be avoided or reduced.
- Greater opportunities to segment the market more effectively and cheaply.
- The possibility of creating a truly global market.
- To complement and support the physical retail network where present.

8.6.4 Internet marketing strategies

The following options, derived in part from the work of Dholakia and Rego (1998), can be adopted:

- Ignore it.
- Develop a basic site.
- Use the site to direct customers to high street or other locations.
- Link the site with a more traditional mail order operation, i.e. as an ordering mechanism.
- Use it to support dialogue with customers, i.e. in the area of customer complaints.
- Use it as a sales tool in its own right.
- Offer an individual service, thus making the individual the basis of segmentation and relationship marketing more of a reality.

In broad terms the strategic option(s) taken will be determined by the level of retailer commitment in terms of cost, linkages to existing retail formats and involvement with customers. This indicates perhaps that the greatest number of strategic options is available to well-established and well-funded clothing retailers. To obtain a current overview of strategies, positioning and segmentation issues the reader is recommended to visit a range of the growing number of websites.

In spite of its undoubted growth in recent years, there is still in, the industry, a degree of scepticism over its long-term impact; perhaps best summed up by one Chief Executive of an upmarket classic menswear retailer quote in the October 2005 Mintel report on Menswear Retailing.

'In reality the Internet is just a more efficient way of catalogue shopping which never got over 9–10% of clothing spending'.

8.7 The 'grey market'

Previously a number of clothing retailers, including some major supermarket groups, had obtained high-profile, high-margin fashion brands from a variety of sources other than the brand owner, the so-called grey or parallel market. The retailers benefited in terms of increased footfall and extra sales, often at better margins together with increased publicity. Their customers had the opportunity to purchase expensive brands at a considerable discount. However, the brand owners or rather their usual stockists lost sales at the normal margin price, but perhaps more importantly the brand may risked losing credibility. This potential devaluation of the brand equity, the brand owners argued, represented a considerable loss on their investment in research and development and marketing support in creating and maintaining the brand, and can act as a disincentive to developing new brands or products.

The victory of Levi Strauss over Tesco in the European Court and China joining the World Trade Organization has virtually eliminated this problem. However the selling of fake merchandise remains a problem particularly for upmarket fashion brands.

8.8 Retail marketing effectiveness

Obviously the overall measure of success is long-term profitability. A subgoal of this is usually to increase sales in relative terms on an

Table 8.1 Entrant to buyer conversion

Segment	Entrants (%)	Buyers (%)	Conversion from entrant to buyer (%)
Fashion	7	4	16
Fashion-aware	23	18	21
Classic	9	14	42
Mainstream	42	51	37
Downstream	19	13	28

Source: Drapers Record 18-7-87.

annual or a seasonal basis. Other indicators are sales per square foot and sales per employee. Selling a lower proportion of merchandise at reduced margins is also an indication of effective marketing as well as astute buying.

Another indicator is the conversion rate, or the number of customers who buy as a proportion of the total number who enter the store. The conversion varies by consumer segment, as shown in the example of a menswear retailer (Table 8.1).

A low conversion rate may be due to a variety of factors such as inappropriate price points, unattractive merchandise, or staff lacking product knowledge and selling skills.

As much of the marketing effort in the industry comes from the retail sector, the large retailers invest considerable money and effort in market research (see Chapter Four) to measure its effectiveness.

8.9 Summary

At the conclusion of this chapter the reader should be able to:

- understand the importance of the UK fashion retailing business;
- describe the retailer's relationship with the manufacturing sector;
- explain the importance of imports and exports to the UK fashion retail industry;
- outline the structure of the industry;
- indicate how retail marketing effectiveness can be assessed.

Further reading

Bitner, M.J. (1992), Servicescapes: the impact of physical surroundings on customers and employers, *Journal of Marketing*, Vol. 56, pp. 57–71.

Cox, R. and Brittain, P. (2004), *Retailing: An Introduction*, 5th Edition, FT Prentice Hall, London.

Davies, G. (1991), *What Next?* Arrow Books, London.

Dholakia, U.M. and Rego, L.L. (1998), An empirical investigation of web page effectiveness, *European Journal of Marketing*, Vol. 32, No. 7/8, pp. 724–736.

Fashion Multiples (2008), Verdict Research, London.

Fernie, J. *et al.* (2004), *Principles of Retailing*, Butterworth-Heinemann, London.

Harris, D. and Walters, D. (1992), *Retail Operations Management*, Prentice Hall, London.

Marciniak, R. and Willans, J.R. (2008), Fashion Retailing, Blackwell, London.

Retailing (1999), Verdict Research, London.

Chapter Nine
Fashion Marketing Communications

9.1 Introduction

Promotion, widely regarded as the fourth P of marketing, is now being renamed marketing communications to which perhaps reflect its growing importance and increased profile within the marketing mix.

In this chapter the role and scope of marketing communications will be explained, with an emphasis on fashion marketing communications. Fashion is different!

9.1.1 Defining marketing communications

The definition of marketing developed by the Chartered Institute of Marketing is widely regarded as a useful one:

> Marketing is the management process responsible for identifying, anticipating and satisfying consumer requirements profitably.

Communication, from the Latin communis (a oneness of thought), is defined as 'imparting or – an exchange of information' (*Oxford Dictionary*).

If we combine the definitions of marketing and communication we might define marketing communications as:

> A management process responsible for communicating with customers in order to inform and satisfy their needs and wants.

Therefore the focus of marketing communications is still on the consumer, but with the additional dimension of statisfying the consumer's need for information. It may perhaps be useful to reiterate that consumers cannot be 'persuaded' to buy something they do not want or need. The skill in marketing communications, just as in marketing, lies in understanding the consumer and informing them about the benefits of your product above any other competing offers. The starting point of this mutually beneficial exchange must be informing them of your fashion offer.

9.1.2 The historical background

Marketing communications goes back a long way. The earliest example of a promotional tool may well have been the town crier who would literally call out in the streets the availability of goods or services of a seller. This would presumably have been an effective method of promotion as the general populace had low literacy levels, and the media (newspapers, for example) were therefore non-existent.

Visual symbols, for example, an image of a needle and thread for a tailor, might have been painted above the shop premises. The traditional sign for a barber's shop, a red- and- white-striped pole symbolizing blood and bandages, still remains today as a legacy of the time when barbers also doubled as dentists and surgeons.

Today we find that visual symbols are an integral part of modern marketing communications, perhaps reflecting the old saying: 'a picture is worth a thousand words'. This is reinforced by the commonly held belief that we retain 70% of what we see, compared with 30% of what we hear.

Another good example of the usage of visual imagery as a communication tool is the advertisements by Benetton, which relied on controverside images as a tool of brand recollection, separate perhaps from the Benefton product itself.

9.2 The marketing communications environment

Trevor Beattie (1999), one of the gurus of advertising who was responsible for memorable and successful campaigns, including Levi's 501s, said: 'If we whisper, we can't be heard.'

Today's consumer is constantly bombarded by visual stimuli in the form of advertising, logos, junk mail, celebrity gossip magazines, Internet pop ups and so on. It is therefore not surprising that marketing communications have to strive hard to stand out from the crowd. The modern consumer is subjected to a much more complex array of messages and media in an increasingly competitive retail environment when compared to the consumer of the past. Furthermore, modern marketing communications must take into account the fact that today's consumer is more sophisticated and discerning than the consumer of the past. It is no longer sufficient to say that your product is the best. In today's competitive retail environment where competing products are quite similar, the consumer wants to be entertained as well as informed – this is sometimes called infotainment. Marketing communications must give the consumer a reason to purchase your product over other similar products, and creating a strong brand with an equally strong brand identity may be a way of succeeding in the competitive retail marketing environment. Nowhere is this more important than in the highly competitive and saturated fashion market, where very similar products vie for the consumer's attention.

9.3 The traditional approach to promotion

9.3.1 Communication theory

Communication theory suggests the following fairly straightforward model of communication:

Sender → Message → Receiver

The sender is the producer or seller of the goods; the message is what the sender wishes to say, which may be encoded in symbols (visuals/music); and the receiver is the consumer or the target market. However, it is not always this simple, as the receiver may not receive the intended message or interpret (decode) it in the way the sender intended. When the message is obscured or misunderstood it is called noise; this is some sort of interference. Marketing communications is not an exact science; measuring and evaluating the effectiveness of a message in terms of feedback is not always a simple process.

Another model that marketers use to describe the process of communication is AIDA:

A	Awareness
I	Interest
D	Desire
A	Action

This model suggests a linear process whereby the consumer moves from unawareness of the product to awareness, then takes an interest in the product, which in turn leads to desire for the product, which results in an action – a purchase.

In many texts on marketing communications the promotional mix is traditionally listed as:

- advertising;
- sales promotion;
- public relations;
- personal selling.

Furthermore, each of these tends to be explained with examples from a diverse range of industries. It is the aim of this chapter to explore each aspect of the promotional mix in relation to fashion.

9.3.2 An integrated approach to marketing communications

According to McGoldrick (2002), the marketing communications objectives should be clearly defined at the outset. They may be some or all of the following:

- develop new customers;
- increase expenditure by existing customers;
- increase store traffic;
- increase product sales;
- develop the store image.

Therefore, the overall strategy of the organization should be the starting point of all marketing communications. This should in turn follow what is known as an integrated approach, where each and every communication from the organization has the same 'handwriting'. A more comprehensive definition of integrated marketing communications (IMC) is:

> IMC is a concept of marketing communications planning that recognizes the added value of a comprehensive plan that evaluates the strategic roles of a variety of communications disciplines (e.g. general advertising, direct response, sales promotion and public relations) ... and combines these disciplines to provide clarity, consistency and maximum communications impact.

Therefore at the outset organizations should ask themselves:

- What do we want to achieve?
- How should we achieve this? (perhaps most importantly)
- How can we measure success?

The organization may well use its internal capabilities to initiate a campaign; however, it is becoming more recognized that the services of an agency are required to develop a creative campaign and buy media space.

9.3.3 Developing and communicating a brief

A brief is an outline of the objectives that the company wants to achieve with its marketing communications. The fashion company may well have established, usually by some research, that a campaign is needed to do one or a combination of the following:

◆ Confirm with present consumers that theirs is a credible brand and therefore prevent the customers from straying into the outlets of a competitor who may have a high-profile campaign. This might be the 'follow-my-leader' campaign prompted by the competition.
◆ Introduce a new product range/brand. This might be when a retailer launches an accessory collection, or a childrenswear offer, or opens a new outlet in a new city.
◆ To inform potential consumers that the brand has changed in some way. This might be a repositioning campaign.

The company will communicate 'the brief' to a number of agencies and they will then 'pitch' for the account, normally by making a presentation to the company outlining their marketing communications plan in terms of:

◆ creative treatment (the encoding of the message in symbols, e.g. visuals/music);
◆ media strategy (which channels of communication would be appropriate, bearing in mind the target market, e.g. MTV, *Vogue*);
◆ evaluation (feedback mechanisms to measure the success of the campaign).

This means that the agency should have the capability to deliver all these aspects of a campaign and have personnel involved in

◆ creativity (graphics, copywriting, etc.);
◆ media planning (access to space);
◆ research (before, during and after the campaign).

There has been a great deal of consolidation in the advertising agency sector in the recent past, including mergers and acquisitions within both the domestic and overseas sectors. This strengthens the capabilities of the agency to provide a complete package to the client and can facilitate integration of the various elements of the campaign. One recent developments is advertising agencies launching fashion only subdivisions, e.g. J. Walter Thompson (JWT) has created LABEL@JWT dedicated to the fashion sector. This implies advertising agencies have recognized that fashion requires a different approach and treatment in comparison with everyday commodities.

9.3.4 An integrated approach

Fashion brand retailers are increasingly looking towards an integrated approach to their marketing communications strategies which can give some synergy and also cost economies.

If every aspect of the promotional mix is integrated then the effect is likely to be stronger and long lasting as the imagery and treatment, i.e. the handwriting, is consistent every time it is used – be it in an advertisement, on the web, in a store, or on the letter head. It becomes distinctive and is:

- Recognizable
- Repeated
- Reinforced
- Reiterated
- Recalled.

9.3.5 Case study example

A middle market retailer of women's, men's and children's clothing launched a marketing communications campaign which comprised of a series of television, magazine, and cinema advertisements. The garments featured in the advertisements were made available to the press via the retailer's public relations department. The public relations department also informed the store personnel, via briefing sheets, of the exact details of the garments (by code number, colour and size availability) which were to be featured in magazines and in the intermissions of specific popular television programmes and cinema films. These were further detailed by region in relation to stores within each region. The programmes and films were itemized, as were the approximate timings of the advertisements.

The briefing notes also alerted staff to the in-store layouts and visual merchandising treatments that were to support the external communications. As one member of staff commented: 'We knew what was being advertised and when, and could direct customers to it on the shop floor.' According to senior management, areas which had underperforming stores now found new customers.

9.4 Fashion advertising

Above the line (paid-for) advertising in fashion is relatively low in comparison with other goods e.g. FMCGs – fast moving consumer goods, which probably reflects the fact that less money is spent by consumers on fashion than on food, transport, leisure, fuel, housing, etc.

Fashion companies in the middle market, where the majority of fashion is purchased, have traditionally relied on their stores, i.e. their physical presence in the market place, being a showcase for their products. However, as competition has increased, this marketing tool (the store itself) has not had as much impact. If the consumer does not see or visit your store because they think it is not the store for them, then their physical presence alone is not enough. Fashion stores therefore advertise in order to stand out from very similar stores carrying similar merchandise.

International upper market fashion brands like Chanel, Louis Vuitton, Versace etc., are heavily reliant on advertising to maintain brand awareness. We will now consider the communication channels which are available to fashion companies.

9.4.1 Television advertising

This is the most expensive method of advertising because it reaches the maximum number of people. However, for fashion retailers it is not always cost-effective as the fashion consumer or the target market may not see the advertisement. Also, it may be lost among other non-fashion advertisements, and a short three-minute commercial cannot always show the full range of items available. Television advertising is, however, a useful medium for brand image creation. For many fashion companies, targeting specific programmes which are likely to be watched by the target market may give some precision and an opportunity for the promotion of international brands such as Levi's and Nike.

9.4.2 Outdoor advertising

Ambient media denotes advertising on billboards, the Underground, street furniture, taxis, etc. It is relatively inexpensive, and its main advantage is that it can be highly targeted to transport users within the area of the fashion stores. A disadvantage is that it cannot give a lot of information as people will only have a moment to glance at it, and it must not be too distracting in content as it could cause people to lose concentration.

9.4.3 Magazine advertising

Advertising in magazines is by far the most effective method of above the line advertising, as it can be fine-tuned to the target market of the magazine. Magazines provide media packs, which outline their target market and pricing strategy. For example, *Vogue* is renowned as a style bible all over the world and has a very clearly defined target market: 'To be in *Vogue* is to be in fashion.'

The media pack gives demographic details on the age profile, social classification, income level and education of its core readership, and a lifestyle profile is provided for their potential advertisers. The *Vogue* reader 'is style conscious … enjoys an affluent, active lifestyle', dining out, pursuing cultural activities, taking frequent holidays and, of course, shopping at upmarket stores, and spending on clothes.

In addition, there are very specific comparisons with other magazines and instructions and costs associated with advertising in the publication. There is also an offer to bring advertisers together with complementary products to share the costs of a *Vogue* promotion; this is co-operative advertising and can be useful for advertisers who cannot afford the full cost (sourced from the *Vogue* Media Pack).

A fashion brand/retailer can be fairly confident when advertising in specific magazines that they can match their target market with the magazine target market and therefore not waste the advertising budget.

Launched in the UK in 2004, Grazia is a weekly glossy which features the very latest in not only fashion, but also celebrity lifestyle. This magazine and other celebrity-focused publications have had a major impact on the fashion marketing communications mix, which will be discussed later in this chapter.

9.4.4 Radio advertising

Radio advertising is not used very much by the fashion industry, since it is difficult to communicate the brand image by sound. The exception to this might be to alert listeners to a sale event – department stores that have a one-off extended trading period or 12-hour event happening that very same day use the radio to stimulate drivers to go into town.

9.5 Sales promotion

This method of promotion revolves around offering a discount on merchandise on production of a coupon often given away in a magazine. The cost of this obviously requires budgeting into the original promotional strategy, but provides a method of immediate feedback on the success of the promotion and would perhaps turn new or occasional shoppers into regular purchasers.

Owing to the seasonal nature of fashion, mid-season and end-of-season sales are the most frequent methods of sales promotion and an effective way of reducing the stockholding in order to make space for new merchandise; however due to the rise of the 'fast fashion' phenomenon, which is the consumers' constant demand for newness, stores are often in continual markdown.

9.6 Public relations

In fashion marketing, public relations (PR) is a very effective method of promotion; however, this method of communicating the fashion brand or a particular item is not always obvious to the untrained eye.

According to Harrison (1995), there is no universally accepted definition of PR, and perhaps this reflects its relatively new and still developing role within marketing. We might use the Institute of Public Relations (IPR) definition as a useful description of the role and responsibility of PR: 'Public Relations is about reputation – the result of what you do, what you say and what others say about you'.

In essence PR can be seen as managing the corporate identity. This can simply be getting goods into the public arena at one end of the spectrum, or at the other extreme, refuting any adverse publicity that the company may face. Therefore, it is important for an organization to have a PR department in place in order to be prepared for adverse reactions from the press or public. PR, if used effectively, can be seen as the guardian of the corporate reputation.

In fashion marketing, PR may be done by an in-house department, or by an external agency. It might be suggested therefore that PR should aim to:

- raise or confirm the profile of the brand/retailer;
- place products in the public arena;
- enhance other parts of the promotional mix;
- communicate with influential media.

In fashion marketing, PR is responsible for ensuring that magazines have merchandise to feature in fashion shoots, comparative offers and editorial features. This is a role 'behind the scenes' that is not always immediately apparent. Editorials are usually taken from press releases and may be very credible to the reader as an editorial is not an advertisement on behalf of the company, but an endorsement by an influential style leader. The success of PR can be measured using the value of how much the amount of space generated would have cost if it had been a traditional advertisement. The space is calculated using advertising rates and is known as 'rate-card value'. PR companies can demonstrate to their clients how much 'free' publicity has been generated using this method.

Of course, the brand has little control over how the product may be used in an editorial piece – it may be criticized as having the worst value for money in a comparison with other competitive products. However, this is a risk that has to be taken, and close relationships between PR and magazine companies exist to limit damage to brands' reputations.

Other responsibilities of PR are also in event management, which could include arranging fashion shows, gala events, exhibitions and sponsorship deals. This makes it sound like a very glamorous career, but of course there is crisis management to consider, especially when the brand (or a celebrity by association) gets bad publicity. Contrary to the popular saying not all publicity is good publicity, as the bad tends to get repeated before any good news. For example, despite increased sales and a high-profile advertising campaign the previous fortunes of the company are often reported in the press:

'… once ailing, M&S stages a come back …'

9.7 Celebrity endorsement and sponsorship

PR also has an important role to play in the use of celebrities by brands. Celebrity endorsement is a particularly powerful form of promotion and is increasingly being used by companies. Linking a well-known personality with the brand can give many benefits. If a well-known personality endorses a product or wears a brand through a sponsorship deal, we may well understand that they are being paid to promote the product. However, the effect is one of credibility, particularly if the personality is admired, in which case they imbue the product with their attributes of good taste, attractiveness, etc. Endorsement can give credibility to a brand that advertising alone cannot give. If a brand is linked with a personality who is outstanding or popular in their chosen field of endeavour, then the brand and the personality will begin to share similar characteristics, and the identity of the brand and the person become linked and begin to share similar characteristics. Sportswear brands have used celebrity endorsements to great effect in matching the brand with the personality.

The major disadvantage of this is if the endorser 'falls from grace', by being accused of some scandal or wrong doing, then the product with which they are linked will inevitably suffer a similar fate, and can become tainted with the same public disapproval. One of the worst things a celebrity endorser can do is publicly announce they don't wear or use the product with which they are linked. Overexposure is also a problem when the celebrity has too many products to endorse. It then seems as if they cannot possibly be in this for anything than the money, and this loses credibility for the brands involved. Sometimes the celebrity is bigger than the brand and viewers remember the celebrity but not the product with which they were connected. Contracts may overcome some of the disadvantages and problems for brands when linking up with people who are, only human after all. Levi's overcame this by using Flat Eric, a puppet!

9.7.1 Case studies – choosing the right celebrity

An own label retailer with a strong brand and market share was considering using celebrity endorsement for an advertising campaign. In order to establish which celebrities out of a large number would be suitable, they undertook some market research. The faces of the celebrities were shown to customers within the store environment and customers were asked to match the store personality to the celebrity personality. From this research there were five clear winners among the celebrities, and these five were subsequently used in an advertising campaign.

Kate Moss has become one of the most famous models in the world since she shot to fame for Calvin Klein, shortly after being discovered in an airline check-in queue. However, as has been widely documented – whether accurate or not – an alleged revelation of substance abuse led to a number of her high-profile brand contracts being terminated. For example, H&M as a brand aimed at impressionable youth rapidly withdrew their support for her, but many including Rimmel which is positioned as an edgy London brand were to continue their affiliation. Indeed it would now appear that Kate Moss has more contracts than she had before. At the time of writing she is the face of Dior, Louis Vuitton, Belstaff and Burberry among others. It will be interesting to observe how this continues. Indeed, in Autumn 2006, she teamed up with TopShop to launch her own fashion range.

Sienna Miller is widely attributed with popularizing the 'boho' look in summer 2005. Many retailers had failed to spot the trend and were left to play a very swift game of catch up, which gave them the expertise to use fast fashion techniques. This demonstrates the power that a celebrity being photographed by paparazzi and appearing in weekly gossip columns can have on the fashion supply chain.

It is often prohibitively expensive for companies on a limited budget to use a top model or celebrity so they may look for one who is tipped to become a star in the future, this is known as 'seeding', and worked well for Eva Herzegovina and Wonderbra. However, if the 'star' does not materialize, the brand will not get the coverage either.

The casual clothing brand Criminal used Steven Marks a self-confessed drug smuggler as an ironic figurehead for its publicity.

David Beckham is an example of a celebrity who has become a brand in his own right.

When selecting a suitable celebrity, fashion marketers try to achieve a match between the characteristics of the brand image they wish to project and the perceived qualities of the celebrity. In practice this is often accomplished by the use of focus groups who discuss their impressions of both celebrities and brands.

9.8 Personal selling

In fashion marketing the role of the sales assistant generally varies according to the type of outlet.

Fashion outlets for the youth market tend to be self-service as the 'fashion enthusiasts' are quite happy to select, try on and purchase garments without much help or interference. However, the older consumer may require a personal service in terms of advice and alterations. Therefore, the type of sales assistant recruited by a fashion company tends to attract and reflect the target market in terms of age, size, demographics and lifestyle; although legislation against age discrimination may counterbalance this exact reflection of the brand by employees.

9.8.1 Personal shoppers become personal stylists

This type of service is offered by upmarket retailers and is now increasingly a feature of the mass market. A selection of merchandise is provided from which the customer can make a selection in some privacy and comfort. It is also popular for the busy, time constrained, working executive or for a special-occasion purchaser. As in the cult of celebrity, everyone wants their own personal stylist and stores are catering to this demand by providing a stylist service. TopShop was the first fashion chain to pick up on the trend.

9.8.2 Direct marketing

Direct marketing can be the purest form of one-to-one personal communication if it is used correctly, but all too often it tends towards the unimaginative mass mail out and misses golden opportunities. How many times have you received a mail shot which seems to take no account of your previous purchase history (you've never bought childrenswear from them, which might suggest you don't have children), and furthermore, they have spelt your name incorrectly? This does not engender confidence that it is the personalized invitation it purports to be.

One shining example of how to use direct marketing effectively is that of the retailer Boden, which by being a predominantly mail order business, has enabled them to hone their skills in this area.

Credit card and loyalty schemes allow brands/retailers to create databases which can provide direct marketing opportunities. Stores use the store card details of their customers to invite shoppers to launch events. Mobile phone and e-mail alerts direct to customers can be a strong reminder of the brand.

9.9 Visual merchandising to visual marketing

In fashion marketing communications, one of the most important tools is the retail environment itself and deserves to have its own separate place in the promotional mix.

There is no single definition of what visual merchandising is, combining as it does for different commentators, different parts of the total retail environment experience. However, this one can be utilized as a broad approach to a definition:

> Visual merchandising is the physical representation and communication cue of the brand or retailer, through creative grouping and presentation of merchandise in windows and in the store.

Visual merchandising is seldom just window display, as the store design and layout also plays a role in the creative treatment of the retail experience. The window, however, is a stage on which the retailer 'struts its stuff' as it is normally the first thing that the customer comes into contact with and this attracts the audience.

Visual merchandising, and store design and layout are now becoming widely regarded as important promotional tools to differentiate fashion store images in a crowded environment. Store designers often incorporate elements of the design process into promotional tools such as in-store graphics, but more are now visible in wrapping materials, carrier bags, T-shirts (which are then carried and worn), and become a powerful and free promotional tool out on the streets.

However, visual merchandising cannot be separated from the rest of the marketing mix. No amount of creativity and promotion can sell merchandise that customers do not want. But assuming that the product, price and place elements of the mix are correctly assembled to match the target market, visual merchandising as a part of the promotional mix is an attractive component of store presentation.

Since it is said that we retain 70% of what we see, compared with only 30% of what we hear or read, then it would be fair to assume that the visual representation of the brand must be an important tool in fashion marketing communications.

Store windows attract customers at a distance and they carry a number of subtle messages which customers use in order to decide whether to enter or not. New and on trend merchandise, the style of the mannequins, the styling of the garments all indicate to potential customers whether this is their type of store. Once inside the store, displays can be used effectively as signage so as to avoid too many written messages. However there is one fixture in stores that has recently become a feature and that is the 'fast fashion' fixture, often labelled with a sense of urgency:

◆　Get it before it goes!
◆　Buy it now or regret it later!

The fixture and the signage provide the busy but 'fashion enthusiast' consumer with a short cut communication to the latest deliveries. A small number of garments are on this fixture which signals exclusivity and rarity, although thousands may exist in the apparel pipeline, this encourages an impulse purchase based on the premise that the opportunity may not arise again.

9.9.1 Store design and layout

There exists a whole industry based on store design and layout. However the psychology of attracting customers, via design and visual merchandising, is by no means an exact science.

Zara, in particular, presents a designer type environment which suggests exclusivity by using a lot of space in between merchandise, yet has affordable middle market pricing.

Even money retailers are recognizing the value of presenting an aesthetically pleasing environment, which in turn encourages customers to stay longer and inevitably spend more than they intend. But they also attract the bargain hunter with a pile it high, sell it cheap offer, which is consequentially an untidy image by the close of business, but it would appear that customers are prepared to forgo a cleanly merchandised environment for a keen price.

Visual merchandising can of course be used to discourage the 'wrong' target market; stores who do not put the prices of garments in the window suggest high prices. Closed, heavy doors, buzzer entry systems, small windows (like Tiffany jewellers) and uniformed 'greeters' are all visual cues to some people to stay away. In general, the bigger the price signs the cheaper the stock, and vice versa.

Layouts in fashion are different in different types of stores. A department store will use a hard surface 'race track' around the perimeter with carpeted areas at each brand concession to slow the footfall and encourage browsing. A 'boutique' layout may look haphazard, but is meant to stop and delight the customer at every turn. A 'supermarket' type of layout is suitable for large value, discount, out of town (i.e. premium priced floor space) stores where trolleys are used.

Colour, music and fragrance are all used to attract and to some extent control the customer's response and experience by activating their full range of senses. Colours can be either exciting or restful – busy environments use dramatic colours like red to signal sales, vibrancy, etc., whereas more leisured shopping environments with more expensive prices promote calm by using restful colours. It all depends how long you want customers to stay. Music with a fast-tempo has the same effect, it promotes a fast shop; whereas classical music promotes a leisurely stroll. Fragrances developed by brands and retailers are sold alongside the clothes. If a customer identifies with the brand and its values it is likely they will buy into the fragrance by association.

9.9.2 Visual marketing

Visual merchandising is much more than just 'dressing dummies'. It presents customers with a vision of what garments might look like on them before they have tried them on, and is therefore a stepping stone to a purchase. It offers ideas of how to achieve the desired look, and encourages extra sales of items especially accessories.

Visual merchandising could therefore be renamed Visual Marketing, reflecting that it combines with the product, price, place and promotion and further underlines its importance in the fashion business.

9.10 International marketing communications

Increasingly, as fashion brands/retailers expand beyond their domestic boundaries, their marketing communications have to translate visually and literally into international markets.

Marketing communications strategies must therefore be capable of international standardization or adaptation in order to benefit from economies of scale, e.g. one advertisement that can be used globally rather than the expensive multiple generations of advertisement for different markets.

This puts considerable strain on the creative treatment of international promotional material, and has led to criticism over a lack of innovation. The future internationalization plans of a company may need consideration when generating ideas for brand names and strap lines. An example of this is the brand name Next, which is difficult to pronounce in some languages, and their advertising strap line, which was innovative and imaginative in the English language: 'Bringing fabric to life', but translated badly into most foreign languages as a rather confusing combination of 'resuscitating dead material': not exactly the image with which the company wished to be associated!

Since so many companies are operating globally now, it is not surprising that their logos (visual communication cues) are popular, rather than relying on heavy text which may need translation. The Burberry plaid speaks for itself, as does the interlinked Cs of Chanel and the Nike swoosh. And rather than, including a text that signals a company's presence,

London   Paris   New York

in a discreet place on an advertisements, a website address is now the norm, which obviously gives far more detail and lists all their locations in whatever language is required.

Observers of Vogue in a variety of markets and languages will see that their advertisements are the same the world over, relying on strong imagery and brand handwriting rather than text.

9.11 Ethics in marketing communications

Legal constraints in terms of advertising have been introduced by most governments on the grounds of deception and false representation; however, the extent to which advertising is controlled varies between countries. Advertising to children is completely banned in Sweden.

In the UK, the advertising industry is self-regulatory, which in essence means that the industry controls itself and there should therefore be no offensive advertising or false claims made. However, this is not always the case, and there are instances when perhaps for shock tactics a company will flout the rules. The self-regulatory system means that it is the responsibility of the consumer to complain about an advertisement (in the UK). Even one single complaint will be investigated and if the panel agrees then the advertisement must be modified or withdrawn.

If advertising agencies suspect that their creative treatment may cause some offence or is controversial in the UK they can approach the regulatory bodies and gain some advice. Some companies may just go ahead with the campaign and hope for the best.

The Advertising Standards Authority (ASA) has some case studies on fashion brands (www.asa.org.uk) which demonstrate the process from complaint to compliance. The brands range from Opium, Harvey Nichols to Diesel, Gucci and of course the ubiquitous French Connection (fcuk).

9.12 Evaluating the effectiveness of marketing communications

The issue of evaluating the effectiveness of any promotional effort is an area that generates a great deal of debate among academics and practitioners alike.

Some campaigns are reasonably easy to evaluate in terms of increased sales. However, the problem lies in measuring success over a longer period and the effectiveness of different elements of marketing communications. Was it the advertisements on television or the money-off vouchers in magazines that was responsible for increased sales? Research is the key tool to use to establish answers to these types of question.

In the UK there are a number of agencies involved in the collection and analysis of data on consumers' viewing and recall habits in the case of advertising. More difficult and expensive to calculate are the changes in attitude towards a brand over time. This requires research before, during and after promotional effort. Some methods of measuring brand awareness can be carried out before, during and after a campaign, this type of research tends to be qualitative and can be done by the company itself, an independent market research company, or a media agency.

Recall tests question whether the brand is salient (uppermost) in the consumer's mind, the recall can be related to present/previous advertising or can just be a question of when did you last shop in 'XXXX'?

The brand personality of a store can be ascertained by a number of variables as a means of comparison with the competition, in advertising evaluations these might include:

- Exciting advertisements ~ versus ~ boring advertisements
- Different from the rest ~ versus ~ the same as the rest
- Strong image/handwriting ~ versus ~ weak image/handwriting.

Just showing advertisements to respondents without the brand name visible and assessing their recognition will answer some of these questions.

Respondents can be asked 'If this brand was a person what sort of personality would it have?' This can give interesting insights into the perception of the brand.

Like most research into consumer behaviour this area is fraught with complications, conflicting opinions and evidence. It can however yield some useful results if undertaken and applied to a marketing problem correctly.

9.13 New directions in fashion marketing communications

Whilst the demise of traditional communication channels has been widely reported, it is highly unlikely that they will disappear. Rather, they will change, develop and integrate with other tools as part of the route to the customer. It will be a test of the skills and a recognition of opportunities for marketing communicators to monitor and adapt to opportunities and changes in the fashion environment.

9.13.1 Media proliferation and direct marketing opportunities

The Internet has allowed fashion brands/retailers to establish a presence, communication channel and transactional websites. The Internet allows companies to be international, even global, without the costs normally associated with this strategy, i.e. setting up stores overseas.

Vogue, *Marie Clare*, *Elle* and *Cosmopolitan*, and the celebrity inspired titles of Hello, OK and Grazia, along with satellite and cable television channels, have crossed international boundaries and therefore provide opportunities for international marketing communications for global fashion brands.

Mobile telephones (GSM) and e-mail have facilitated text message (SMS) alerts to those who sign up for it. Digital technology, whilst in its infancy, is widely regarded as the next most important method for reaching target markets.

As Seen on Screen, www.asos.com, gives the fashion consumer a direct opportunity to buy what the celebrities have been spotted wearing.

Viral marketing is beginning to take off as it is such an easy medium to employ. Simply send your favourite advertisement to your friends, and in no time the advertisement has travelled the world at a little or no expense. Tracking these advertisements give companies an opportunity to test consumer reaction before launching an orchestrated campaign – it is said that the Levi's 'Flat Eric' campaign was born this way.

Product placement is a subtle form of promotion where brands are featured in films or television programmes. Although it is shortly to be deregulated in Europe, it is not yet clear how important this will become, but having established that the consumer finds PR and celebrity endorsement more credible than traditional advertising channels, it is likely to be a strong tool.

There is some evidence that user generated word of mouth, usually associated with Internet chat rooms or blogs, is becoming an increasingly popular medium similar to viral marketing, but the content is customer centric. Although companies could, in theory, join in the debate, the unregulated nature of this medium could be a problem in terms of corporate image.

9.14 Summary

This chapter has aimed to establish that fashion is different when considered in the context of the promotional mix. Fashion has caught up with the pack by moving away from an over-reliance simply on store presence. In an increasingly competitive marketing environment and looking towards an integrated approach to marketing communications, we might call this 'bathing in the brand', where every aspect has a unique handwriting or signature which cannot be mistaken for another store. This is where the store environment, graphics, display and advertising are in the same style and send a cohesive message regarding image and the product on offer. As fashion becomes increasingly global, the marketing communications may need to reflect or overcome cultural, language and geographical differences.

Useful websites

www.asa.org.uk
www.asos.com
www.brandrepublic.com
www.brandchannel.com

Further reading

Harrison, S. (1995), *Public Relations: An Introduction*, Routledge, London.

McGoldrick, P.J. (2002), *Retail Marketing*, McGraw-Hill, Maidenhead.

Milligan, A. (2004), *Brand It Like Beckham*, Cyan, London.

Pringle, H. (2004), *Celebrity Sells*, John Wiley and Sons, Chichester.

Shimp, T.A. (1999), *Advertising, Promotion and Supplemental Aspects of Integrated Marketing Communications*, Dryden Press, London.

Tungate, M. (2005), *Fashion Brands: Branding Style from Armani to Zara*, Kogan Page, London.

Yadin, D. (2000), *Creative Marketing Communications*, Kogan Page, London.

Yeshin, T. (2001), *Integrated Marketing Communications (CIM 2001)*, Butterworth-Heinemann, Oxford.

Chapter Ten
Fashion Marketing Planning

10.1 Introduction

Putting all aspects of a marketing mix together to achieve the goals of the organization is the most important fashion marketing task. Activities must be planned, co-ordinated and effectively implemented, and the results monitored. This chapter deals with the fashion marketing planning process, beginning with a broad overview of the process of planning fashion marketing, and continuing with the central role of the mission statement and marketing objectives.

The analysis of marketing activities and the marketing environment by a marketing audit are described. A synopsis is given of SWOT (strengths, weaknesses, opportunities and threats) analysis, a crucial underpinning to the development of a fashion marketing strategy. Consideration of strategic alternatives follows with reference to earlier material on segmentation and competitor analysis.

The chapter concludes by presenting a framework for producing a fashion marketing plan and examines some important issues concerned with the implementation of plans.

10.2 The planning process and objectives

10.2.1 The planning process

A marketing strategy is a specification of those markets the firm wishes to target with marketing activities and how competitive advantages are to be created and achieved. A marketing strategy is developed within the broader framework of corporate strategy and goals. The focus of this chapter will naturally be upon fashion marketing plans, but the whole context of the fashion marketing planning

Mission statement
↓
Corporate objectives
↓
Marketing objectives
↓
Marketing audit
↓
Marketing strategy
↓
Marketing plan
↓
Implementation
↓
Evaluation and control

Figure 10.1 The fashion marketing planning process.

process should be kept in mind. Figure 10.1 shows the broader view of the process.

Fashion marketing planning has been described as a process. It is a continuous activity and if undertaken correctly should be self-improving. The process requires the setting and communication of standards, effective implementation or corrective action and timely feedback on performance. The starting point in the process is taken from the marketing objectives, although, as noted above, these are subject to wider corporate decisions.

10.2.2 The mission statement

The mission statement should begin by asking what business is the firm in and what kind of business would it like to be in? Normally this should be defined sufficiently broadly to allow flexibility but still be specific, for example, providing fashionable eveningwear and accessories rather than selling dresses. It also should be defined in terms of customer need, bearing in mind the firm's strengths in relation to the competition. Mission statements should be short and inspiring for company employees; they provide reasons for the firm's survival and growth and are a touchstone for judging corporate behaviour and development. Mission statement should be communicated to all interested stakeholders in the firm, employees, suppliers, customers and shareholders. They are in effect an enduring sense of purpose for the organization.

For example River Island has the aim of providing 'design choice and value' as part of the mission statement. The company also has a full range of operating principles that derive from the broad mission statement and these are communicated in the annual report and are used in advertising copy and personnel communication initiatives. As its mission statement Levis Strauss has 'People love our clothes and trust our company. We will make the most appealing and widely worn casual clothing in the world. We will cloth the world.' Part of the Mango mission is 'Dressing the urban and modern woman, meeting her daily needs, is the formula which we have analysed, adapted and applied to each country we operate in.'

10.2.3 Marketing objectives

These will be more specific than the broad mission statement and will include quantified data such as profit levels, number of new business customers and market share. As shown in Figure 10.1, marketing objectives derive from corporate objectives. The latter are broader and include all aspects of the company's operations such as production, personnel and safety, as well as marketing objectives.

Marketing objectives should be clear, written, measurable and attainable, but still challenging. They also should be specific and stated in relation to time constraints. Two examples of marketing objectives are: 'Our aim is to increase sales turnover from £31.3 million to £35.7 million in the next financial year, and to increase the gross profit margin by 5.2%' and 'to increase the share of sales via our corporate website from 4.3% of sales turnover to 8.5% within the next six months.'

10.3 Marketing audits and SWOT analysis

10.3.1 A marketing audit

To achieve marketing objectives the current situation must be analysed. Periodic reviews of the marketing goals, operations and performance of fashion companies are known as marketing audits. The concept is very similar to financial audit, but unfortunately the former are carried out less frequently than the latter. The marketing audit involves a set of detailed questions that are asked to determine the status of the firm in relation to its objectives, customers, competition and marketing environment. One of the main reasons for a marketing audit is to identify areas where corrective action may be needed. The marketing audit is usually organized into two main categories covering the firm's internal and external environment.

The audit of the external marketing environment covers the items identified in Chapter Two. Common frameworks adopted for the external marketing audit include LEPEST or STEPLE analyses, both of which cover Legal, Environmental, Political, Economic, Social and Technological aspects of the environment. The framework in Chapter Two elaborates on the above factors and distinguishes between controllable and partially controllable variables that require monitoring and analysis. The external audit should examine current activity and projected trends in both macro- and micro-marketing environments. It is imperative that all assumptions are made explicit in the audit, so that later modifications can be made to facts about developing events. For example, an assumption about forecast inflation rates for the next 12 months will have an impact upon the company's pricing policy. Thus data from the Retail Price Indices can be used later, if necessary, to revise plans. Likewise, anticipated changes in the bank rate will impact upon consumer purchasing power and thereby impact upon sales of garments.

The scope of an internal marketing audit would cover detailed analysis of sales, profits and market share data by product life and product range. As with the external audit a series of questions are asked about objectives, activities and achievement. For example, the adequacy of the size of the sales force may be assessed in relation to changing distribution trends or the frequency of product line deletions may be examined. The audit also may question how prices are set, the sufficiency of data about competitors' prices or the effectiveness of dealing with customer complaints. The whole range of marketing activities are subject to audit and are judged against customers' perceptions and marketing objectives.

10.3.2 SWOT or situational analysis

The outcome of a marketing audit is usually a detailed document specifying achievements and suggesting, where necessary, corrective action. Another use of the audit is the construction of a SWOT analysis, which is also known as a situational assessment of the firm. The SWOT, in essence, is the key issue emerging from the audit.

SWOT analysis considers both internal and external factors about either the whole company or a particular fashion product line or range in relation to customers, competitors and trends in the marketing environment. Strengths and weaknesses concern internal factors and opportunities and threats concern external factors. Figure 10.2 shows some components of a SWOT analysis.

Obviously the marketing audit is a good starting point to prepare a SWOT analysis; however, not all companies undertake regular marketing audits. The first marketing audit is invariably the most difficult for

Internal	Strengths	Weaknesses
	e.g. Functional areas Design expertise Location Facilities/size	
External	Opportunities	Threats
	e.g. Competitor promotions Market trends in fabrics, etc. Customer attitudes to 'green' issues Intermediary activity Regulatory changes, etc.	

Figure 10.2 Strengths, weaknesses, opportunities and threats.

most companies as benchmarks or experience may be unavailable. Subsequent audits can begin with the preceding audit and marketing plan.

A few guidelines are given below to enable the preparation of a simple SWOT analysis. The SWOT should be concise and specific, and communicate the key issues facing the firm. The items identified should be related to each other and not simply an *ad hoc* collection that does not point to future action. A clearly written analysis is helpful when it points to solutions or direct consequences. For example, 'A new outlet of a large competitor threatens our childrenswear department. Allow for a potential slowdown in sales turnover of 8–10% in next 12 months.' The alternative for the above childrenswear department may be to change the marketing mix to meet the threat more directly.

An important dimension of the SWOT analysis is the need for objectivity. This argument equally applies to the marketing audit. Fashion marketers charged with producing a marketing plan can sometimes be too close to the firm to be objective, as identifying certain weaknesses can be construed as admitting past failures. Outsiders, such as marketing consultants, can bring a broader and more objective perspective, but they are expensive and they take time to get to know the operations and procedures of the particular firm. At times, it can be most useful to employ a manager from another department or branch of the same company or a retired senior executive to bring objectivity coupled with company knowledge to help with the SWOT analysis.

10.4 Marketing strategy

10.4.1 Strategic choice and marketing tactics

If the marketing objective describes 'What' has to be achieved, then the marketing strategy details 'How' the objectives are to be achieved.

Marketing strategy consists of important long-term decisions to which the competition cannot react quickly. It is the relationship of the firm with its environment. As marketing is an activity that is closely concerned with that environment, there is often considerable similarity between the corporate and marketing strategies within a firm.

The terms strategy and tactics need to be distinguished. Strategy is doing the right thing and is ultimately the search for effectiveness. Tactics are doing things right; they lead to efficiency. Unfortunately, some firms who apparently do not believe in planning have allowed short-term tactics to override strategy, as shown in the discussion of promotional pricing in Chapter Seven. Therefore, deciding upon the correct strategy and moving in the right direction are important for firms and require considerable effort.

The SWOT analysis shows how the fashion firm will fare in the future and this should be compared with the marketing objectives that were established earlier. Often there will be a gap between objectives and the current situation and the larger the gap the more risky or adventurous the marketing plan must be.

From the SWOT analysis the firm should be able to make detailed assessment of the competition, its own distinctive strengths and which market segments to aim for.

10.4.2 Assessment of the competition

A framework for assessing the competition is the same as the one used for the SWOT analysis, and some sample items are shown below:

- employment statistics and levels of expertise;
- organizational structure;
- number and location of distribution outlets;
- manufacturing capacity and flexibility;
- links with intermediaries;
- market share statistics;
- key products and services offered;
- promotional expenditure and impact;
- customer service levels;
- market segments targeted and trends;
- price levels;

◆ growth status – whether contracting, stable or growing;
◆ particular challenges to the firm;
◆ areas of vulnerability from the firm;
◆ environmental policies.

10.4.3 Selecting marketing segments

Market segmentation involves identifying separate market entities, with different needs and characteristics, so that the firm may specialize the product offering or marketing programme by segment or target.

Market segmentation was discussed in detail in Chapter Five along with consideration of a positioning statement for the firm. Segmentation strategies, such as concentration and multi-segment strategies, were also described. Examination of the company's resources and the assessment of the competition, as determined in the sections above, should help to decide the precise strategy. Segment size, identification, profitability, access and stability also should be considered at this stage.

10.4.4 Determining a marketing strategy

The Ansoff matrix can be a useful tool to aid in the development of marketing strategy. A version of the matrix applied to fashion marketing is shown in Figure 10.3.

In the main, strategies are considered that offer new products or services to existing customers as in quadrant 2 or the same products or services to new market segments as in quadrant 3. High-risk

	Fashion product or service	
	Existing	New
Fashion markets — Existing	1 Consolidation or market penetration	2 Fashion product or service development
Fashion markets — New	3 Fashion market development	4 Diversification

Figure 10.3 The Ansoff matrix applied to fashion.

options should only be considered if the planning gap, identified above, is achievable given company resources. The higher the quadrant number in the figure, the riskier the option.

Consolidation can be seen as a risk-aversive strategy; however, under certain circumstances it can be a shrewd move. When the market is in recession or the company is facing restructuring, for example, a consolidation strategy may be the best option. Market penetration is simply achieving a greater share of existing markets and may be gained by offering comparative advantages in pricing or services or by more effective advertising.

Market development concerns the marketing of existing products in new markets. Thus a small fashion retailer may open another store in a new city or a clothing manufacturer may start exporting to Japan. Donna Karan offered online shopping for DKNY products in 2005. Sometimes market development may be evident when a new use for an existing product is found. For example, Harris Tweed has been used in a range of trainers produced by Nike as well as being used for trim in braces and belts.

Fashion product or service development is the mainstay of most fashion marketing firms, although the rate of introduction of new market offerings varies considerably. This strategic option has been extensively discussed in Chapters Five and Six.

Diversification is where new products are developed for new markets. The degree of difference from existing markets and products can range from marginal to massive, and the greater the difference the larger the risk. A minor form of diversification for fashion firms is vertical integration where, for instance, a manufacturer sets up or buys some retail outlets or *vice versa*. A company manufacturing men's suits which enters the formal womenswear market would be making a relatively small change in direction and some expertise in design, manufacture and marketing may be transferable.

The most common move for fashion companies is into fragrance markets, Ted Baker and Guess? being two such examples. Where there are totally unrelated products and markets in a diversification move, the organization is called a conglomerate. The licensing arrangements of some larger French fashion houses make them appear like conglomerates with home furnishing, sunglasses, cutlery, shampoo, cigarette lighters and dozens of other non-clothing items all sold under the same brand name. The main benefit of diversification is to spread the risk of trading across more than one market.

Having selected the correct marketing strategy to pursue attention must be paid to more detailed planning. A marketing plan must be devised with specific marketing mix(es) for the selected target market(s).

10.5 The fashion marketing plan

The fashion marketing plan is a document that details marketing action for a specified period. It states what has to be done when, how and with what effect. The plan gives details of the marketing strategy and how the firm will achieve its marketing objectives. The plan also allocates responsibilities and resources, schedules major activities and enables senior management to monitor the implementation of the fashion marketing strategy.

There are variations in how a plan should be structured. These variations are minor and usually just reflect the house style of the fashion firm. The following sections cover the main components of a marketing plan.

10.5.1 Summary for senior management

This is self-evident and usually concentrates on profits, sales and resources. Many companies suggest that the summary should produced on a single side of a paper.

10.5.2 Marketing objectives

These should be stated concisely and be related to the mission statement. A number of related marketing objectives may be grouped such as promotional objectives.

10.5.3 Situational analysis or SWOT

As noted above, the SWOT should be related to the competition and produce a coherent and related set of recommendations.

10.5.4 Marketing analysis

This is an assessment of market segment options, the competition, the marketing environment and major trends.

10.5.5 Marketing strategy

This is a statement of how objectives will be met by reference to segmentation and positioning of the product.

10.5.6 Marketing mix programmes

This section should detail product, price, distribution and promotional activities. This is probably the most detailed part of the plan as it states what is to happen along with the scheduling and co-ordination of activities. The plan should also show the allocation of tasks, accountability for implementation and costs of the activities.

10.5.7 Forecast results and budgeting

The forecast sales and profits from the plan should be given along with market share data and other relevant quantifiable criteria. Some firms place the expected results in Section 10.5.2. To facilitate calculations and comparisons, it is helpful to place revenue and profit data with information on costs and budgets. Some approaches to budget setting were described in Chapter Nine. The total budget is derived from the marketing mix programme costs mentioned above.

10.5.8 Resourcing and implementation issues

This item is to outline any staffing or physical resources that may be needed to enable the plan to be effected. For example, the introduction of a marketing database, for direct mail activities aimed at regular customers, may have major implications for staff training in information technology and the purchase and maintenance of computer equipment. Possible resistance from staff or fashion intermediaries to certain strategic changes should also be identified, along with recommended action to overcome or minimize negative effects. For example, the importation of garments made in a country that generates polarized political opinion may meet opposition from sections of the workforce or certain active consumer groups.

10.5.9 Marketing control and evaluation

Measurement of the plan is essential so that corrective action can be taken if necessary. Given the objectives and expected results specified above, this section of the plan details the frequency and nature of measurements to be taken. Mechanisms for comparing actual with planned results and the reporting procedures must be shown. Some plans incorporate contingency corrective action in the event of deviations from the plan.

10.6 Implementation and organizational issues

10.6.1 Planning horizons

The time scales for fashion marketing plans vary considerably. All plans are related to the fashion calender, usually two seasons, as noted in Chapter

Planning helps in anticipating and avoiding proble

Figure 10.4   The value of planning – an irony.

Six. They are also linked to the target market and the nature of the product life cycle. Chapter Six also describes product life cycles from the high-fashion fad to the fashion classic and these are major factors in the time scales adopted in the fashion marketing plan. All planning may be carried out for a variety of purposes, but one should strive never to forget its most basic function which is demonstrated in Figure 10.4.

Most fashion firms will have long-range plans lasting from three to five years or longer, medium-term plans for one to three years and short-term plans that may over one season or up to a year.

All three types of plan need to be co-ordinated, therefore short-term plans become part of medium-term plans, and so on. The more complex and changeable the marketing environment that the firm faces, the greater the tendency to need long-range plans and to review fully and update those plans regularly. Except for a very small minority of firms supplying stable items of clothing, possibly functional classic items such as uniforms, most fashion firms are confronted by a volatile and competitive marketing environment.

10.6.2 Organizational culture

Another factor influencing marketing planning is the organizational culture of the firm. As noted in Chapter One, fashion is about change and many managers, in coping with the demands of immediacy, adopt a short-term perspective. Large parts of the fashion industry do appear to lurch from one deadline to another, with the conse-quence that many managers concentrate on dealing with daily mat-ters and short-term issues. Given the high failure rate of fashion firms and the constant uncertainty in the market, many managers feel that long-term planning is of limited value compared with concentrating on doing immediate tasks well. Another factor inhibiting long-range planning is the mobility of staff within the fashion sector. High labour turnover and headhunting (staff poaching) activities can mean that staffing changes can jeopardize the planning process and the security of marketing plans from the competition.

The establishment of a marketing plan, particularly in a rapidly changing environment, can mean a substantial change of resources within the marketing department of a fashion firm. For example, the decision to place more emphasis on support for retailers via in-store promotion and merchandising may mean a reduction in the advertising and publicity budgets. These changes also may mean staff redeployment or redundancies that can demoralize staff and lead to reduced enthusiasm for implementation of the plan. The lesson to be learned is that encouraging participation in the marketing planning process and concern for, and communication with, those involved in implementation is crucial for success.

10.6.3 Internal marketing

Internal marketing is the process of encouraging employees in all functional areas to have a customer focus and do their best to help deliver a good customer experience. A number of writers, e.g. Hulbert *et al.* (2005) and Dunmore (2002), argue that this aspect of a marketing plan is vital if objectives are to be achieved. Much marketing activity depends on the co-operation of other functional areas within the firm and without their support many projects may not be either completed or auctioned on time. Different departments have their own plans and a prime task of senior management to co-ordinate the various plans. However, fashion marketers do have a clear interest in making sure colleagues in other functional areas understand the rationale for the marketing plan and their supporting role within it. Thus the marketing plan needs to be 'sold' within the firm before it can be fully realized.

10.6.4 Management styles

The previous sections argue that planning for the long term, within the fashion sector, is difficult. It is important to note that long-term plans are essential for survival and growth, and that means commitment from senior management to long-term planning. The approaches adopted by some fashion executives can be summarized by the management styles shown below:

- *Management by conjecture*: i.e. Why worry about the future?
- *Management by crisis*: i.e. Let's deal with problems when they arise.
- *Management by subordinates*: i.e. Each fashion marketer does their own thing.
- *Management by prayer*: i.e. Things will get better, we hope!

The flaws in each style above are easily spotted. The approach advocated in this text is management by objectives, as described in an earlier section.

All fashion firms should plan for the long term. The resources and energy they allocate to that process are a function of the target market, organizational culture, product life cycles, the particular marketing environment and the commitment from senior management. A prudent approach for many fashion firms seems to be to plan on a rolling principle so that short-term plans always exist and they are reviewed and modified appropriately to meet new circumstances and challenges.

10.7 Summary

This chapter has dealt with further marketing planning, covering:

- the organizational mission;
- marketing objectives;
- marketing strategy.

Strategic alternatives were further examined in relation to:

- marketing audits;
- SWOT analysis.

Strategic marketing plans can be constructed more easily in the light of the information thus obtained. The chapter concluded by emphasizing the importance of adequate long-range planning in the context of organizational culture, internal marketing and management styles.

Further reading

Baker, M.J. (2007), *Marketing Strategy and Management*, 4th Edition, Palgrave Macmillan, Basingstoke.

Dibb, S. and Simkin, L. (2008), *Marketing Planning: A Workbook for Managers*, Thomson Learning, London.

Dunmore, M. (2002), *Inside Out Marketing: How to Create an Internal Marketing Strategy*, Kogan Page, London.

Gilligan, C. and Wilson, R.M.S. (2003), *Strategic Marketing Planning*, Butterworth-Heinemann, Oxford.

Hulbert, J.M. *et al.* (2005), *Total Integrated Marketing: Breaking the Bounds of the Function*, Kogan Page, London.

Kotler, P. and Armstrong, G. (2008), *Principles of Marketing*, 12th Edition, Pearson/Prentice Hall, Harlow.

McDonald, M. (2007), *Malcolm McDonald on Marketing Plans: Understanding Marketing Plans and Strategy*, Kogan Page, London.

Westwood, J. (2005), *The Marketing Plan Workbook*, Kogan Page, London.

Wood, M.B. (2007), *The Essential Guide to Marketing Planning*, Financial Times/Prentice Hall, Harlow.

Glossary of Fashion Marketing Terms

Advertising is persuasive and/or informative non-personal communications paid for by a clearly identifiable sponsor.

Break-even analysis shows the relationship between fixed costs, variable or marginal costs, total costs, sales revenue and output or volume.

Causal research is used to determine the relationship between variables, e.g. the relationship between advertising and repeat purchases.

Concessions also known as shops-within-shops, can be defined as space leased by the host retailer to another retailer, wholesaler or manufacturer from which to sell its merchandise.

Consumer behaviour provides a framework for identifying consumer needs and target markets, and enables the anticipation of consumer responses to marketing action.

Cost-plus pricing is simply calculating the cost of raw materials, labour and overheads, and adding an amount to cover profit in order to arrive at the selling price.

Demographics is the study of changes in the size and make-up of the population.

Descriptive research provides an accurate description of the variables uncovered by the exploratory research.

Exploratory research is an attempt to uncover any variables that may be relevant to the research project as well as an investigation of the environment in which the research will take place.

Family life cycle is an attempt to classify people according to the age of head of household, marital status, and the age and number of children.

Fashion is about continuous change, clothing and related products and services, and the exercise of creative design skills. Fashion is a current mode of consumption behaviour applied specifically to clothing products and related services.

Fashion classics can usually be seen as the midpoint compromise of any style, i.e. total look or composite effect. Colour and pattern may vary, but the classic customer does not seek the satisfaction of a new seasonal experience in the way that the fashion and fad counterparts do.

Fashion fads will meteorically rise in popularity only to suffer an abrupt decline as they become adopted. As a fad becomes fashionable it also becomes unfashionable.

Fashion marketing is the application of a range of techniques and a business philosophy that centres upon the customer and potential customer of clothing and related products and services in order to meet the long-term goals of the organization.

Fashion marketing concept attempts to embrace the positive aspects of high concern for design, customers and profit by recognizing the interdependence of marketing and fashion design personnel.

Fashion marketing plan is a document that details marketing action for a specified period. The plan gives implementation details of the marketing strategy and states how the firm will achieve its marketing objectives.

Fashions usually have a slower rise to popularity, plateau with continuing popularity and then decline gradually; often this cycle relates to a season, whether autumn/winter or spring/summer.

Franchising is a contractual relationship between franchiser and franchisee in which the franchiser offers, or is obliged to maintain, a continuing interest in the business of the franchisee in such areas as knowledge and training; wherein the franchisee operates under a common trade name, format or procedure owned by or controlled by the franchiser, and in which the franchisee has made or will make a considerable capital investment in his business from his own resources.

Geodemographics are systems derived from statistical analysis of census variables to discover residential areas, usually census enumeration districts, that are linked to purchasing behaviour and media usage.

Innovation is anything the consumer perceives to be new, and could include an 'old' product introduced into a new market.

Intergated Marketing Communications is a concept of marketing communications planning that recognizes the added value of a comprehensive plan that evaluates the strategic roles of a variety of communications disciplines (e.g., general advertising, direct response, sales promotion and public relations) ... and combines these disciplines to provide clarit, consistency and maximum communications impact.

Lifestyle or **psychographics** is a classification of consumers based on activities, interests and opinions (AIOs).

Markdown is where profit is expressed as a percentage of the sale price.

Market-based pricing is founded on market research to find the optimum selling price which then acts as the main driving force upon cost containment via design and quality control effort.

Market penetration pricing tries to capture a large market share by charging low prices. The low prices charged stimulate purchases and can discourage competitors from entering the market as the profit margins per item are low.

Market research is used to refer to research into a specific market, investigating such aspects as market size, market trends, competitor analysis, and so on.

Market segmentation is where the larger market is heterogeneous and can be broken down into smaller units that are similar in character.

Market skimming pricing charges high initial prices and then only reduces prices gradually, if at all. A skimming price policy is a form of price discrimination over time.

Marketing is both a way of thinking about the firm from the perspective of the customer or potential customer, and a management process concerned with anticipating, identifying and satisfying customer needs to meet the long-term goals of the organization.

Marketing analysis is an assessment of market segment options, the competition, the marketing environment and major trends.

Marketing audit involves sets of detailed questions that are asked to determine the status of a firm in relation to its objectives, customers, competition and marketing environment.

Marketing environment is all the influences beyond the control of fashion companies that affect marketing action. It includes consideration of the social, cultural, technological, economic and political contexts within which fashion marketing occurs.

Marketing intermediaries are the main channels that help to get fashion products and services from the manufacturer to the consumer.

Marketing mix describes the specific combination of marketing variables used by a fashion marketer to meet the needs of specific groups of customers known as target markets. It comprises decisions made about products, prices, promotion, services and distribution that are assembled in a coherent and profitable way to represent what the firm is offering to the consumer.

Marketing research covers investigation into all aspects of the marketing of goods or services, such as product research and development, pricing research, advertising research and distribution research, as well as all the aspects of market analysis covered by market research.

Marketing strategy is a specification of those markets the firm wishes to target with marketing activities and how competitive advantages are to be created and achieved.

Markets are places for buying and selling, for exchanging goods and services, usually for money. To constitute a market there should be a genuine need, the customer(s) should be willing and able to buy the fashion product, and the aggregate demand should be sufficient to enable a supplier to operate profitably.

Markup is where profit is expressed as a percentage of costs.

Mass marketing assumes that all customers in a market are the same. It is based on the idea that customer needs do not vary and that the company can offer a standardized marketing mix that meets the needs of everyone.

Multi-Fibre Agreement (MFA) came into existence in 1974 as a temporary expedient and is basically a framework for regulating trade in fibres, fabrics and clothing between developing low-cost countries and the industrialized countries.

Multiples are businesses with at least ten outlets selling predominantly one merchandise group, e.g. clothing or shoes.

Niche marketing is where a clearly defined segment is targeted with a narrow product range.

Opinion leadership refers to the degree of influence exerted in a given choice situation.

Perception is the process whereby buyers select, organize and interpret simple stimuli into a meaningful and coherent picture of the world.

Personal selling is interpersonal promotion carried out by the sales staff of a retailer, wholesaler or manufacturer.

Positioning is to do with the perception by the target market of the firm and its marketing mix. Positioning is how customers see the market, although that perception may have been influenced by marketing action.

Price is the point at which exchange between buyer and seller takes place, where supply and demand are equal. Price is the amount of money that is exchanged for fashion products and/or services.

Product can be defined as anything that can be offered in the marketplace that might satisfy a need. Products may be classified as convenience, shopping or specialty goods.

Product life cycle is based on the proposal that all products have a finite 'life cycle' that can be plotted over a given period using the biological analogy of growth, development and decline.

Product mix or **product range** is the assortment of fashion products that a company offers for sale at any point in time.

Promotional mix is the particular combination of promotional methods and media used by an organization to achieve its marketing communication goals. It includes advertising, sales promotions, public relations and selling.

Publicity is media coverage that is not paid for and has a mass audience and a high level of credibility.

Public relations aims to establish and maintain a favourable image through a pre-planned, long-range programme by communicating with its publics, including consumers, suppliers, shareholders, trade customers, employees, unions, government, pressure groups and the local community.

Sales promotion involves promotional activities that add value to fashion products or induce consumers or intermediaries to buy or provide an incentive for channel effectiveness.

Sampling involves selecting a small number of people from the larger survey population whose characteristics, attitudes and behaviour are representative of the larger group.

Social class refers to divisions of people according to their economic position in society, whether they are aware of that position or not.

SWOT (strengths, weaknesses, opportunities and threats) analysis considers both internal and external factors about either the whole company or a particular fashion product line or range in relation to customers, competitors and trends in the marketing environment.

Variety chain stores sell a variety of merchandise. In the UK, the four major variety chain stores with a significant clothing turnover are Bhs, Marks and Spencer, Little-woods and, to a lesser extent, Woolworths.

Index